GREAT
BASEBALL
STORIES

GREAT
BASEBALL
STORIES

CRESCENT BOOKS
NEW YORK • AVENEL

This 1995 edition published by Crescent Books,
distributed by Random House Value Publishing, Inc.
40 Engelhard Avenue, Avenel, New Jersey 07001

Random House
New York • Toronto • London • Sydney • Auckland
ISBN 0 517 12068 2

A CIP catalog record for this book
is available from the Library of Congress

8 7 6 5 4 3 2

Printed and bound in the USA

CONTENTS

BASEBALL
Anonymous

The ball once struck off,
Away flies the boy
To the next destined post
And then home with joy

Baseball Is a Dream
That Can't Go Away

PHIL HERSH

THE FIELD WHERE *the boy played pickup baseball games every day was called, in simple elegance, Big Hill. The hill began about 40 feet behind third base and rose, with almost no incline, to the road that ran along its crest. The strong right-handed batters in the neighborhood began to hit balls onto the road when they were about 10 years old, but they never seemed to hit passing cars.*

The boy was righthanded, too, but he wasn't very strong. It wasn't until he was 12 that he reached the heights nearly everyone he played with had already attained. The first ball he hit onto the road smacked against the side window of a car, which immediately stopped. The driver ran down Big Hill and grabbed the boy and a friend and dragged them to the police station. A police officer asked the boy what had happened and he said, 'I hit a home run.' He would never forget how that sounded.

Once again, the joyous noise of baseball was briefly silenced. Once again, baseball has not only suffered that foolishness but has beaten it with a resounding grand slam.

You could see the game's triumph in the people lined up at the 'future games' ticket window Thursday morning at Comiskey Park. There was suddenly no reason for doubt about the immediate future of the game, but there never was, really. You could see that in the eyes of a 6-year-old boy, one of the few people in the ball park a couple of hours before the irregularly scheduled doubleheader was to begin.

The boy was sitting next to the White Sox dugout and watching batting practice, the only practice in sports anyone but a coach does watch. He was wearing a tiny uniform jersey that said 'Fisk 72' on its back. When the large man wearing a uniform that said 'Fisk 72' on its back emerged from the dugout, the boy's mouth opened and his eyes got wide.

'The essence of the professional game in the United States of America,' wrote Robert Creamer, author of the best biography of Babe Ruth 'is a small boy looking with absolute rapture at a grown man.'

That essence hadn't been spoilt by Black Sox scandals, white drug scandals, artificial stadiums, unnatural turf, unreal salaries or surreal uniforms. It wasn't spoiled by a two-day strike in which rich old men failed to regain control of the game from rich young men who once were indentured servants. It would not have been spoiled even if the strike lasted far longer.

The game persists, so solidly woven underneath the fabric of American society that it can retain the romantic quality of the 19th Century while the country hurtles pell-mell into the 21st. The men who play the game remain dream weavers.

Baseball is the only game you can see on the radio.

Baseball is the only game you can see yourself playing.

'Any schnook can play it, and they do play it, at all levels, whether it is stickball in the streets or rockball in the country,' says Carlton Fisk, the White Sox catcher.

'Because everybody has or can or could play it, they live their dreams through ball players. Baseball is the only sport they do that in. Oh, I'm sure people go one-on-one in their minds, Larry Bird against Doctor J, but most don't really imagine themselves in the situation. Basketball is a game for exceptional physical specimens. Baseball is for everyday people.'

What better example of that could there be than Pete Rose, who is too short, too slow, too old and too much in love with the game to let any of that stop him from becoming one of its immortals? His is the apotheosis of everyman, chronicled daily in type so small that it would reduce other news to insignificance. Baseball is a game that thrives on statistical minutiae; putting it in bigger type would be aggrandizement as ridiculous as the Roman numerals tacked onto the end of the Super Bowl.

'It is on the radio and in the newspapers everyday, the only game you can follow on that basis, from whatever arm's length you choose,' says White Sox pitcher Tom Seaver. 'It is always there.'

It is *every* day. That is why people take it so badly when it is interrupted. Suddenly, baseball is gone, and the dream is a nightmare. Fans become angry at the players, but they are only a convenient target because of their large salaries. What the people are really mad about is the change in the rhythms of their lives.

'Some people respond like jilted lovers,' Seaver says. 'The first reaction is out of hate or revenge. If they still have a love for it, which a fan does for baseball more than for its players, they will miss it.'

Baseball officially goes from April to October, which is more than half of every year, and unofficially the rest of the year. Think about that: What else, other than family or job, can occupy someone's attention for such an extended period of time? The game becomes a habit; the ritualization of such habits, as Sinclair Lewis said of George Babbitt's daily choice of clothes, is 'of eternal importance, like baseball.'

It disappeared for a week in 1972, almost two months in 1981 and a couple of days this past week. It was missed far more each one of those days than football was during its nine-game strike three years ago. Football is a passing fancy. Baseball is the only game whose season knows none.

'The gods decree a heavyweight title match only once in a while and a national election only every four years, but there is a World Series with every revolution of the earth around the sun,' wrote French-born historian Jacques Barzun. 'And in between, what varied pleasures long drawn out!'

The build-up to the biggest game in professional football, the Super Bowl, is unnaturally long. At least a week goes by between ordinary games. That is one of the reasons why football writers have the worst—or at least the most difficult—assignment on a daily newspaper. All week long, they have to write about nothing. The day of the game, they have to write about something even the coach can't analyze until he has seen the films.

'Baseball is a game of complex simpleness, or simple complexity,' Fisk says. 'People can get involved with its workings and strategies more than any other sport.'

As a strategist, a baseball manager acts his role before an audience of educated critics. At football games, only those aliens born with headphones growing out of their ears can argue that a trap play wouldn't work against a hexadexamexaflexa defense. Nearly everyone in a ball park can debate the merits of a suicide squeeze.

'It starts out being a very easy game to explain, and then the fans who get into the game realize how much more is going on,' says White Sox Manager Tony LaRussa.

The fourth game of last year's National League playoffs will be remembered always for its dramatic ending—Steve Garvey's two-run homer in the ninth. But its purest baseball moment occurred three innings earlier, when the game was tied and the Padres' Kevin McReynolds was on first base with one out.

The batter, Carmelo Martinez, hit a ground ball that looked like a live grenade, but Cubs shortstop Larry Bowa fielded it and threw to second baseman Ryne Sandberg. As Sandberg crossed second, he was upended by the powerful McReynolds, whose clean, hard slide drove Sandberg's throw to first off-line. First baseman Leon Durham instantly moved in the throw's direction, grabbed it and reached back to tag Martinez.

Double play. End of inning. And so much more—a perfect distillation of professionals at their best, everyone doing his job well. Martinez had hit the ball hard, but it was the ground ball pitcher Warren Brusstar had tried to make happen; Bowa had fielded the ball cleanly, but not fast enough to save Sandberg from peril; McReynolds had slid the way a man must to break up a double play, but Durham's instinctive reaction had prevented it. This description lasted longer than the play. It was only an instant, its result plain and simple, its individual components clearly visible, the chain connecting them beautiful in its intricacy.

'Baseball is a kind of collective chess with arms and legs under play in sunlight,' wrote Barzun, who taught for 50 years at Columbia University.

Baseball has satisfied the intellectual and the mindless, the yuppie and the hippie, the writer and the reader. The president of Yale, a scholar of romance languages, has thought out loud that becoming American League president would be a lateral move. More distinguished authors have tried their hand at describing this game—some with needless pomp, others with remarkable circumstance—than any other. What better modern stories have been written than Gay Talese's profile of Joe DiMaggio or John Updike's description of Ted Williams' last game, the latter filled with distracting but necessary statistical footnotes?

'Say this much for big league baseball,' wrote American historian Bruce Catton, 'it is beyond question the greatest conversation piece ever invented in America.'

It is the link between fathers and sons—and now, thankfully, fathers and daughters—because they are talking about the same game. Its true marvel is that the same 6–4–3 double play involving the Cubs, who have been a team since 1876, and Padres, who did not exist until 1969, could have been made 24 or 50 or 100 years ago, by men whose gloves were tatterdemalion, whose fields were unfenced, whose strength and size were less than that of most high school ball players today.

The critical dimension that Alexander Cartwright conceived for his New York Knickerbockers in 1846, that the distance from home to second and first to third should be '42 paces' or 126 feet, has changed only 15 inches in 139 years. The pitcher's mound has not moved since 1893. The grounder to deep short still produces a bang-bang play at first base, whether the runner is Ty Cobb or Rickey Henderson, the shortstop Honus Wagner or Alan Trammell. Walter Johnson's fastball and Dwight Gooden's fastball ride the same express train to home plate.

'It is the unchanged item in a changing world, the one stable factor in a lot of people's lives,' Fisk says.

To say baseball, as an enterprise, is the same as it was 30 years ago is impossible. It has moved west, expanded twice, become a bastard son of the entertainment industry. And yet the game, as a game, is comfortingly constant. Sure, the strike zone was shrunk in 1969 and the designated hitter added in 1973, both out of a well-intentioned desire to add scoring, but those are not important. It is not the number of runs scored, but how they are scored and prevented, that is the fundamental interest of baseball.

'On a fair and beautiful October day about 1820, two distinguished Maine citizens each selected a team of neighborhood men to play a match game of 50 scores,' the Bangor Whig reported. 'A referee was selected and empowered to decide all questions. With the score 45 to 40 darkness intervened, and the outcome was decided by pitching pennies.'

Even inflation can't account for the outcome of the mind games baseball's management and players now choose to play with each other every five years. The hundreds of millions of dollars involved have apparently become a pox on both their houses. Working men once sympathized with players who fought pitched salary battles against the robber barons who ran the game. Now they find themselves on the side of owners with whom they have never had anything in common, people for whom the game is merely a ledger item. 'The rich are different from you and me', Hemingway told Fitzgerald, but we needed to harbor the illusion that ball players weren't, that they were doing what we always wanted to, enjoying a life where work was child's play.

'The one thing that you have to understand,' Seaver says, 'is that this game is still a way we make a living and pay for our children's education and the rest. Ideally, you would like to keep that all behind the scenes, but the financial aspects of baseball are there.

'We don't go on the field thinking about how much money we're making by playing. When we sit around as a group and discuss aspects of our industry and how that affects us, we're simply wearing a different hat.'

We don't want to hear that coming from Tom Seaver. We want to hear him talk of the joys of the old ball parks, which he does with eloquence. We want to see him only in a baseball cap, jumping into Fisk's arms after winning his 300th game last Sunday. That Seaver sensibly thinks of his bottom line as well as his pitching line seems a sacrilege.

We accept heroes with feet of clay; Babe Ruth was a womanizer, a glutton and a boozer, and that has oddly enhanced his deserved reputation as baseball's greatest player. Why, then, do we find it harder to accept heroes whose solid feet are firmly grounded?

Illusions die hard. We want this to be a simpler world, one with no grays, and we want baseball to embody it. A baseball writer whose boyhood hero was Henry Aaron wanted to crawl into a hole the night that Aaron called the press box in the middle of a game to harangue the official scorer about a call that deprived him of a base hit. That churlish behavior had demeaned only Aaron, not the game; it would not stop another child from looking in rapture at another player, unknowing that the image might later be shattered by a personal scandal or a collective strike to preserve salaries some would call already outrageous.

The paradox is that those salaries are helping baseball, by helping it draw the best athletes. How ironically satisfying that must seem to Bill Veeck, who worried about what once were declining numbers of good black athletes in the sport. Ten years ago, a remarkable athlete like Tennessee's Condredge Holloway would choose, without question, to pursue a football career in Canada rather than a baseball career in the United States. This year, Auburn's Bo Jackson, a Heisman Trophy candidate and hard-hitting outfielder, knows he might get richer and have a longer—and less perilous—career in baseball.

Making money, after all, is as American as apple pie. Why else would a television program that lets the rich and famous flaunt their lifestyles be watched so widely by people who are neither, except in their dreams?

'Whoever wants to understand the heart and mind of America had better learn about baseball, its rules and realities,' Barzun wrote.

In 1907 the Spalding Commission resolved a dispute over the origins of baseball in favor of the jingoistic and mythical theory that Abner Doubleday, a West Point graduate and military hero, had invented it. The committee also decided, with equal disregard for facts, that 'Base Ball had its origin in the United States.' So what if, as baseball historian Fred Lieb pointed out, the New York Times' long obituary for Doubleday in 1893 did not contain the word 'baseball'? To say, officially or officiously, that baseball is American does no harm to a game which, although it had English roots, has grown into more than just a national pastime.

Baseball is the game that brought a rainbow of joy after the racial storms that devasted Detroit in 1968 and New York the following year. The reality of those cities and this country's worst problems did not change, of course, but at the darkest moments even a brief shift in mood is important. It is like the walk down the darkened tunnels of an old ball park. Beyond them is a world where mean and chaotic streets suddenly are transformed into a pastoral landscape, where the sun or the sodium vapor bulbs make the grass as green as grass should always be. The light at the end of those tunnels is magical, and the first sight of it can never be stricken from our minds.

Field of Dreams

W. P. KINSELLA

THERE IS AN aura of mystery, a definite difference about the game to be played tonight. The opposing team, gray and ephemeral as dandelion fluff, does not consist of the usual opponents, who often appear to be identical to the players from the previous game, with only a change of uniform and adjusted batting stances.

Fittingly, it is Eddie Scissons who first notices the difference.

'That's Three Finger Brown!' he says, pointing to the shadowy pitcher warming up on the sidelines. 'Check his number! Check his number!' he shouts. But none of us know Three Finger Brown's number offhand.

'Look at the infield!' Eddie crows. 'Tinker-to-Evers-to-Chance. Do you boys have any idea how lucky you are?'

It does seem to me that the cloudlike infielders have the bear-cub insignia grinning from their ghostly uniforms. But what kind of game is it?

Shoeless Joe avoids my questions when I lean down to talk to him. He doesn't reiterate what I already understand—that there are things it is better not to know—but changes the subject, discussing, amongst other things, Moonlight Graham's .300 batting average since he joined the team.

As the game begins, Eddie gathers us around him like a group of disciples and regales us with the history of each Chicago Cub. He launches into baseball stories of all kinds, as if he were playing a game of free association.

'Got a daughter living in Seattle, I have. When I visited her, she took me to a game—sent me to a game is more like it. She convinced a neighbor boy to drive me there and back by giving him a free ticket. The Kingdome in Seattle is like playing baseball in your cellar. Why, they'd hit the ball toward first or third base and it would hit a seam in the AstroTurf and skip off into a corner, while the runner went tearing around the bases. And the sound doesn't carry. You can't hear the bat make contact, and even when the fans cheer, you can't hear them. It was like looking at a TV game with the sound turned down.' He stops to chuckle, and his eyes take on their now-familiar faraway expression.

'We had a shortstop when I was in the minors, can't remember his name, but he used to carry twelve rocks in his hip pocket—scatter them out when he left the field, and he'd pick them up when he came out for the next inning. He'd sit on the bench and watch the face of the shortstop when lazy grounders suddenly hopped over his head like pin-pricked frogs. Stony! That was what he was called! I should have remembered.'

'When I was growing up,' Eddie goes on, 'why I used to watch a catcher named Gordon Sims; played for Omaha in, I think it was a Class A league. My uncle used to take me up there once or twice a summer. Oh, but that catcher was great; built low to the ground and hard as a locomotive. They used to tell stories about how once the pitcher forgot to duck a throw to second and Sims threw the ball right through him, and got the runner out. It might have been true, 'cause I've never seen anybody rifle the ball the way he could. My uncle said he was gonna be in the Bigs in no time. But he never made it—just disappeared. The next summer when we went to Omaha we stayed in the same hotel as the Kansas City team, and my uncle buttonholed the Kansas City manager and asked if he knew what happened to Gordon Sims. 'You mean Crazy Sims,' said the manager. 'He developed a thing about throwing the ball back to the pitcher, or to second base for that matter. He'd catch the ball and then he wanted to hand the ball to a bat boy and have him walk it back to the mound. You can guess how long he lasted with that attitude—not that they didn't try to talk him out of it. The Omaha team even paid to send him off to the Mayo Clinic in Minnesota for a week. He was back planting corn on his papa's farm in Iowa, last anyone heard of him.'

Going into the eighth inning, the Cubs are ahead by four runs, but after a walk, a single, and Swede Risberg's double off Three Finger Brown, the lead is reduced to three. A walk to the catcher loads the bases, and Frank Chance, who manages as well as playing first base, dispatches Three Finger Brown to the dugout and signals to the bullpen for a left-handed pitcher.

'My God,' says Eddie Scissons as he watches the new pitcher lope
in from right field. Eddie stands, whacking his cane on the edge of
the bleacher. Karin, who has been dozing in my lap, springs to life.

'Now pitching for the Chicago Cubs, Kid Scissons.' The words rever-
berate around the stadium, as if it were a hollow gourd.

'I told you,' Eddie says. 'Didn't I tell you?' He looks around. 'Where
is that brother-in-law of yours now?'

In front of us, Kid Scissons, a swath of blond hair cascading over
his forehead, his body solid, pure, and hard as birch, warms up on
the pitcher's mound.

His style is awkward, his left arm whipping out toward first base
like a shepherd's crook when he delivers the ball. As I watch, I remember
Eddie telling us how left-handed pitchers came to be called southpaws.
'Back in the early days, Chicago's West Side Park, as you might expect,
faced west, so anyone who pitched left-handed was doing so with his
southmost hand, or south paw. And that's all there was to it. Most
mysterious-sounding things have simple explanations.'

I look over at Jerry and assume he shares the tingly feeling that dominates my senses.

On the field, Eddie runs the count to 3–2 on Buck Weaver, then walks
him. The lead is narrowed to two. I stare at Eddie Scissons, sitting,
clutching his serpent-head cane, mouth open in awe like an orphan
sitting in front of a clown.

Kid Scissons throws two balls to Shoeless Joe.

'Throw a curve,' says Eddie. 'Throw the curve, dammit, it's my best
pitch.'

Kid Scissons does throw the curve, and it hangs over the plate as
big as a cantaloupe, and Joe swats it over the third baseman's head.
It lands soft as a balloon along the foul line, and lies there while the
third baseman races back and the left fielder charges in. When the dust
settles, Joe stands on second, Buck Weaver on third, and the score is
tied. Chance instructs Kid Scissons to walk Fred McMullin, to load the
bases.

'Buzzard's luck,' says Eddie. 'He can't kill nothing, and nothing will
die for him.'

For a second, it looks as if the strategy of loading the bases, to make
a force play possible at every base, has paid off. With the count 2–2,
Chick Gandil raps the ball sharply, but it takes one hop and ends up
in Kid Scissons's glove. Noisy Kling, the Cub catcher, stands solid as

an iron statue on home plate, his glove extended, waiting for the ball and the force out, waiting to double up Gandil at first. But Kid Scissons is not thinking. He has already turned to look at second, where he has a play, but, instead of throwing, he looks back at first, then to second again, where it is now too late to force McMullin. He looks desperately at first again, and throws, but too late to catch the speeding Gandil. Everyone is safe and the Cubs trail. The catcher is still standing on home with his glove extended. He kicks the dust disgustedly and yells toward the pitcher's mound. Frank Chance says a couple of words to Kid Scissons, and the pitcher's head snaps straight, as if he has taken a jab to the chin. On the bleacher, Eddie pulls his cap lower over his eyes and concentrates.

The next batter, Happy Felsch, drives the ball deep to left center field on the first pitch.

'Go for it! Damn you, stretch your legs,' shouts Eddie, who stands suddenly, his hair escaping from under his cap. The hair is yellow-white like an old dog's. The center fielder can't reach the ball and it rolls to the wall as Happy Felsch slices around the bases, pulling in at third standing up.

Kid Scissons stands dejectedly on the mound. He has not even backed up the play at third. Frank Chance does not walk to the mound, he just signals for a right-hander from the bullpen and points to the dugout. Kid Scissons walks off the field, head bowed, amid occasional boos and a smattering of half-hearted applause. As Kid Scissons slumps onto the bench in the dugout, Eddie Scissons sinks slowly to his bleacher seat, looking devastated.

After the game, Eddie disappears into his room and does not come out until nearly noon the next day, and then his voice is hollow as he asks me if I will drive him to Iowa City. As he gets in and out of the car, his body makes dry sounds like pages of newspaper in a breeze. We make two or three stops in Iowa City, ending up at his apartment, where I expect him to say goodbye. Instead he goes in, and returns with a shopping bag crammed with clothes, carrying his overcoat over his arm.

Dusk and the trappings of magic have not yet lowered onto and around my ballpark. The Iowa wind dominates today. The cornstalks bend ominously, rustling like plastic pompons. The wind is stroking, gusting, warm, living, a pervasive sign.

As I approach the field, I see Eddie Scissons standing alone on the bleacher. He has taken off his cap and is facing into the wind, his hair blown back like snow drifted against a fence. He is speaking, gesturing alternately with his free hand and the hand holding the serpent-headed cane.

Even though the wind is dry and toast-warm, I see that Eddie is wearing the same sleet-gray overcoat he wore when I first met him on the street in Iowa City. But under the coat he is wearing his Chicago Cub uniform, the material new as white envelopes, the blue stripes looking as if they have been freshly drawn by a felt pen.

I stand along the left-field line and stare up at him. He gestures broadly, making a point, but the wind floats his words away. Suddenly, as if the park has been inundated with butterflies and flower petals, the scene changes. The grandstands and floodlights appear, and the players file in through the gate in the center-field wall. They materialize out of the cornfield, as if from some unseen locker room. The sounds and smells of baseball are all about me. I peek over my shoulder and see that Richard has been trailing me, that Jerry and Annie and Karin are crossing from the house to the ballpark. Eddie leans down and whacks his cane on the edge of a board, to attract Shoeless Joe's attention. He speaks briefly with Joe, who in turn calls the other players closer. Eventually, we all gather on the left-field grass, staring up at Eddie standing on the bleacher, wild and wind-blown, looking for all the world like an Old Testament prophet on the side of a mountain.

'I take the word of baseball and begin to talk it. I begin to speak it. I begin to live it. The word is baseball. Say it after me,' says Eddie Scissons, and raises his arms.

'The word is baseball,' we barely whisper.

'Say it out loud,' exhorts Eddie.

'The word is baseball,' we say louder, but still self-consciously. I look down at Annie, who shrugs her shoulders. Karin claps her hands as the rhythm of Eddie's voice flows into her blood. The baseball players exchange aggrieved glances.

'The word is what?'

'Baseball . . .'

'Is what?'

'Baseball . . .'

'Is what?' As his voice rises, so do ours.

'Baseball!'

He pauses dramatically. 'Can you imagine? Can you imagine?' His voice is filled with evangelical fervor. 'Can you imagine walking around with the very word of baseball enshrined inside you? Because the word of salvation is baseball. It gets inside you. Inside me. And the words that I speak are spirit, and *are* baseball.'

He shakes his head like a fundamentalist who can quote chapter and verse for every occasion.

'The word healed them, and delivered them from destruction. The word makes the storm a calm, so that the waves thereof are still.' He looks around wildly.

'Your mother should be here,' I whisper to Annie. She digs her small, pointed elbow into my ribs.

'As you begin to speak the word of baseball, as you speak it to men and women, you are going to find that these men and women are going to be changed by that life-flow, by the loving word of baseball.

'Whenever the word of baseball is brought upon the scene, something happens. You can't go out under your own power, under your own light, your own strength, and expect to accomplish what baseball can accomplish.

'We have to have the word within us. I say you must get the word of baseball within you, and let it dwell within you richly. So that when you walk out in the world and meet a man or woman, you can speak the word of baseball, not because you've heard someone else speak it but because it is alive within you.

'When you speak the word, something will begin to happen. We underestimate the power of the word. We don't understand it. We underestimate all that it can accomplish. When you go out there and speak the word of baseball—the word of baseball is spirit and it is life.

'I've read the word, I've played it, I've digested it, it's in there! When you speak, there is going to be a change in those around you. That is the living word of baseball.'

The players shuffle their feet. Some move away a little, but then it is as if Eddie's voice pulls them back in.

'As I look at you, I know that there are many who are troubled, anxious, worried, insecure. What is the cure? Is it to be found in doctors and pills and medicines? No. The answer is in the word, and baseball is the word. We must tell everyone we meet the true meaning of the word of baseball, and if we do, those we speak to will be changed by the power of that living word.'

'Can you say the word?'

'Baseball,' we chant, and our voices rise toward Eddie Scissons like doves on the warm Iowa wind.

'The word is what?'

'Baseball.'

'Is what?'

'Baseball.'

'Praise the name of baseball. The word will set captives free. The word will open the eyes of the blind. The word will raise the dead. Have you the word of baseball living inside you? Has the word of baseball become part of you? Do you live it, play it, digest it, forever? Let an old man tell you to make the word of baseball your life. Walk into the world and speak of baseball. Let the word flow through you like water, so that it may quicken the thirst of your fellow men.'

Late that night, I am sitting in the dark at the kitchen table when Eddie joins me. He wears a nightgown that looks as if it may have been made from a Chicago Cub road uniform.

'You're afraid to talk to him,' he says, pulling out a chair, leaning heavily on his serpent-head cane as he takes a seat.

I know immediately that he is talking about the catcher.

I nod to show Eddie that I do indeed know who he is referring to, and that I am indeed afraid.

'I heard somebody say once, "Success is getting what you want, but happiness is wanting what you get."' He lays one of his large hands out on the oilcloth-covered table before me. 'You saw what happened to me. I got what I wanted, but it wasn't what I needed to make me happy.'

'But you still . . .'

'Believe.' Eddie finishes the sentence for me. 'It takes more than an infinite ERA to shake my faith,' he chuckles, not unhappily.

'It's just that the implications are so immense,' I say.

'They don't have to be, Ray. I know I'm sounding like I'm trying to be the wise old rascal, and I suppose I am. But you were so excited when you told us about the idea of your catcher appearing. Since he has, all you do is sneak around your own ballpark looking at your shoes.'

'Just go up to the man and tell him you admire the way he catches a game of baseball.' Outside the window, the moon is whitish and hangs like a sickle of ice. 'Share what you've got in common,' he goes on.

'Talk about the small ballparks he took you to as a kid, where kids played with mongrel dogs under the bleachers and farmers scuffed their boots on the boards and kept one eye on the sky. Tell him your name is Ray, and introduce him to Karin—for her sake, not his, because someday she'll be old enough to understand and appreciate what you did.

'The right chemistry will be there, it can't help but be. You both love the game. Make that your common ground, and nothing else will matter.' Eddie smiles at me, the cool summer moon reflected in his pale eyes.

'But how can I do it and not give away what I know?' I think of a picture of a group of baseball players standing in front of a bleacher in a small town in Montana. It was taken by my mother with an old-fashioned Kodak box camera made of heavy black cardboard. The ballplayers in the picture are all but indistinguishable, but my mother used to point one out and say, 'That's Daddy,' and if I looked closely, I could see the square cut of his jaw, could recognize him by the way he liked to stand with his left hand resting on his hip.

'Of course you can do it,' says Eddie. 'You're awfully good at keeping secrets. I should know.' But I hardly hear him, for I am thinking of the man I knew in Montana, John Martin Duffy Kinsella—a name as Irish as shamrocks, a name that derives from the word *peninsula* and was, until the mid-1800s, O'Kinshella. He was an affectionate, sentimental man who sang songs about The Wearin' o' the Green, and about the patriot he was named for, John Martin Duffy.

'Of course you can do it,' Eddie says again. 'You have to do it. How many people get a chance to do it? I've got a sneaking feeling that the magic has been here all the time, that *it* was what drew me out here from Chicago, not the teaching job. But I was like a key with one tooth missing. I didn't have what it took to let the genie out of the bottle. Maybe that's why I stopped you on the street.'

Spikes of moonlight decorate the table as Eddie reaches across and clasps my hand. 'I'm counting on you. And in more ways than one. I guess you know that there weren't any baseball boys. That was all malarkey, like everything else I told you . . . '

'I understand,' I say. And I hope I do.

'Once you meet him, it will be like the last inning of a perfectly played ball game—you'll pray for extra innings so you'll never have to go home. You'll see.' He rises and makes his way to the stairs, and seems to float upward into the moon-spangled darkness.

I sit alone, recalling a conversation I had with Salinger.

'That catcher's good. Look at how fast he comes up with the ball,' Jerry said one day. 'He has an arm like a catapult. Is he really? . . .'

'He is.'

'Does he know?'

'Of course not. He's a young man from North Dakota named Johnny Kinsella, who has just broken into the majors with the White Sox. I'm not even a glint in his eye.'

'And you can't tell him?'

'That's why I haven't even approached him. I'm afraid I'll give myself away.'

'It must be painful for you.'

'You're a master of understatement. But if you were him, would you want to know what I know?'

'No mere apple could equal the temptation. But no, I wouldn't. It would destroy anyone to know his own future.'

'I know I have to put what I'm aware of in perspective. He's young and rugged and unafraid and full of hope. It should be enough for me, to see him doing what he loves best.'

Salinger nodded his head in agreement.

'But I saw him years later, worn down by life. Think about it. I'm getting to see something very special.'

It was after noon when Salinger decided to ask Eddie if he wanted to play hearts. When he got no answer to his knock, he opened the door and found Eddie dead. Eddie must have had a premonition, for he had changed into his Chicago Cub uniform. His cap, glove, and brand-new spikes were laid out beside the bed.

It is more difficult than you might expect to dispose of a dead body, especially when you find you know virtually nothing about the deceased. We knew that Eddie's daughters were scattered about America in Seattle, Boston and Pheonix, but we did not know how to contact even one of them. Some kind men from the Johnson County Sheriff's Department finally took charge of the situation, after asking me a number of pointed questions about why I had the body of a ninety-one-year-old stranger in a Chicago Cub uniform in my guest bedroom. Eddie's body ended up at Beckman-Jones Funeral Home in Iowa City. His daughters were notified by the proper authorities, and each dutifully booked passage to Cedar Rapids Airport. I could picture the flight paths of their airplanes sectioning a map of the United States into triangles and rectangles as they rushed home.

Annie and I make a duty call on them at Eddie's tiny apartment, where the three of them have holed up on arrival. They are middle-aged women, severe as suffragettes, who inspect us critically and ask our religious affiliation. I tell them only that Eddie was homesick for the farm and that we had invited him to spend a few days with us. They sniff disdainfully each time their eyes land on one of Eddie's baseball artifacts that line the mantel and windowsill, or when they see one of the Chicago Cub programs that are thumb-tacked to the walls of both living room and bedroom. I don't mention my interest in baseball, but tactfully inform them of Eddie's desire to be buried in his Cub uniform.

'I know,' replies one who is wearing a crocheted hat. 'He wrote each of us at least a dozen times to tell us that.' She scowls and sniffs.

'The coffin will be closed, of course,' says a second daughter, whose hair looks as if it has been stained with blueberries.

The following day the phone rings.

'Mr Kinsella?'

'Yes.'

'This is Gladys Vickery speaking.'

'Yes.'

'I used to be Gladys Scissons. We met briefly yesterday.'

'We did.'

'Well, I'm calling from the lawyer's office. My father added a strange clause to his will—just last week, in fact. I think it is preposterous, but Mr Embury says I should at least check with you . . .'

'Go on.'

'At the end of his will, he added, "I want to be buried in Ray Kinsella's cornfield." Just like that. No explanation or anything.'

'No one else would understand,' I said.

'Do you understand?'

'We had a mutual interest in baseball.'

'Oh,' she says in a knowing voice. 'Did he fill you full of his awful stories? You know, he never played for . . . '

'It's all right, I can afford the space. Your father can be buried here.'

'I'll have Mr Embury draw up a contract. We'll pay you the same as the cemetery.'

'That won't be necessary.'

There is a long silence, then I hear her aside to the lawyer. 'He says he wants him buried there. Must be as crazy as Daddy was.'

The daughters decide not to attend the burial. I am able to convince them that they would not want to muddy their shoes in a cornfield. The hearse that delivers Eddie's coffin is painted an apple green, with black stripes along the sides like swaths of ribbon. The two attendants, who could easily serve as mannequins in a formal-shop window, are anxious to see the body planted. We let them wheel the coffin as far as the baseball stadium. Their eyes race back and forth in gloomy faces, and it takes great self-control for them not to ask questions. They place the coffin on the ground beside the grave. Jerry and I insist that we will lower the coffin into the grave at a more appropriate time. The dolorous attendants, who speak like English butlers with midwestern voices, reluctantly agree.

We are not dishonoring Eddie's last request. Yesterday, as Salinger and I headed for the cornfield behind left field, shovels in hand, we saw to our surprise that the ballplayers were holding a workout.

'We'd like to be part of it,' Shoeless Joe Jackson said with great sincerity. 'He loved the game as much as anyone can, and we'd like to pay our last respects.'

'But out there you can't?' I said, nodding toward the spaces beyond the fence, where the corn rustles greenly.

Joe nodded. The others were behind Joe, silent and subdued.

'What happens to you when you go through that door? It's not fifty yards to the gravesite,' I said. But Joe and the others only smiled sadly, enigmatically.

'If you can't come to the grave, then suppose we bring the grave to you?' said Jerry.

'That would be most considerate,' said Shoeless Joe, and the others nodded solemnly.

I looked at the blade of my nearly new shovel, the black paint barely scratched, and I thought of the labor, the love, the passion I'd expended to make the field. I looked in horror at Salinger for suggesting such a thing.

But he looked back at me with a level brown gaze, and the players stared silently at me, and Shoeless Joe walked wordlessly across the outfield, slowly, his magnificent bat, Black Betsy, wavering in front of him like a metal detector, like a divining rod.

And the place where he stopped was in deep left field, where the grass is most lush, the grain of it like expensive carpet, the color dark and luxurious as ripe limes.

The wind whispered through the empty stands, and heavy clouds roiled across the sky. Salinger had lowered the stars and stripes and the Iowa flag to half-mast on the flagpole in center field. Both flags snapped crisply in the breeze.

'All right,' I said resignedly. And as I did, I felt the greatest tenderness toward Eddie Scissons. He may have exaggerated a little, but he did it with class. I hope people will be able to say the same about me after I'm gone. 'But let me make the first cut,' I said, and placed the shovel on the ground and stepped down on it. I felt it slip into the earth easily, as if I were spading chocolate pudding.

Now, as the varnished coffin sits beside the grave, I recall the service that afternoon in Iowa City—a closed-coffin service in which a minister from a church Eddie had never attended ranted and chanted and raged over his coffin. His words were, I suppose, in some way a comfort for the daughters who had engaged him, but he said not one thing about Eddie, except that he had lived a long life and produced three fine God-fearing daughters.

Well, old buddy, I think, whatever happens, whether you stay buried here beneath a baseball field or whether it all gets leveled out and planted in corn, there's no finer resting place in the world.

'I think we should open the coffin,' I say aloud. No one objects. It takes Salinger and me a while to find the hidden snaps with which the undertakers have fastened it. Inside, Eddie, capless, his white mane trimmed and hair-sprayed into place, the cosmetics of the dead making him look younger than I have ever seen him, lies resplendent in his Chicago Cub uniform. His cap rests on his folded hands, his feet are encased by his new cleats, his glove lies at his side below his right-hand. One of the daughters must have remembered that he was left-handed.

'Yes, it's Eddie Scissons,' I say.

'Dead as Billy-be-damned,' says Salinger, playing his part.

'It's all right to bury him now,' I say, as the players file by the coffin, caps in hands. 'There *are* baseball boys, Eddie. There always have been.' And as I look around me, I have the feeling that if I were to go to Iowa City tomorrow, go to the public library or the university library, find the reference section, and pick up a copy of the *Baseball Encyclopedia* and turn to page 2006, I would find right at the bottom of the page, right after the entry for Hal Schwenk, who played for the 1913 St Louis Browns, and right before the entry for Jim Scoggins, who played for the 1913 Chicago White Sox, a listing under Eddie's name that would look like this:

KID SCISSONS   Scissons, Edward Sebastian—BL TL 6′ 2″ 195 lbs.
                B. Nov. 12, 1887 Kearney, Neb.
                D. July 28, 1979 Iowa City, Iowa.

And under that would be the details of Eddie's three seasons as a relief pitcher for the Cubs: his won-and-lost record, number of innings pitched, ERA, strikeouts, bases on balls, and batting record. I have the feeling. I have the feeling.

When it is finished, when the coffin has been lowered by the ball-players, and the ropes retrieved, the grave filled in, the excess earth, which was piled on tarpaulins, removed, the top of the grave convex as a pitcher's mound, I look at Joe Jackson and start to speak.

'I've played on worse,' says Joe, reading my mind, and I picture him hopping over the gopher-riddled outfield of one of the Textile League ballparks in South Carolina, one of the fields where he began, and where he ended, his playing days.

The Milk Pitcher

HOWARD BRUBAKER

THE FULLERS NAMED their son 'Philip' after his maternal grandfather. That was an error in judgment because the time came when the name Phil Fuller aroused chuckles and snickers among the pleasure-loving faces of the countryside. At the age of one Phil had practically settled upon red as the best color for hair. Some time in his third year the truth was established that he was left-handed. When given something he did not want, he threw it away with violence.

This act seemed to set up pleasurable emotions in his young soul. His simple face widened into a grin, and before long he was heaving things around for the sheer love of heaving.

At four, Phil sprouted a genuine freckle on his nose, the forerunner of a bumper crop, and even his prejudiced mother had to admit that his ears were large for his age.

The youth spent his fourth summer in the society of a Jersey calf named Lily, who was tethered in the orchard. Phil had nothing to do except to throw green apples at a tree with his left hand, and Lily's time was also her own. The child learned not to wince when she licked his pink nose with her rough tongue, and the calf put up with some pretty rowdy conduct too. Both infants cried when separated for the night. The tender attachment between Phil and Lily was the subject of neighborhood gossip as far away as the Doug Morton place at the bend of Squaw Creek.

When Phil was six, he threw a carriage bolt from the wagon shed into the water trough, and he laughed so boisterously over this feat that Mr Harrington heard the noise while passing in a light spring wagon.

Phil had a misguided sense of humor. It seemed to him that throwing things was the world's funniest joke. As he picked up a stone and let it fly, the freckles on his face arranged themselves into a pleasure pattern, his features widened, and he grinned expansively, showing vacant spots where he was changing teeth.

By this time his love for the cow stable had become a grand passion. Horses, dogs, cats, and pigs meant rather less in his young life than they do to most farm boys, but cows meant more. Phil attended all the milkings with his father, dealt out bran, and threw down hay. He wandered in and out among bovine legs without fear; hoofs, horns, and teeth had no terrors for him. He was soon old enough to drive the cattle to pasture and bring them back.

At the age of eight he was probably the ablest red-headed cowboy and left-handed stone-thrower in Clinton Township. At this date in history he had drunk enough milk to float a battleship and thrown enough stones, sticks, bones, horeseshoes, apples, corncobs, and baseballs to sink one. He was now the owner in fee simple of Lily's knock-kneed daughter, Dolly. This white-faced blond flapper followed Phil around with adoration and bleated at the barnyard gate until her playmate came home from school.

That fount of knowledge was Clinton Township, District No. 5, known locally as Tamarack School. There he absorbed a reasonable quantity of booklore and learned to pitch a straight ball with speed and control. He is still remembered in educational circles as the southpaw who hurled the Tamarackers to glorious victory over the Squaw Creek outfit, while unveiling the broadest grin ever seen on the lot and issuing many unnecessary noises. Although he had a lot of influence over a baseball, he could not make his face behave.

Baseball was the great joy of Phil's school years. Every spring when the frost came out of the ground his flaming head sprang up on the soggy field like a tulip. He had never learned to bat well, but he was a thrower of great ability and a laugher and yeller of great audibility. In school when asked to give the boundaries of Baluchistan he could scarcely make the teacher hear, but on the diamond his disorderly conduct was noted and deplored as far away as Grandma Longenecker's cottage.

The game uncorked his inhibitions and released his ego. His habitual shyness vanished and gave place to vociferous glee. He did frolicsome things with his feet, his arms went round like a windmill wheel, sometimes he burst into what he wrongly believed to be song. Miss Willkans, the teacher, testified that Phil had easily the worst singing voice that had attended District No. 5 in her time—which would be nineteen years if she lived through this term, as seemed highly unlikely.

Inevitably there came an afternoon in late May when Phil's career as a Tamaracker had run its course. He twisted a button almost off his new coat, whispered a graduating piece about Daniel Webster, took his books and his well-worn right hand glove and went back to the cows.

At five o'clock the following morning the fourteen-year-old Phil became the vice president and general manager of the dairy department of the Fuller farm. His father was overworked, help was scarce and expensive, and the graduate of Tamarack was judged strong enough to handle the job. He milked all the cows that summer, cleaned the stalls, helped to get in the hay and fill the silo. He ran the separator, he churned, he carried skim milk to the pigs. The end of the summer found him a stocky lad of rather less than normal height but with a rank growth of feet, arms and ears. He had the complexion of a boiled beet and hair exactly the shade of a two-cent stamp. His hands were large and fully equiped with freckles, calluses, bumps, cracks, warts, knuckles, and rough red wrists.

Phil could lift with one hand Dolly's new calf, Molly; he could throw a ten-pound sledgehammer over the hay barn; he could sing like a creaky pump, and he shattered all known speed records from the stable to the dining room. He was an able performer with the table fork as well as with the pitchfork.

In September he took all these assets and liabilities and his first long pants and went to Branford to live with Aunt Mary and Uncle Phineas and attend high school. As he was winding up his affairs preparatory to his great adventure, it was clear that he had something on his mind. It came out one night at supper in the hiatus between the fifth and sixth ears of Golden Bantam.

'It's too bad you don't keep a cow,' he said, apropos of nothing.

'Oh, sakes alive, child!' Mother exclaimed in surprise. 'They wouldn't want to be bothered with a cow.'

Phil's ears went red. He polished off his corncob and returned to the attack. 'They wouldn't need to be bothered much. They have no horse any more, and there's room in the barn, I could feed her and milk her and everything. I bet Aunt Mary would be glad to have lots of nice milk and cream. We could tie her behind the buggy and take her in with us.'

'Tie who—Aunt Mary?' asked Father with ill-timed facetiousness.

'Dolly,' said Phil.

A dozen objections were raised and disposed of. Aunt Mary and Uncle Phineas were consulted by telephone, and after the first shock they agreed to the outrageous plan. And thus it came about that Phil Fuller was the first case in recorded history of a boy who went to Branford High School accompanied by a private and personal cow.

During those first months of strangeness and homesickness, Dolly was his comfort and his joy, his link with the familiar. He brushed and polished that blond cow until her upholstery was threadbare, pampered her with choice viands and clean bedding, scrubbed and whitewashed the interior of the old barn, put in window sashes to give Dolly more sunlight and a better view. Often when the day was fair he led her around the block to take air and see a little city life.

At six o'clock of a dark, bitter morning the neighbors could hear distressing noises issuing from Phineas Rucker's lantern-lit barn, and they knew from sad experiences of the past that another day was about to dawn and the red-headed Fuller boy was singing to his heart's true love.

Dolly was now in the full flush of her splendid young cowhood and home was never like this. Phil plied her with experimental mixtures—beet pulp, ground oats, cottonseed meal—and carefully noted the results. The contented cow responded gratefully to this treatment. Before long she exceeded the needs of the Rucker family and Phil was doing a pleasant little milk business with the neighbors. His immaculate barn, his new white overalls, his vocal excesses, and his free street parades all helped trade. The milk inspector passed Dolly with high honors, and doctors recommended her for ailing babies. Presently she was one of Branford's leading citizens, a self-supporting twenty-quart cow, commanding a premium of three cents over the market price. Phil had discovered his life work.

His second great discovery did not come until spring. On a blustery March day he was out on the diamond behind the high-school building, warming up his left wing and chuckling over his favorite joke, when Mr Huckley, chemistry teacher and baseball coach, came along.

'Southpaw, eh!' he demanded. 'Let's see what you've got, Fuller.'

Phil gave a brief exhibition of his wares with Dinky Doolittle holding the catcher's glove.

'Plenty of steam and good control,' the teacher said, 'and your footwork is terrible. Now show us your curve.'

'I haven't got any,' Phil answered. 'Nobody ever showed me how to pitch a curve.'

'Somebody will now,' Mr Huckley said. 'Whether you can do it or not is another question.'

That was the beginning of a beautiful friendship and a new era in the life of Philip Fuller.

Mr Huckley had pitched on the team of Athens University, of which he was a graduate. He liked Phil, admired his able hands, his abnormally developed forearms, his keen joy in the game. The coach saw great possibilities in this piece of raw material, and he spent a patient hour teaching Phil some of the rudiments of curve pitching and in time they achieved a perceptible out-curve. At the height of his exultation, the boy pulled out a nickle-plated watch and said:

'I ask you to excuse me now. It's time to milk my cow.'

After a week of such instruction, Mr Huckley handed down this decision: 'You have the makings of a good pitcher, Phil, if you're willing to learn. You have a couple of fine qualities and not over twenty-five or thirty serious faults.'

Phil's ears flushed with pleasure and embarrassment.

'Well, maybe I can get shut of some of them—I mean those—faults. I've got four years to do it in.'

'Right-o. You have good control of your fast one, you have a nice little out, and you have the worst style of windup these eyes have ever seen.'

Four years of study, dairying, and baseball, with summers of hard work on the farm, made Phil a different boy—different and yet curiously the same. His shoulders were broader, his arms stronger, but he did not add many inches to his stature. He knew more mathematics, science, and history, but Latin was still Greek to him. Although he took on some of the manners and customs of his town contemporaries, he still had the gait of one walking over a plowed field. In time he learned to talk with girls without being distressed, but as a social light he was a flickering flame in a smoky chimney. He was a conspicuous success on the barn floor but a brilliant failure on the dance floor. His voice changed, but not for the better. His matin song to Dolly now sounded like a bullfrog with a bad attack of static. He wrote a creditable little rural farce for the senior dramatic class and further distinguished himself as the worst actor on the American stage.

Though much ridiculed, he was universally liked and genuinely respected. On the ball field he was a source of low comedy to friend and foe because of the eccentric behavior of his face and feet, but in his succeeding seasons on the mound he pitched the Branford High School out of the cellar position into respectable company, into select society, and finally, in his senior year, into the state championship, of the small-town division.

At the joyfest in the assembly hall in celebration of this final triumph, Phil was forced to make a speech. He fixed his eyes upon his third vest button and informed it in confidence that it was Mr Huckley who had made him what he was today—which wasn't so very much.

When his turn came, the chemist and coach arose and told the world a great secret about this Phil Fuller, who had now pitched his last game for dear old BHS. Phil, he said, owed his success as a pitcher to his having been brought up in a cow barn. Constant milking had developed his forearm muscles to surprising strength, and the knots and knobs on his good left hand had enabled him to get a spin on the ball that produced his deadliest curves.

'I therefore propose,' he said, 'that Phil's girl friend, Dolly, be elected an honorary member of the team.'

This motion was seconded with a will and carried with a whoop, and Dolly became, as far as anyone could learn, the only cow that ever belonged to a ball club.

'Phil has told you,' Mr Huckley went on, 'that he got some help from my coaching. If so, he has chosen a rotten way to pay his debt. Instead of going to a high-class and fancy culture factory like Athens, he has decided to enter Sparta Agricultural College. Athens and Sparta are deadly enemies in athletics, and some day Phil may use what I taught him against my own alma mater. There is no use trying to keep Phil from running after the cows; but this is a sad blow to me. I didn't raise my boy to be a Spartan.'

It was the county agricultural agent who had first put Sparta into Phil's head. The boy had naturally assumed that his education would cease with high school, but this Mr Runkleman came into Dolly's palatial quarters one day and spoke an eloquent piece in favor of his own Sparta.

'A boy who intends to be an expert dairy farmer,' he said in part, 'ought to learn all there is to know on the subject. You have a natural gift for taking care of cows, but what you don't know about scientific dairying would fill a ten-foot shelf.'

'That's so,' Phil answered, 'but I haven't got much money.'

'You don't need much money. Lots of the boys are working their way through. I'll guarantee that you get a job in the college dairy barn. The work will pay your board, teach you the practical side, and you'll meet the nicest cows in the world.'

This was a weighty inducement, and one crisp day in late September found Phil knocking at the door of the higher education. He was a youth of five feet five with fiery hair and complexion, with ears that stuck out like red semaphores; a homely, awkward, likable boy, full of hope, inexperience, diffidence and whole raw milk. His only regret was that he could not take Dolly with him to college.

Because of Mr Runkleman's hearty recommendation, he got his job in the dairy barn, and he took a room in a house near by. His days sped by in a new kind of eternal triangle—boardinghouse, dairy and classroom—and he was happy in all three places.

Every morning at the ghastly hour of four he trudged through windy blackness to the big concrete barn. Now followed several hours of milking, feeding, currying, and stable cleaning in company with half a dozen other cow students, then home to breakfast and to class. In the late afternoon there was a repetition of these chores, followed by dinner, some study, and an early bed. Such was the wild college life of this flaming youth.

Football, the great autumn obsession, meant little to him. Basketball was more fun, but a habitual early riser makes a poor customer of night life. In fact, Phil made up his mind that, for the first year, he would waste no time on athletics.

Sibyl Barnett Samboy, the wife of Kenneth Samboy, director of Sparta athletics, said after Phil had been introduced to her at the freshman reception: 'That's the first time I ever shook hands with a Stillson wrench.'

Although he honestly intended to keep out of baseball, the first warm afternooon in March brought on an attack of the old spring fever. There was no harm, he thought, in getting out a ball and glove and tossing a few to Spider Coppery behind the barn while waiting for milking time. Before long it was a regular practice among the 'cowboys' to beguile their idle moments with playing catch and knocking up flies, and presently there was talk of forming a team to play a game with the students of the horticultural department, otherwise the 'greenhouse gang'.

An insulting challenge was given and taken, and the game took place on a pleasant Saturday.

This contest was held upon the old ball grounds. The new stadium was built upon a better site, and the former athletic grounds with their little grandstand were given over to the general use of the students. Samboy was a firm believer in athletics for everybody. He loved to stir up little wars between classes, dormitories, fraternities, and departments. Often these little home-brew contests developed and uncovered talent for the college teams.

Along about the fifth inning of this ragged ball game, an uninvited guest appeared among the handful of spectators in the grandstand. Phil was on the mound at the time.

So Mr Samboy's eyes were gladdened by the sight of a stocky, freckled, red-headed southpaw who burned them over with power, who laughed from head to foot and uttered unfortunate noises.

Samboy talked with him after the game, poked his nose into his past and urged him to try for the college team.

Phil protested that he was too busy with his classes and his cows. It was a long argument, but Samboy won.

'Report to Donnigan on Monday,' said the director, 'and tell him I suggested that he look you over. Every coach has a free hand with his own team, you know, but if he turns you down let me know and I'll give you a tryout on the freshman team. I'll speak to Professor Wetherby, if you like, and ask him to let you shift hours at the dairy while you're trying your luck on the diamond.'

'You don't suppose'—Phil was visibly embarrassed—'there wouldn't be any danger of me losing that job— or anything? I wouldn't do that for all the baseball there is.'

'Not a chance, Fuller. We don't give fellows positions here because they are good athletes, but we don't fire 'em either.'

H. B. Donnigan—'Hard-boiled Donnigan'—had learned his trade under the great Tim Crowley, of the Eagles. Donnigan's big-league days were over and he was making a living coaching college teams. He used the Crowley method and the Crowley philosophy. All ball players were worms and should be treated as such.

He had spent his boyhood among the tin cans and bottles of a vacant lot in New York's gas-house district, and he never really believed that ball players could be grown in the country.

One trouble with his policy was that it did not work at all. It was rumored that when his contract expired at the end of the season, Samboy would let him go. A sense of his failure did not improve the coach's technique—or his temper. It was to this man-eating tiger that Samboy had cheerfully thrown the red-headed rookie from the cow barn.

'And now who let you in?' was Hard-boiled Donnigan's address of welcome.

'Mr Samboy said would you please look me over.'

The phrase was perhaps an unfortunate one. The coach did exactly that.

'All right. Tell him I've done it, and if you're Lillian Gish, I'm Queen Marie.'

'I'm a pitcher—southpaw.' Phil's hard-earned grammar fled in this crisis. 'I done good in high school.'

'Oh, all right, stick around,' said the testy coach. 'When I get time, I'll see if you've got anything.'

He seemed to forget all about Phil—who had not the slightest objection. The boy had a bad case of stage fright, partly from Donnigan's ill nature, but more from the immensity of the empty stadium. He had almost made up his mind to sneak back to his beloved cows when he realized that he was being addressed.

'Hey, you—carrots—come out to the box and pitch to the batters.' Donnigan took his place behind the plate. 'Murder this guy,' he muttered to Risler, a senior and captain of the team.

Risler murdered, instead, the bright April sunshine in three brutal blows. The old miracle had happened again. The moment Phil took hold of the ball and faced the batter he forgot his fears, he remembered only that throwing a baseball was the greatest fun in the world.

'Hey, wipe that grin off your map,' yelled the coach. 'What do you think this is, a comic opery?'

Phil controlled his features with an effort while two more batters showed their futility. Donnigan handed his catcher's glove to Swede Olson.

'Gimme that stick,' he growled. 'You birds belong in a home for the blind!'

There were two serious mistakes that Phil could make in this crisis and he made them both without delay. He struck out Hard-boiled Donnigan and he laughed. Of course he knew better than to ridicule the coach, but there was something irresistible about the way Donnigan lunged for that last slow floater.

'All right, now you've done your stuff, get out!' yelled the offended professional. 'And stay out, I can't monkey with a guy who won't take his work seriously. Laugh that off.'

A few snickers were thrown after the defeated candidate, but the players knew that Donnigan had commited a manager's unpardonable sin of turning down a promising recruit on a personal grudge—and he knew that they knew.

As for Phil, he left the stadium with genuine relief. The more he saw of Donnigan, the better he liked cows. He had kept his promise to Samboy; now he would just sink out of sight and stick to business.

In reply to an inquiry, Samboy got a letter from Mr Huckley stating that, in the opinion of an old Athens pitcher, Phil Fuller was the best that Branford High School had ever produced. The director showed this tribute to Donnigan.

'Oh, that's the sorrel top. He hasn't got anything but a giggle.'

'Are you sure, Hank? We could use a good southpaw.'

'I know, but he ain't the answer. This Athens bird is trying to frame us.'

'I'll wish him on the freshmen then.'

'Sure—give the kid a chanst, Ken,' said Donnigan with affected good will. 'He might show something if he ever gets over the idea it's all a big wheeze.'

Phil was heartily welcomed into the freshman squad. In the presence of Samboy he performed ably in a practice game. His fast ball, well-controlled curve, and change of pace made the inexperienced batters helpless, and his strange conduct landed him in the public eye with a bang.

The college comic paper, *The Cut-up*, had a fine time over Phil. It discovered that the eccentric left-hander was a cowbarner, and it almost died of laughter at this joke. 'Phil Fuller the Milk Pitcher' was the title of the piece. He was one of the wide-open faces from the wide-open spaces, the wit said, and sure winner of the standing broad grin. Also, he proved the truth of the old saying, 'Little pitchers have big ears.'

But the result of the publicity was that the crowd at the freshman-sophomore game was the largest of the season. Among those present were old President Whitman, Professor Wetherby, and Mr and Mrs Kenneth Samboy.

The assembled underclassmen laughed until they ached at the grinning, gesticulating, noisy southpaw with the red-thatched roof. They greeted his queer, awkward windup with a yell invented by the sophomore cheer leader, a long, rhythmic 'so—o—o, boss.' But when he had won the game handily for the freshmen, the jeers turned to cheers.

Sibyl Samboy looked at her husband.

'And why,' she asked, 'is this infant phenomenon not on the varsity?'

'Hank can't see him somehow, and if I butt in, it upsets my whole system of government. Personally I'd pitch him in a game or two to season him and then try him on Athens. But it isn't worth a rumpus, Sib. After all, Fuller will be with us a long time yet and Donnigan won't.'

'Poor old Hank! I wonder what he's got against the boy.'

'It's incompatibility of temperament, I guess. Hank thinks baseball is cosmic, and Phil thinks it's comic.'

'And you,' said Sibyl, 'I think you're a wisecracker on *The Cut-up*.'

In the next issue of that little weekly there was a marked difference in tone. The fresh cowboy, it said, was showing ability as well as risibility. It was time Donnigan tried him out on the team.

There was something inevitable about the Phil Fuller movement. Donnigan did not want him on the team, Samboy was committed to keep his hands off, and Phil himself had no craving to appear in that big stadium. But the team was limping through a disastrous season and there were signs of disaffection among the players. The crowds dwindled, finances were suffering, and the all-important Athens game, the schedule's climax, was approaching like the day of doom.

Donnigan resisted as long as he could, but schooled as he was in the professional game, he recognized one power greater than players, managers, or owners—the customers. And when white-haired Doctor Whitman called him into the president's office and intimated ever so gently that it might be just as well to give the public what it wanted, he gave in.

He did not surrender, but he retreated inch by inch. He gave Phil a uniform and let him practice with the team and learn the signals, then put him in at the end of a game that was already hopelesssly lost. On the eve of the Athens contest he announced that he would pitch Hagenlaucher with Graybar and Fuller in reserve.

Any contest with the traditional foe always brought out the largest crowd of the season, but this year there was a novelty in the situation. The freshmen were out in full force prepared to make an organized nuisance of themselves on behalf of their favorite character. When he appeared on the field for practice, they gave him a tremendous ovation.

Just before the game started, Phil realized that somebody was calling to him from the edge of the stand. To his great delight, this proved to be Mr Huckley, who had traveled all the way from Branford to see the game.

'Phil,' he said, 'if you get a chance today, I want you to do your darnedest.'

'I'd kinda hate to play against Athens after all you did for me.'

'I know. That's why I spoke. Forget all that, Phil. If they put you in, pitch as you did last year against Milltown, Three Falls, Oderno, and Jefferson. Good luck!'

'Thank you, Mr Huckley. I'll meet you right here after it's over. I've got something to tell you.'

As he took his seat on the bench his smile faded and he lapsed into gloom. 'He's scared stiff,' thought Donnigan. 'I won't dare to stick him in if Haggy blows.'

But Hagenlaucher was not blowing up; he was pitching his best game of the season. The Athens moundsman was doing well, too, and there was promise of a tight pitchers' battle. But in time the game grew looser, the pitchers faltered. Haggy was getting wabbly.

The score stood 6 to 5 in favor of the visitors in the fifth when the umpire made the momentous announcement. 'Greenwich batting for Hagenlaucher.' At the same moment Graybar and Fuller left for the bull pen to warm up. The next inning would see a new face in the box.

Whose face? That was what all Sparta wanted to know; that was what Samboy wanted to know as he stepped out of the stand and walked up to Donnigan.

'Graybar,' said the coach. 'Fuller is scared to death. I guess he's got a yellow streak.'

Samboy hesitated. The teams were changing sides now and the embattled freshmen were booming in unison, like a base drum: 'Phil! Phil! Phil!'

'All right, you're the doctor, Hank. But I'll go and talk to the boy.'

The new pitcher did his best, but he was a broken reed. A base on balls, a single, and a hit batter filled the bags, with nobody out, and the air was full of disaster. Captain Risler stepped to the box as if to steady the wobbly pitcher; Swede Olson, the catcher, joined this conference, which was further enriched by the presence of the lanky first baseman, Keeler.

Now Graybar handed the ball to Risler, who made a sign toward the bench. There was an instant of suspense, and then out of the dugout appeared the gaudy head of Phil Fuller.

An avalanche of sound slid down upon the field. From the freshman bloc came the long rhythmic yell, 'So—o—o, boss.' In the general confusion, Hard-boiled Donnigan was scarcely seen emerging from the dugout. He seemed to shrink before the wave of noise, then he disappeared through an opening out of the field, and out of the athletics department of Sparta.

Scarcely anyone in the audience knew that Donnigan had not ordered the change of pitchers, nor had Samboy. It was Risler, backed by Olson, Keeler, and the whole team. It was mutiny, it was rebellion.

But this was not the familiar Phil Fuller who had laughed and danced his way into the hearts of the fans. This was a serious Phil, a gloomy Phil. Life was now real, life was earnest. He took his long, queer windup and he threw the ball high, far too high. Olson made a jump for the ball, missed it, and landed in a heap. Before he could recover the ball, two runs had come over and Athens rocked with laughter.

But so, to the amazement of the universe, did Phil Fuller. It suddenly seemed to the misguided youth that it was the funniest thing in the world that he should have thrown away a ball and let in two runs. The infield laughed in imitation. Philip was himself again.

Now the tension under which the team had been working suddenly relaxed as if a tight band had snapped and brought relief. The nervous, eager, do-or-die spirit suddenly disappeared, leaving the natural instinct of youth to have a good time. With the utmost ease the pitcher and the infield disposed of the next three batters and in their half of the inning they began their climb toward victory.

It was a strange, exciting hilarious game. Phil had never played in such fast company before or faced such a murderous array of bats. He was in hot water half a dozen times, but he never lost the healing gift of laughter.

And the team played as if baseball came under the head of pleasure.

Samboy said to Risler, who sat beside him on the bench in the eighth:

'Whether we win or lose, this is the answer. We're going to build a new idea and a new style of play around that southpaw. You watch our smoke for the next three years, Rissy.'

'Just my luck, Ken. In about fifteen minutes I'm through with college baseball forever.'

'Well, don't you regret what you did today. I can't officially approve it, but—there goes Phil fanning again.'

Samboy now addressed the departing warriors.

'All right, boys—last frame and two to the good. All you have to do is hold 'em.'

Now it appeared that Phil had been saving the finest joke of all for the end. The season was over and he could take liberties with his arm. He dug his warts and bumps and calluses into the horsehide and proceeded to retire the side with three straight strike-outs, nine rowdy laughs, two informal dances, and an incredible noise that was a hideous parody on song.

But it was an altered and sobered Phil who found his old coach after the game and received his fervent congratulations.

'Were you worried, Phil?' Mr Huckley asked.

'Yes, but I was glad they let me play. I had so much fun I forgot my trouble.'

'What trouble, Phil?'

'Well, I got a letter from Father this morning and my Dolly is terribly sick. Seems she got hold of an old paint can some place. Cows like to lick paint, you know, and it's deadly poison. They don't think Dolly will live. Maybe I left a can of paint somewhere myself. That's what bothers me.'

'Listen, Phil. I was supposed to tell you but you got away too quick. Your father telephoned me this morning. Dolly's out of danger. She's doing fine.'

'Oh, boy!' cried Phil and his eyes shone with tears.

Down in the field the Sparta students, led by the band, were circling the stadium in that parade of victory that must follow every triumph over Athens.

'There'll be plenty more ball games,' said Phil, 'but there'll never be another cow like Dolly.'

Babe Ruth: One Of A Kind

RED SMITH

GRANTLAND RICE, the prince of sportswriters, used to do a weekly radio interview with some sporting figure. Frequently, in the interest of spontaneity, he would type out questions and answers in advance. One night his guest was Babe Ruth.

'Well, you know, Granny,' the Babe read in response to a question, 'Duke Ellington said the Battle of Waterloo was won on the playing fields of Elkton.'

'Babe,' Granny said after the show, 'Duke Ellington for the Duke of Wellington I can understand. But how did you ever read Eton as Elkton? That's in Maryland isn't it?'

'I married my first wife there,' Babe said, 'and I always hated the goddamn place,' He was cheerily unruffled. In the uncomplicated world of George Herman Ruth, errors were part of the game.

Babe Ruth died twenty-five years ago and his ample ghost has been with us all summer and he seems to grow more insistently alive every time Henry Aaron hits a baseball over a fence. What, people under fifty keep asking, what was this creature of myth and legend like in real life? If he were around today, how would he react when Aaron at last broke his hallowed record of 714 home runs? The first question may be impossible to answer fully; the second is easy.

'Well, what'd you know!' he would have said when the record got away. 'Babe loses another! Come on, have another beer.'

To paraphrase Abraham Lincoln's remark about another deity, Ruth must have admired records because he created so many of them. Yet he was sublimely aware that he transcended records and his place in the American scene was no mere matter of statistics. It wasn't just that he hit more home runs than anybody else, he hit them better, higher, farther, with more theatrical timing and a more flamboyant flourish. Nobody could strike out like Babe Ruth. Nobody circled the bases with the same pigeon-toed, mincing majesty.

'He was one of a kind,' says Waite Hoyt, a Yankee pitcher in the years of Ruthian splendor. 'If he had never played ball, if you had never heard of him and passed him on Broadway, you'd turn around and look.'

Looking, you would have seen a barrel swaddled in a wrap-around camel-hair topcoat with a flat camel-hair cap on the round head. Thus arrayed he was instantly recognizable not only on Broadway in New York but also on the Ginza in Tokyo. 'Baby Roos! Baby Roos!' cried excited crowds, following through the streets when he visited Japan with an all-star team in the early 1930s.

The camel-haired coat and cap are part of my last memory of the man. It must have been in the spring training season of 1948 when the Babe and everybody else knew he was dying of throat cancer. 'This is the last time around,' he had told Frank Stevens that winter when the head of the H. M. Stevens catering firm visited him in the French Hospital on West 30th Street, 'but before I go I'm gonna get out of here and have some fun.'

He did get out, but touring the Florida training camps surrounded by a gaggle of admen, hustlers and promoters, he didn't look like a man having fun. It was a hot day when he arrived in St Petersburg, but the camel-hair collar was turned up about the wounded throat. By this time, Al Lang Stadium had replaced old Waterfront Park where he had drawn crowds when the Yankees trained in St Pete.

'What do you remember best about this place?' asked Francis Stann of the *Washington Star*.

Babe gestured toward the West Coast Inn, an old frame building a city block beyond the right-field fence. 'The day I hit the adjectival ball against that adjectival hotel.' The voice was a hoarse stage whisper; the adjective was one often printed these days, but not here.

'Wow!' Francis Stann said. 'Pretty good belt.'

'But don't forget,' Babe said, 'the adjectival park was a block back this way then.'

Ruth was not noted for a good memory. In fact, the inability to remember names is part of his legend. Yet he needed no record books to remind him of his own special feats. There was, for example, the time he visited Philadelphia as a 'coach' with the Brooklyn Dodgers. (His coachly duties consisted of hitting home runs in batting practice.) This was in the late 1930s when National League games in Philadelphia were played in Shibe Park, the American League ground where Babe had performed. I asked him what memories stirred on his return.

'The time I hit one into Opal Street,' he said.

Now, a baseball hit over Shibe Park's right-field fence landed in 20th Street. Opal is the next street east, just a wide alley one block long. There may not be five hundred Philadelphians who know it by name, but Babe Ruth knew it.

Another time, during a chat in Hollywood, where he was an actor in the film *Pride of the Yankees*, one of us mentioned Rube Walberg, a good left-handed pitcher with the Philadelphia Athletics through the Ruth era. To some left-handed batters there is no dirtier word than the name of a good left-handed pitcher, but the Babe spoke fondly:

'Rube Walberg! What a pigeon! I hit twenty-three home runs off him.' Or whatever the figure was. It isn't in the record book but it was in Ruth's memory.

Obviously it is not true that he couldn't even remember the names of his teammates. It was only that the names he remembered were not always those bestowed at the baptismal font. To him Urban Shocker, a Yankee pitcher, was Rubber Belly. Pat Collins, the catcher, was Horse Nose. All redcaps at railroad stations were Stinkweed, and everybody else was Kid. One day Jim Kahn, covering the Yankees for the *New York Sun*, watched two players board a train with a porter toting the luggage.

'There go Rubber Belly, Horse Nose and Stinkweed,' Jim said.

Don Heffner joined the Yankees in 1934, Ruth's last year with the team. Playing second base through spring training, Heffner was stationed directly in the line of vision of Ruth, the right fielder. Breaking camp, the Yankees stopped in Jacksonville on a night when the Baltimore Orioles of the International League were also in town. A young reporter on the *Baltimore Sun* seized the opportunity to interview Ruth.

'How is Heffner looking?' he asked, because the second baseman had been a star with the Orioles in 1933.

'Who the hell is Heffner?' the Babe demanded. The reporter should, of course, have asked about the kid at second.

Jacksonville was the first stop that year on the barnstorming trip that would last two or three weeks and take the team to Yankee Stadium by a meandering route through the American bush. There, as everywhere, Ruth moved among crowds. Whether the Yankees played in Memphis or New Orleans or Selma, Alabama, the park was almost always filled, the hotel overrun if the team used a hotel, the railroad depot thronged. In a town of 5,000 perhaps 7,500 would see the game. Crowds were to Ruth as water to a fish. Probably the only time on record when he sought to avert a mob scene was the day of his second marriage. The ceremony was scheduled for 6 a.m. on the theory that people wouldn't be abroad then, but when he arrived at St Gregory's on West 90th Street, the church was filled and hundreds were waiting outside.

A reception followed in Babe's apartment on Riverside Drive, where the 18th Amendment did not apply. It was opening day of the baseball season but the weather intervened on behalf of the happy couple. The party went on and on, with entertainment by Peter de Rose, composer-pianist, and May Singhi Breen, who played the ukulele and sang.

Rain abated in time for a game next day. For the first time, Claire Ruth watched from a box near the Yankees' dugout, as she still does on ceremonial occasions. Naturally, the bridegroom hit a home run. Rounding the bases, he halted at second and swept off his cap in a courtly bow to his bride. This was typical of him. There are a hundred stories illustrating his sense of theater—how he opened Yankee Stadium (The House That Ruth Built) with a home run against the Red Sox, how at the age of forty he closed out his career as a player by hitting three mighty shots out of spacious Forbes Field in Pittsburgh, stories about the times he promised to hit a home run for some kid in a hospital and made good, and of course the one about calling his shot in a World Series.

That either did or did not happen in Chicago's Wrigley Field on October 1, 1932. I was there but I have never been dead sure of what I saw.

The Yankees had won the first two games and the score of the third was 4–4 when Ruth went to bat in the fifth inning with the bases empty and Charley Root pitching for the Cubs. Ruth had staked the Yankees to a three run lead in the first inning by hitting Root for a home run with two on base. Now Root threw a strike. Ruth stepped back and lifted a finger. 'One.' A second strike, a second upraised finger. 'Two'. Then Ruth made some sort of sign with his bat. Some said, and their version has become gospel, that he aimed it like a rifle at the bleachers in right center field. That's where he hit the next pitch. That made the score 5–4. Lou Gehrig followed with a home run and the Yankees won, 7–5, ending the Series the next day.

All the Yankees, and Ruth in particular, had been riding the Cubs unmercifully through every game, deriding them as cheapskates because in cutting up their World Series money the Chicago players had voted only one-fourth of a share to Mark Koenig, the former New York shortstop who had joined them in August and batted .353 in the last month of the pennant race. With all the dialogue and pantomine that went on, there was no telling what Ruth was saying to Root. When the papers reported that he had called his shot, he did not deny it.

A person familiar with Ruth only through photographs and records could hardly be blamed for assuming that he was a blubbery freak whose ability to hit balls across the county lines was all that kept him in the big leagues. The truth is that he was the complete ballplayer, certainly one of the greatest and maybe the one best of all time.

As a lefthanded pitcher with the Boston Red Sox, he won 18 games in his rookie season, 23 the next year and 24 the next before Ed Barrow assigned him to the outfield to keep him in the batting order every day. His record of pitching 29⅔ consecutive scoreless innings in World Series stood 43 years before Whitey Ford broke it.

He was an accomplished outfielder with astonishing range for his bulk, a powerful arm and keen baseball sense. It was said that he never made a mental error like throwing to the wrong base.

He recognized his role as public entertainer, and understood it. In the 1946 World Series the Cardinals made a radical shift in their defense against Ted Williams, packing the right side of the field and leaving the left virtually unprotected. 'They did that to me in the American League one year,' Ruth told the columnist, Frank Graham. 'I coulda hit .600 that year slicing singles to left.'

'Why didn't you?' Frank asked.

'That wasn't what the fans came out to see.'

He changed the rules, the equipment and the strategy of baseball. Reasoning that if one Babe Ruth could fill a park, sixteen would fill all the parks, the owners instructed the manufacturers to produce a livelier ball that would make every man a home-run king. As a further aid to batters, trick pitching deliveries like the spitball, the emery ball, the shame ball and the mud ball were forbidden.

The home run, an occasional phenomenon when a team hit a total of twenty in a season, came to be regarded as the ultimate offensive weapon. Shortstops inclined to swoon at the sight of blood had their bats made with all the wood up in the big end, gripped the slender handle at the very hilt and swung from the heels.

None of those devices produced another Ruth, of course, because Ruth was one of a kind. He recognized this as the simple truth and conducted himself accordingly. Even before they were married and Claire began to accompany him on the road, he always occupied the drawing room on the team's Pullman; he seldom shared his revels after dark with other players, although one year he did take a fancy to a worshipful rookie named Jimmy Reese and made him a companion until management intervened; if friends were not on hand with transportation, he usually took a taxi by himself to hotel or ball park or railroad station.

Unlike other players, Ruth was never seen in the hotel dining room or sitting in the lobby waiting for some passerby to discard a newspaper.

Roistering was a way of life, yet Ruth was no boozer. Three drinks of hard liquor left him fuzzy. He could consume great quantities of beer, he was a prodigious eater and his prowess with women was legendary. Sleep was something he got when other appetites were sated. He arose when he chose and almost invariably was the last to arrive in the clubhouse, where Doc Woods, the Yankee's trainer, always had bicarbonate of soda ready. Before changing clothes, the Babe would measure out a mound of bicarb smaller than the Pyramid of Cheops, mix and gulp it down.

'Then,' Jim Kahn says, 'he would belch. And all the loose water in the showers would fall down.'

The man was a boy, simple, artless, genuine and unabashed. This explains his rapport with children, whom he met as intellectual equals. Probably his natural liking for people communicated itself to the public to help make him an idol.

He was buried on a sweltering day in August 1948. In the pallbearers' pew, Waite Hoyt sat beside Joe Dugan, the third baseman. 'I'd give a hundred dollars for a cold beer,' Dugan whispered.

'So would the Babe,' Hoyt said.

The Young Pitcher

ZANE GREY

KEN WARD dug down into his trunk for his old baseball suit and donned it with strange elation. It was dirty and torn, and the shoes that went with it were worn out, but Ken was thinking of what hard ball playing they represented. He put his overcoat on over his sweater, took up his glove and sallied forth.

A thin coating of ice and snow covered the streets. Winter still whistled in the air. To Ken, in his eagerness, spring seemed a long way off. On his way across the campus he saw strings of uniformed boys making for Grant Field, and many wearing sweaters over their every-day clothes. The cage was situated at one end of the field apart from the other training quarters. When Ken got there he found a mob of players crowding to enter the door of the big barn-like structure. Others were hurrying away. Near the door a man was taking up tickets like a doorkeeper of a circus, and he kept shouting: 'Get your certificates from the doctor. Every player must pass a physical examination. Get your certificates.'

Ken turned somewhat in disgust at so much red tape and he jostled into a little fellow, almost knocking him over.

'Wull! Why don't you fall all over me?' growled this amiable individual, 'For two cents I'd hand you one.'

The apology on Ken's lips seemed to halt of its own accord.

'Sorry I haven't any change in these clothes,' returned Ken. He saw a wiry chap, older than he was, but much smaller, and of most aggresive front. He had his mouth turned down at the corners. He wore a disreputable uniform and a small green cap over one ear.

'Aw! don't get funny!' he replied.

Ken moved away muttering to himself: 'That fellow's a grouch.' Much to his amazement, when he got to the training house, Ken found that he could not get inside because so many players were there ahead of him. After waiting an hour or more he decided he could not have the physical examination at that time, and he went back to the cage. The wide door was still blocked with players, but at the other end of the building Ken found an entrance. He squeezed into a crowd of students and worked forward until stopped by a railing.

Ken was all eyes and breathless with interest. The cage was a huge, open, airy room, lighted by many windows, and, with the exception of the platform where he stood, it was entirely enclosed by heavy netting. The floor was of bare ground well raked and loosened to make it soft. This immense hall was full of a motley crowd of aspiring ball players.

Worry Arthurs, with his head sunk in the collar of his overcoat, and his shoulders hunched up as if he was about to spring upon something, paced up and down the rear end of the cage. Behind him a hundred or more players in line slowly marched toward the slab of rubber which marked the batting position. Ken remembered that the celebrated coach always tried out new players at the bat first. It was his belief that batting won games.

'Bunt one and hit one!' he yelled to the batters.

From the pitcher's box a lanky individual was trying to locate the plate. Ken did not heed a second glance to see that this fellow was no pitcher.

'Stop posin', and pitch!' yelled Arthurs.

One by one the batters faced the plate, swung valiantly or wildly at the balls and essayed bunts. Few hit the ball out and none made a creditable bunt. After their turn at the bat they were ordered to the other end of the cage where they fell over one another trying to stop the balls that were hit. Every few moments the coach would yell for one of them, any one, to take a turn at pitching. Ken noticed that Arthurs gave a sharp glance at each new batter, and one appeared to be sufficient. More and more ambitious players crowded into the cage, until there were so many that batted balls rarely missed hitting some one.

Presently Ken Ward awoke from his thrilling absorption in the scene to note another side of it. The students around him were making game of the players.

'What a bunch!'

'Look at the fuzzy gosling with the yellow pants!'

'Keep your shanks out of the way, Freshie!'

'Couldn't hit a balloon!'

Whenever a batter hit a ball into the crowd of dodging players down the cage these students howled with glee. Ken discovered that he was standing near Captain Dale and other members of the barred varsity.

'Say, Dale, how do the candidates shape up?' asked a student.

'This is a disgrace to Wayne,' declared Dale bitterly. 'I never saw such a mob of spindle-legged kids in my life. Look at them! Scared to death! that fellow never swung at a ball before—that one never heard of a bunt—they throw like girls?—Oh! this is sickening, fellows. I see where Worry goes to his grave this year and old Wayne gets humbled by one-horse colleges.'

Ken took one surprised glance at the captain he had admired so much and then he slipped farther over in the crowd. Perhaps Dale had spoken the truth, yet somehow it jarred upon Ken's sensitive nature. The thing that affected Ken most was the earnestness of the uniformed boys trying their best to do well before the great coach. Some were timid, uncertain; others were rash and over zealous. Many a ball cracked off a player's knee or wrist, and more than once Ken saw a bloody finger. It was cold in the cage. Even an ordinarily hit ball must have stung the hands, and the way a hard grounder cracked was enough to excite sympathy among those scornful spectators, if nothing more. But they yelled in delight at every fumble, at everything that happened. Ken kept whispering to himself: 'I can't see the fun in it. I can't!'

Arthurs dispensed with the bunting and ordered one hit each for the batters. 'Step up and hit!' he ordered, hoarsely. 'Don't be afraid—never mind that crowd—step into the ball and swing natural.

. . . Next! Hurry, boys!'

Suddenly a deep-chested student yelled out with a voice that drowned every other sound.

'Hard luck, Worry! No use! You'll never find a hitter among those misfits!'

The coach actually leaped up in his anger and his face went from crimson to white. Ken thought it was likely that he recognised the voice.

'You knocker! You knocker!' he cried. 'That's a fine college spirit, ain't it? You're a fine lot of students, I don't think. Now shut up, every one of you, or I'll fire you out of the cage . . . And right here at the start you knockers take this from me . . . I'll find more than one hitter among those kids!'

A little silence fell while the coach faced the antagonistic crowd of spectators. Ken was amazed the second time, and now because of the intensity of feeling that seemed to hang in the air, Ken felt a warm rush go over him, and that moment added greatly to his already strong liking for Worry Arthurs.

Then the coach turned to his work, the batting began again, and the crack of the ball, the rush of feet, the sharp cries of the players mingled once more with the laughter and caustic wit of the unsympathetic audience.

Ken Ward went back to his room without having removed his overcoat. He was thoughtful that night and rebellious against the attitude of the student body. A morning paper announced the fact that over three hundred candidates had presented themselves to Coach Arthurs. It went on to say that the baseball material represented was not worth considering and that old Wayne's varsity team must be ranked with those of the fifth rate colleges. This, following Ken's experience at the cage on the first day, made him angry and then depressed. The glamour of the thing seemed to fade away. Ken lost the glow, the exhilaration of his first feelings. Everybody took a hopeless view of Wayne's baseball prospects. Ken Ward, however, was not one to stay discouraged long, and when he came out of his gloom it was with his fighting spirit roused. Once and for all he made up his mind to work heart and soul for his college, to be loyal to Arthurs, to hope and believe in the future of the new varsity, whether or not he was lucky enough to win a place in it.

Next day, going early to the training quarters, he took his place in a squad waiting for the physical examination. It was a wearisome experience. At length Ken's turn came with two other players, one of whom he recognized as the sour-complexioned fellow of the day before.

'Wull, you're pretty fresh,' he said to Ken as they went in. He had a most exasperating manner.

'Say, I don't like you a whole lot,' retorted Ken.

Then a colored attendant ushered them into a large room in which were several men. The boys were stripped to the waist.

'Come here, Murray,' said the doctor. 'There's some use in looking these boys over, particularly this husky youngster.'

A tall man in a white sweater towered over Ken. It was the famous trainer. He ran his hands over Ken's smooth skin and felt his muscles.

'Can you run?' he asked.

'Yes,' replied Ken.

'Are you fast?'

'Yes.'

Further inquiries brought from Ken his name, age, weight, that he had never been ill, had never used tobacco or intoxicating drinks.

'Ward, eh? "Peg" Ward,' said Murray, smiling. 'Worry Arthurs has the call on you—else, my boy, I'd whisper football in your ear. Mebbe I will, anyhow, if you keep up your studies. That'll do for you.'

Ken's companions also won praise from the trainer. They gave their names as Raymond and Weir. The former weighed only one hundred and twenty two, but he was a knot of muscles. The other stood only five feet, but he was very broad and heavy, his remarkably compact build giving an impression of great strength. Both replied in the negative to the inquiries as to use of tobacco or spirits.

'Boys, that's what we like to hear,' said the doctor. 'You three ought to pull together.'

Ken wondered what the doctor would have said if he had seen the way these three boys glared at each other in the dressing room. And he wondered, too, what was the reason for such open hostility. The answer came to him in the thought that perhaps they were both trying for the position he wanted on the varsity. Most likely they had the same idea about him. That was the secret of little Raymond's pugnacious front and Weir's pompous air; and Ken realized that the same reason accounted for his own attitude toward them. He wanted very much to tell Raymond that he was a little grouch and Weir that he looked like a puffed-up toad. All the same Ken was not blind to Weir's handsome appearance. The sturdy youngster had an immense head, a great shock of bright brown hair, flashing grey eyes, and a clear bronze skin.

'They'll both make the team, I'll bet,' thought Ken. 'They look it. I hope I don't have to buck against them.' Then as they walked towards the cage Ken forced himself to ask genially: 'Raymond, what're you trying for? and you, Weir?'

'Wull, if it's any of your fresh business, I'm not trying for any place. I'm going to play infield. You can carry my bat,' replied Raymond, sarcastically.

'Much obliged,' retorted Ken, 'I'm not going to substitute. I've a corner on that varsity infield myself.'

Weir glanced at them with undisguised disdain. 'You can save yourselves useless work by not trying for my position. I intend to play infield.'

'Wull, puff-up, now, puff-up!' growled Raymond.

Thus the three self-appointed stars of the varsity bandied words among themselves as they crossed the field. At the cage door they became separated to mingle with the pushing crowd of excited boys in uniforms.

By dint of much squeezing and shoulder work Ken got inside the cage. He joined the squad in the upper end and got in line for the batting. Worry Arthurs paced wildly to and fro yelling for the boys to hit. A dense crowd of students thronged the platform and laughed, jeered, and stormed at the players. The cage was in such an uproar that Arthurs could scarcely be heard. Watching from the line Ken saw Weir come to bat and stand aggressively and hit the ball hard. It scattered the flock of fielders. Then Raymond came along, and, batting left-handed, did likewise. Arthurs stepped forward and said something to both. After Ken's turn at bat the coach said to him: 'Get out of here. Go run the track. Do it every day. Don't come back until Monday.'

As Ken hurried out he saw and felt the distinction with which he was regarded by the many players whom he crowded among in passing. When he reached the track he saw Weir, Raymond, and half a dozen other fellows going round at a jog-trot. Weir was in the lead, setting the pace. Ken fell in behind.

The track was the famous quarter-mile track upon which Murray trained his sprinters. When Ken felt the spring of the cinder-path in his feet, the sensation of buoyancy, the eager wildfire pride that flamed over him, he wanted to break into headlong flight. The first turn around the track was delight; the second pleasure in his easy stride; the third brought a realization of distance. When Ken had trotted a mile he was not tired, he still ran easily, but he began to appreciate that his legs were not wings. The end of the second mile found him sweating freely and panting.

Two miles were enough for the first day. Ken knew it and he began to wonder why the others, especially Weir, did not know it. But Weir jogged on, his head up, his hair flying, as if he had not yet completed his first quarter. The other players stretched out behind him. Ken saw Raymond's funny little green cap bobbing up and down, and it made him angry. Why could not the grouch get a decent cap, anyway?

At the end of the third mile Ken began to labour. His feet began to feel weighted, his legs to ache, his sides to hurt. He was wringing wet; his skin burned; his breath whistled. But he kept doggedly on. It had become a contest now. Ken felt instinctively that every runner would not admit he had less staying power than the others. Ken declared to himself that he could be as bull headed as any of them. Still to see Weir jogging on steady and strong put a kind of despair on Ken. For every lap of the fourth mile a runner dropped out, and at the half of the fifth only Weir, Raymond and Ken kept to the track.

Ken hung on gasping at every stride. He was afraid his heart would burst. The pain in his side was as keen as a knife thrust. His feet were lead. Every rod he felt must be his last, yet spurred on desperately, and he managed to keep at the heels of the others. It might kill him, but he would not stop until he dropped. Raymond was wagging along ready to fall any moment, and Weir was trotting slowly with head down. On the last lap of the fifth mile they all stopped as by one accord. Raymond fell on the grass; Ken staggered to a bench, and Weir leaned hard against the fence. They were all blowing like porpoises and regarded each other as mortal enemies. Weir gazed grandly at the other two; Raymond glowered savagely at him and then Ken; and Ken in turn gave them withering glances. Without a word the three contestants for a place on the varsity then went their several ways.

WHEN KEN presented himself at the cage on the following Monday it was to find that Arthurs had weeded out all but fifty of the candidates. Each afternoon for a week the coach put these players through batting and sliding practice, then ordered them out to run around the track. On the next Monday only twenty-five players were left, and as the number narrowed down the work grew more strenuous, the rivalry keener, and the tempers of the boys more irascible.

Ken discovered it was work and not by any means pleasant work. He fortified himself by the thought that the pleasure and glory, the real play, was all to come as a reward. Worry Arthurs drove them relentlessly. Nothing suited him; not a player knew how to hold a bat, to stand at the plate, to slide right, or to block a ground ball.

'Don't hit with your left hand on top—unless you're left-handed. Don't grip the end of the bat. There! Hold steady now, step out and into the ball, and swing clean and level. If you're afraid of bein' hit by the ball, get out of here!'

It was plain to Ken that not the least of Arthurs's troubles was the incessant gibing of the students on the platform. There was always a crowd watching the practice, noisy, scornful, abusive. They would never recover from the shock of having that seasoned champion varsity barred out of athletics. Every once in a while one of them would yell out. 'Wait, Worry! oh! Worry, wait till the old varsity plays your yanigans!' And every time the coach's face would burn. But he had ceased to talk back to the students. Besides, the athletic directors were always present. They mingled with the candidates and talked baseball to them and talked to Arthurs. Some of them might have played ball once, but they did not talk like it. Their advice and interference served only to make the coach's task harder.

Another Monday found only twenty players in the squad. That day Arthurs tried out catchers, pitchers, and infielders. He had them all throwing, running, fielding, working like Trojans. They would jump at his yell, dive after the ball, fall over it, throw it anywhere but in the right direction, run wild, and fight among themselves. The ever flowing ridicule from the audience was anything but a stimulus. So much of it coming from the varsity and their adherents kept continually in the minds of the candidates their lack of skill, their unworthiness to represent the great university in such a popular sport as baseball. So that even if there were latent ability in any of the candidates no one but the coach could see it. And often he could not conceal his disgust and hopelessness.

'Battin' practice!' he ordered, sharply. 'Two hits and a bunt to-day. Get a start on the bunt and dig for first. Hustle now!'

He placed one player to pitch to the hitters, another to catch, and as soon as the hitters had their turn they took to the fielding. Two turns for each at bat left the coach more than dissatisfied.

'You're all afraid of the ball,' he yelled. 'This ain't no dodgin' game. Duck your nut if the ball's goin' to hit you, but stop lookin' for it. Forget it. Another turn now. I'm goin' to umpire. Let's see if you know the difference between a ball and a strike.'

He changed the catcher and, ordering Ken to the pitcher's box, he stepped over behind him. 'Peg,' he said, speaking low, 'you're not tryin' for pitcher, I know, but you've got speed and control and I want you to peg 'em a few. Mind now, easy with your arm. By that I mean hold in, don't whip it. And you peg 'em as near where I say as you can; see?'

As the players, one after another, faced the box, the coach kept saying to Ken: 'Drive that fellow away from the plate . . . give this one a low ball . . . now straight over the pan. Say, Peg you've got a nice ball there . . . put a fast one under this fellow's chin.'

'Another turn, now, boys!' he yelled. 'I tell you—*stand up to the plate!*' Then he whispered to Ken 'Hit every one of them! Peg 'em now, any place.'

'Hit them?' asked Ken amazed.

'That's what I said.'

'But—Mr Arthurs—'

'See here, Peg. Don't talk back to me. Do as I say. We'll peg a little nerve into this bunch. Now I'll go back of the plate and make a bluff.'

Arthurs went near to the catcher's position. Then he said 'Now, fellows, Ward's pretty wild and I've told him to speed up a few. Stand right up and step into 'em.'

The first batter was Weir. Ken swung easily and let drive. Straight as a string the ball sped for the batter. Like a flash he dropped flat in the dust and the ball just grazed him. It was a narrow escape. Weir jumped up, his face flaring, his hair on end, and he gazed hard at Ken before picking up the bat.

'Batter up!' ordered the coach. 'Do you think this's a tea-party?'

Weir managed by quick contortions to get through his time at bat without being hit. Three players following him were not so lucky.

'Didn't I say he was wild?' yelled the coach. 'Batter up now!'

The next was little Raymond. He came forward cautiously, eyeing Ken with disapproval. Ken could not resist putting on a little more steam, and the wind of the first ball whipped off Raymond's green cap. Raymond looked scared and edged away from the plate, and as the second ball came he stepped wide with his left foot.

'Step into the ball,' said the coach. 'Don't pull away. Step in or you'll never hit.'

The third ball cracked low down on Raymond's leg.

'Oh!—Oh!—Oh!' he howled, beginning to hop and hobble about the cage.

'Next batter!' called Arthurs. And so it went on until the most promising player in the cage came to bat. This was Graves, a light-haired fellow, tall, built like a wedge. He had more confidence than any player in the squad and showed up well in all departments of the game. Moreover, he was talky, aggressive, and more inclined to be heard and felt. He stepped up and swung his bat at Ken.

'You wild freshman! If you hit me!' he cried.

Ken Ward had not fallen in love with any of his rivals for places on the team, but he especially did not like Graves. He did not stop to consider the reason of it at the moment, still he remembered several tricks Graves had played, and he was not altogether sorry for the coach's order. Swinging a little harder, Ken threw straight at Graves.

'*Wham!*' The ball struck him fair on the hip. Limping away from the plate he shook his fist at Ken.

'Batter up!' yelled Arthurs. 'A little more speed now, Peg. You see it ain't nothin' to get hit. Why, that's in the game. It don't hurt much. I never cared when I used to get hit. Batter up!'

Ken sent up a very fast ball, on the outside of the plate. The batter swung wide, and the ball, tipping the bat, glanced to on side and struck Arthurs in the stomach with a deep sound.

Arthurs' round face went red; he gurgled and gasped for breath; he was sinking to his knees when the yelling and crowing of the students on the platform straightened him up. He walked about a few minutes, then ordered sliding practice.

The sliding board was brought out. It was almost four feet wide and twenty long and covered with carpet.

'Run hard, boys, and don't let up just before you slide. Keep your speed and dive. Now at it!'

A line of players formed down the cage. The first one dashed forward and plunged at the board, hitting it with a bang. The carpet was slippery and he slid off and rolled in the dust. The second player leaped forward and, sliding too soon, barely reached the board. One by one, others followed.

'Run fast now!' yelled the coach. 'Don't flinch ... Go down hard and slide light on your hands ... keep your heads up ... slide!'

This feature of cage work caused merriment among the onlookers. That sliding-board was a wonderful and treacherous thing. Most players slid off it as swift as a rocket. Arthurs kept them running so fast and so close together that at times one would shoot off the board just as the next would strike it. They sprawled on the ground, rolled over, and rooted in the dust. One skinned his nose on the carpet; another slid the length of the board on his ear. All the time they kept running and sliding, the coach shouted to them, and the audience roared with laughter. But it was no fun for the sliders. Raymond made a beautiful slide, and Graves was good, but all the others were ludicrous.

It was a happy day for Ken, and for all the candidates, when the coach ordered them out on the field. This was early in March. The sun was bright, the frost all out of the ground, and a breath of spring was in the air. How different it was from the cold gloomy cage! Then the mocking students, although more in evidence than before, were confined to the stands and bleachers, and could not so easily be heard. But the presence of the regular varsity team, practising at the far end of Grant Field, had its effect on the untried players.

The coach divided his players into two nines and had them practise batting first, then fielding, and finally started them in a game, with each candidate playing the position he hoped to make on the varsity.

It was a weird game. The majority of the twenty candidates displayed little knowledge of baseball. Schoolboys on the commons could have beaten them. They were hooted and hissed by the students, and before half the innings were played the bleachers and stands were empty. That was what old Wayne's students thought of Arthurs's candidates.

In sharp contrast to most of them, Weir, Raymond, and Graves showed they had played the game somewhere. Weir at short-stop covered ground well, but he could not locate first base. Raymond darted here and there quick as a flash, and pounced upon the ball like a huge frog. Nothing got past him, but he juggled the ball. Graves was a finished and beautiful fielder; he was easy, sure, yet fast, and his throw from third to first went true as a line.

Graves's fine work accounted for Ken Ward's poor showing. Both were trying for third base, and when Ken once saw his rival play out on the field he not only lost heart and became confused, but he instinctively acknowledged that Graves was far his superior. After all his hopes and the kind interest of the coach it was a most bitter blow. Ken had never played so poor a game. The ball blurred in his tear-wet eyes and looked double. He did not field a grounder. He muffled foul flies and missed thrown balls. It did not occur to him that almost all of the players around him were in the same boat. He could think of nothing but the dashing away of his hopes. What was the use of trying? But he kept trying and the harder he tried the worse he played. At the bat he struck out, fouled out, never hit the ball square at all. Then when Ken was in the field Graves would come down the coaching line, and talk to him in a voice no one else could hear.

'You've got a swell chance to make this team, you have, *not*! Third base is my job, Freshie. Why, you tow-head, you couldn't play marbles. You butter-finger, can't you stop anything? You can't even play sub on this team. Remember, Ward, I said I'd get you for hitting me that day. You hit me with a potato once, too. I'll chase you off this team.'

For once Ken's spirit was so crushed and humbled that he could not say a word to his rival. He even felt he deserved it all. When the practice ended, and he was walking off the field with hanging head, trying to bear up under the blow, he met Arthurs.

'Hello! Peg', said the Coach. 'I'm going your way.'

Ken walked along feeling Arthurs's glance upon him, but he was ashamed to raise his head.

'Peg, you were up in the air today—way off—you lost your nut.'

He spoke kindly and put his hand on Ken's arm. Ken looked up to see that the coach's face was pale and tired, with the characteristic worried look more marked than usual.

'Yes, I was,' replied Ken, impulsively. 'I can play better than I did today—but—Mr Arthurs, I'm not in Graves's class as a third baseman. I know it.'

Ken said it bravely, though there was a catch in his voice. The coach looked closely at him.

'So you're sayin' a good word for Graves, plugging his game.'

'I'd love to make the team, but old Wayne must have the best players you can get.'

'Peg, I said once you and me were goin' to get along. I said also that college baseball is played with the heart. You lost your heart. So did most of the kids. Well, it ain't no wonder. This 's a tryin' time. I'm playing them against each other, and no fellow knows what he's at. Now, I've seen all along that you weren't a natural infielder. I played you at third to-day to get that idea out of your head. Tomorrow I'll try you in the outfield. You ain't no quitter Peg.'

Ken hurried to his room under the stress of a complete revulsion of feeling. His liking for the coach began to grow into something more. It was strange to Ken what power a few words from Arthurs had to renew his will and hope and daring. How different Arthurs was when not on the field. There he was stern and sharp. Ken could not study that night, and he slept poorly. His revival of hope did not dispel his nervous excitement.

He went out into Grant Field next day fighting himself. When in the practice Arthurs assigned him to a right field position, he had scarcely taken his place when he became conscious of a queer inclination to swallow often, of a numbing tight band around his chest. He could not stand still; his hands trembled; there was a mist before his eyes. His mind was fixed upon himself and upon the other five outfielders trying to make the team. He saw the players in the infield pace their positions restlessly, run without aim when the ball was hit or thrown, collide with each other, let the ball go between their hands and legs, throw wildly, and sometimes stand as if transfixed when they ought to have been in action. But all this was not significant to Ken. He saw everything that happened, but he thought only that he must make a good showing; he must not miss any flies, or let a ball go beyond him. He absolutely must do the right thing. The air of Grant Field was charged with intensity of feeling, and Ken thought it was all his own. His baseball fortune was at stake, and he worked himself in such a frenzy that if a ball had been batted in his direction he might have not seen it all. Fortunately none came his way.

The first time at bat he struck out ignominiously, poking weakly at the pitcher's out curves. The second time he popped up a little fly. On the next trial the umpire called him out on strikes. At his last chance Ken was desperate. He knew the coach placed batting before any other department of the game. Almost sick with the torture of the conflicting feelings, Ken went up to the plate and swung blindly. To his amaze he cracked a hard fly to left center, far between the fielders. Like a startled deer Ken broke into a run. He turned first base and saw that he might stretch the hit into a tree-bagger. He knew he could run, and never had he so exerted himself. Second base sailed under him, and he turned in line for the third. Watching Graves, he saw him run for the base and stand ready to catch the throw in.

Without slacking his speed in the least Ken leaped into the air headlong for the base. He heard the crack of the ball as it hit Graves's glove. Then with swift scrape of hands and breast he was sliding in the dust. He stopped suddenly as if blocked by a stone wall. Something hard struck him on the head. A blinding light within his brain seemed to explode into glittering slivers. A piercing pain shot through him. Then from the darkness and a great distance sounded a voice: 'Ward, I said I'd get you!'

THAT incident put Ken out of the practice for three days. He had a bruise over his ear as large as a small apple. Ken did not mind the pain nor the players' remarks that he had a swelled head anyway, but he remembered with slow-gathering wrath Graves's words: 'I said I'd get you!'

He remembered also Graves's reply to a question put by the coach. 'I was only tagging him. I didn't mean to hurt him.' That rankled inside Ken. He kept his counsel, however, even evading a sharp query put by Arthurs, and as much as it was possible he avoided the third-baseman.

Hard practice was the order of the day, and most of it was batting. The coach kept at the candidates everlastingly, and always his cry was: 'Toe the plate, left foot a little forward, step into the ball and swing!' At the bat Ken made favourable progress because the coach was always there behind him with encouraging words; in the field, however, he made a mess of it, and grew steadily worse.

The directors of the Athletic Association had called upon the old varsity to go out and coach the new aspirants for college fame. The varsity had refused. Even the players of preceding years, what few were in or near the city, had declined to help develop Wayne's stripling team. But some of the older graduates, among them several of the athletic directors, appeared on the field. When Arthurs saw them he threw up his hands in rage and despair. That afternoon Ken had three well-meaning, but old-fashioned ball players coach him in the outfield. He had them one at a time, which was all that saved him from utter distraction. One told him to judge a fly by the sound when the ball was hit. Another told him to play in close, and when the ball was batted to turn and run with it. The third said he must play deep and sprint in for the fly. Then each had different ideas as to how batters should be judged, about throwing to bases, about backing up the other fielders. Ken's bewilderment grew greater and greater. He had never heard of things they advocated, and he began to think he did not know anything about the game. And what made his condition of mind border on imbecility was a hurried whisper from Arthurs between innings: 'Peg, don't pay the slightest attention to 'em fat-head grad coaches.'

Practice days succeeding that were worse nightmares to Ken Ward than the days he had spent in constant fear of the sophomores. It was a terrible feverish time of batting balls, chasing balls, and of having dinned into the ears thousands of orders, rules of play, talks on college spirit in athletics—all of which conflicted so that it was meaningless to him. During his dark time one ray of light was the fact that Arthurs never spoke a sharp word to him. Ken felt vaguely that he was whirling in some kind of a college athletic chaos, out of which he would presently emerge.

Towards the close of March the weather grew warm, the practice field dried up, and baseball should have been a joy to Ken. But it was not. At times he had a shameful wish to quit the field for good, but he had not the courage to tell the coach. The twenty-fifth day, the day scheduled for the game with the disgraced varsity team loomed closer and closer. Its approach was a fearful thing for Ken. Everyday he cast furtive glances down the field to where the varsity held practice. Ken had nothing to say; he was as glum as most of the other candidates, but he had heard gossip in the lecture-rooms, in the halls, on the street, everywhere, and it concerned this game. What would the old varsity do to Arthurs's new team? Curiosity ran as high as the feeling toward the athletic directors. Resentment flowed from every source. Ken somehow got the impression that he was blamable for being a member of the coach's green squad. So Ken Ward fluctuated between two fears, one as bad as the other—that he would not be selected to play, and the other that he would be selected. It made no difference. He would be miserable if not chosen, and if he was—how on earth would he be able to keep his knees from wobbling? Then the awful day dawned.

Coach Arthurs met all his candidates at the cage. He came late, he explained, because he wanted to keep them off the field until time for practice. Today he appeared more grave than worried, and where the boys expected a severe lecture, he simply said: 'I'll play as many of you as I can. Do your best, that's all. Don't mind what these old players say. They were kids once, though they seem to have forgotten it. Try to learn from them.'

It was the first time the candidates had been taken upon the regular diamond of Grant Field. Ken had peeped in there once to be impressed by the beautiful level playground, and especially the magnificent turreted grandstand and the great sweeping stretches of bleachers. Then they had been empty; now, with four thousand noisy students and thousands of other spectators besides, they stunned him. He had never imagined a crowd coming to see the game.

Perhaps Arthurs had not expected it either, for Ken heard him mutter grimly to himself. He ordered practice at once, and called off the names of those he had chosen to start the game. As one in a trance Ken Ward found himself trotting out to right field.

A long-rolling murmur that was half laugh, half taunt, rose from the stands. Then it quickly subsided. From his position Ken looked for the players of the old varsity, but they had not yet come upon the field. Of the few balls batted to Ken in practice he muffed only one, and he was just beginning to feel that he might acquit himself creditably when the coach called the team in. Arthurs had hardly given his new players time enough to warm up, but likewise they had not had time to make any fumbles.

All at once a hoarse roar rose from the stands, then a thundering clatter of thousands of feet as the students greeted the appearance of the old varsity. It was applause that had in it all the feeling of the undergraduates for the championship team, many of whom they considered had been unjustly barred by the directors. Love, loyalty, sympathy, resentment—all pealed up to the skies in that acclaim. It rolled out over the heads of Arthurs's shrinking boys as they huddled together on the bench.

Ken Ward, for one, was flushing and thrilling. In that moment he lost his gloom. He watched the varsity come trotting across the field, a doughty band of baseball warriors. Each wore a sweater with the huge white 'W' shining like a star. Many of those players had worn that honoured varsity letter for three years. It did seem a shame to bar them from this season's team. Ken found himself thinking of the matter from their point of view, and his sympathy was theirs.

More than that, he gloried in the look of them, in the trained, springy strides, in the lithe, erect forms, in the assurance in every move. Every detail of that practice photographed itself upon Ken Ward's memory, and he knew he would never forget.

There was Dale, veteran player, captain and pitcher of the nine, hero of victories over Place and Herne. There was Hogan, catcher for three seasons, a muscular fellow, famed for his snap throw to the bases and his fiendish chasing of foul flies. There was Hickle, the great first baseman, whom the professional leagues were trying to get. What a reach he had; how easily he scooped in the ball; low, high, wide, it made no difference to him. There was Canton at second, Hollis at short, Burns at third, who had been picked for the last year's All-American College team. Then there was Dreer, brightest star of all, the fleet hard-hitting center fielder. This player particularly fascinated Ken. It was a beautiful sight to see him run. The ground seemed to fly behind him. When the ball was hit high he wheeled with his back to the diamond and raced out, suddenly to turn with unerring judgement—and the ball dropped into his hands. On low line hits he showed his fleetness, for he was like a gleam of light in his forward dash; and, low by his knees, or on a short bound, he caught it. Ken Ward saw with despairing admiration what it meant to be a great outfielder.

Then Arthurs called 'Play ball!' giving the old varsity the field.

With a violent start Ken Ward came out of his rhapsody. He saw a white ball tossed on the diamond. Dale received it from one of the fielders and took his position in the pitcher's box. The uniform set off his powerful form; there was something surly and grimly determined in his face. He glanced about to his players, as if from long habit, and calling out gruffly: 'Get in the game, fellows! No runs for this scrub outfit!' Then, with long-practiced swing, he delivered the ball. It travelled plateward swift as the flight of a white swallow. The umpire called it a strike on Weir; the same on the next pitch; the third was wide. Weir missed the fourth and was out. Raymond followed on the batting list. Today, as he slowly stepped toward the plate, seemingly smaller and glummer than ever, it was plain he was afraid. The bleachers howled at the little green cap sticking over his ear. Raymond did not swing at the ball; he sort of reached out his bat at the first three pitches, stepping back from the plate each time. The yell that greeted his weak attempt seemed to shrivel him up. Also it had its effect on the youngsters huddling around Arthurs. Graves went up and hit a feeble grounder to Dale and was thrown out at first.

Ken knew the half innings was over; he saw the varsity players throw aside their gloves and trot in. But either he could not rise or he was glued to the bench. Then Arthurs pulled him up, saying 'Watch sharp, Peg, these fellows are right field hitters!' At these words all Ken's blood turned to ice. He ran out into the field fighting the coldest, most sickening sensation he ever had in his life. The ice in his veins all went to the pit of his stomach, and there formed into a heavy lump. Other times when he had been frightened flitted through his mind. It had been bad when he fought with Greaser, and worse when he ran with the outlaws in pursuit, and the forest fire was appalling. But Ken felt he would gladly have changed places at that moment. He dreaded the mocking bleachers.

Of the candidates chosen to play against the varsity Ken knew McCord at first, Raymond at second, Weir at short, Graves at third. He did not know even the names of the others. All of them except Graves, appeared too young to play in that game.

Dreer was first up for the varsity, and Ken shivered all over when the little center fielder stepped to the left side of the plate. Ken went out deeper, for he knew most hard-hitting left-handers hit to right field. But Dreer bunted the first ball teasingly down the third base line. Fleet as a deer he was across the bag before the infielder reached the ball. Hollis was next up. On the first pitch, as Dreer got a fast start for second, Hollis bunted down the first-base line. Pitcher and base-man ran for the bunt; Hollis was safe, and the sprinting Dreer went to third without even drawing a throw. A long pealing yell rolled over the bleachers. Dale sent coaches to the coaching lines. Hickle, big and formidable, hurried to the plate, swinging a long bat. He swung it as if he intended to knock the ball out of the field. When the pitcher lifted his arm Dreer dashed for home base, and seemed beating the ball. But Hickle deftly dumped it down the line and broke for first while Dreer scored. This bunt was not fielded at all. How the bleachers roared! Then followed the bunts in rapid succession, dashes for first, and slides into the bag. The pitcher failed to cover the bag, and the catcher fell over the ball. Every varsity man bunted, but in just the place where it was not expected. They raced around the bases. They made long runs from the first to third. They were like flashes of light, slippery eels. The bewildered infielders knew they were being played with. The taunting 'boo-hoos' and screams of delight from the bleachers were as demoralizing as the illusively daring runners. Closer and closer the infielders edged in until they were right on top of the batters. Then Dale and his men began to bung little infield flies over the heads of their opponents. The merry audience cheered wildly. But Graves and Raymond ran back and caught three of these little pop flies, thus, retiring the side. The old varsity had made six runs on nothing but deliberate bunts and daring dashes around the bases.

Ken hurried in to the bench and heard some one call out 'Ward up!'

He had forgotten he would have to bat. Stepping to the plate was like facing a cannon. One of the players yelled: 'Here he is, Dale! Here's the potato-pegger! Knock his block off!'

The cry was taken up by other players. 'Peg him, Dale! Peg him, Dale!' And the bleachers got it. Ken's dry tongue seemed pasted to the roof of his mouth. This Dale in baseball clothes with the lowering frown was not like the Dale Ken had known. Suddenly he swung his arm. Ken's quick eye caught the dark, shooting gleam of the ball. Involuntarily he ducked. 'Strike' called the umpire. Then Dale had not tried to hit him. Ken stepped up again. The pitcher whirled slowly this time, turning with long, easy motion, and threw underhand. The ball sailed, floated, soared. Long before it reached Ken it had fooled him completely. He chopped at it vainly. The next ball pitched came up swifter, but just before it crossed the plate it seemed to stop, as if pulled back by a string, and then dropped down. Ken fell to his knees trying to hit it.

The next batter's attempts were not as awkward as Ken's still they were as futile. As Ken sat wearily down upon the bench he happened to get next to coach Arthurs. He expected some sharp words from the coach, he thought he deserved anything, but they were not forthcoming. The coach put his hand on Ken's knee. When the third batter fouled to Hickle, and Ken got up to go out to the field he summoned courage to look at Arthurs. Something in his face told Ken what an ordeal this was. He divined that it was vastly more than business with Worry Arthurs.

'Peg, watch out this time,' whispered the coach. 'They'll line 'em at you this inning—like bullets. Now try hard, won't you? *Just try!*'

Ken knew from Arthurs' look more than his words that *trying* was all that was left for the youngsters. The varsity had come out early in the spring, and they had practiced to get into condition to annihilate this new team practically chosen by the athletic directors. And they had set out to make the game a farce. But Arthurs meant that all the victory was not in winning the game. It was left for his boys to try in the face of certain defeat, to try with all their hearts, to try with unquenchable spirit. It was the spirit that counted, not the result. The old varsity had received a bitter blow; they were aggressive and relentless. The students and supporters of old Wayne, idolizing the great team, always bearing in mind the hot rivalry with Place and Herne, were unforgiving and intolerant of an undeveloped varsity. Perhaps neither could be much blamed. But it was for the new players to show what it meant to them. The greater the prospect of defeat, the greater the indifference or hostility shown them, the more splendid their opportunity. For it was theirs to try for old Wayne, to try, to fight, and never to give up.

Ken caught fire with the flame of that spirit.

'Boys, come on!' he cried, in his piercing tenor. *'They can't beat us trying!'*

As he ran out into the field members of the varsity spoke to him 'You green-backed freshman! Shut up! You scrub!'

'I'm not a varsity has-been!' retorted Ken, hurrying out to his position.

The first man up, a left-hander, rapped a hard twisting liner to right field. Ken ran toward deep centre with all his might. The ball kept twisting and curving. It struck squarely in Ken's hands and bounced out and rolled far. When he recovered it the runner was on third base. Before Ken got back to his position the second batter hit hard through the infield toward right. The ball came skipping like a fiendish rabbit. Ken gritted his teeth and went down on his knees, to get the bounding ball full in his breast. But he stopped it, scrambled for it, and made the throw in. Dale likewise hit in his direction, a slow low fly, difficult to judge. Ken overran it, and the hit gave Dale two bases. Ken realized that the varsity was now executing Worry Arthurs's famous right-field hitting. The sudden knowledge seemed to give Ken the blind staggers. The field was in a haze; the players blurred in his sight. He heard the crack of the ball and saw Raymond dash over and plunge down. Then the ball seemed to streak out of the grass toward him, and as he bent over, it missed his hands and cracked on his shin. Again he fumbled wildly for it and made the throw in. The pain roused his rage. He bit his lips and called to himself: 'I'll stop them if it kills me.'

Dreer lined the ball over his head for a home run. Hollis made a bid for a three-bagger, but Ken, by another hard sprint, knocked the ball down. Hickle then batted up a tremendously high fly. It went far beyond Ken and he ran and ran. It looked like a small pin-point of black up in the sky. The white sky suddenly glazed over and the ball wavered this way and that. Ken lost it in the sun, found it again, and kept on running. Would it never come down? He had not reached it, he had run beyond it. In an agony he lunged out, and the ball fell into his hands and jumped out.

Then followed a fusillade of hits, all between second base and first, and all vicious-bounding grounders. To and fro Ken ran, managing somehow to get some portion of his anatomy in front of the ball. It had become a demon to him now and he hated it. His tongue was hanging out, his breast was bursting, his hands were numb, yet he held before him the one idea to keep fiercely trying.

He lost count of the runs after eleven had been scored. He saw McCord and Raymond trying to stem the torrent of rightfield hits, but those they knocked down gave him no time to recover. He blocked the grass-cutters with his knees or his body and pounced upon the ball and got it away from him as quickly as possible. Would this rapid fire of uncertain-bounding balls never stop? Ken was in a kind of frenzy. If he had only time to catch his breath.

Then Dreer was at bat again. He fouled the first two balls over the grandstand. Someone threw out a brand-new ball. Farther and farther Ken edged into deep right. He knew what was coming. 'Let him—hit it!' he panted. 'I'll try to get it! This day settles me. I'm no outfielder. But I'll try!'

The tired pitcher threw the ball and Dreer seemed to swing and bound at once with the ringing crack. This hit was one of his famous drives close to the right-field foul line.

Ken set off with all the speed left in him. He strained every nerve and was going fast when he passed the foul flag. The bleachers loomed up indistinct in his sight. But he thought only of meeting the ball. The hit was a savage liner, curving away from him. Cinders under his flying feet were a warning that he did not heed. He was on the track. He leaped into the air, left hand outstretched, and felt the ball strike in his glove.

Then all was dark in a stunning, blinding crash—.

WHEN KEN WARD came fully to his senses he was being half carried and half led across the diamond to the players' bench. He heard Worry Arthurs say: 'He ain't hurt much—only butted into the fence.'

Ken tried manfully to entertain Worry's idea about it, but he was too dazed and weak to stand alone. He imagined he had broken every bone in his body.

'Did I make the catch—hang to the ball?' he asked.

'No, Peg, you didn't,' replied the coach, kindly. 'But you made a grand try for it.'

He felt worse for failing to hold the ball than he felt over half killing himself against the bleachers. He spent the remainder of that never-to-be-forgotten game sitting on the bench. But to watch his fellow-players try to play was almost as frightful as being back there in right field. It was no consolation for Ken to see his successor chasing long hits, misjudging flies, failing weakly on wicked grounders. Even Graves weakened toward the close and spoiled his good beginning by miserable fumbles and throws. It was a complete and disgraceful rout. The varsity never let up until the last man was out. The team could not have played harder against Place or Herne. Arthurs called the game at the end of the sixth innings with the score 41 to 0.

Many beaten and despondent players had dragged themselves off Grant Field in bygone years. But none had ever been so humiliated, so crushed. No player spoke a word or looked at another. They walked off with bowed heads. Ken lagged behind the others; he was still stunned and lame. Presently Arthurs came back to help him along, and did not speak until they were clear of the campus and going down Ken's street.

'I'm glad that's over,' said Worry. 'I kicked against havin' the game, but 'em fat-headed directors would have it. Now we'll be let alone. There won't be no students comin' out to the field, and I'm blamed glad.'

Ken was sick and smarting with pain, and half crying.

'I'm sorry, Mr Arthurs,' he faltered, 'we were—so—so—rotten!'

'See here, Peg' was the quick reply 'that cuts no ice with me. It was sure the rottenest exhibition I ever seen in my life. But there's excuses, and you can just gamble I'm the old boy who knows. You kids were scared to death. What hurt me, Peg, is the throw down we got from my old team and from the students. We're not to blame for rules made by fathead directors. I was surprised at Dale. He was mean, and so were Hollis and Hickle—all of 'em. They didn't need to disgrace us like that.'

'Oh, Mr Arthurs, what players they are!' exclaimed Ken. 'I never saw such running, such hitting. You said they'd hit to right field like bullets, but it was worse than bullets. And Dreer! . . . When he came up my heart just stopped beating.'

'Peg, listen,' said Worry, 'Three years ago when Dreer came out on the field he was greener than you, and hadn't half the spunk. I made him what he is, and I made all of 'em—I made that team, and I can make another.'

'You are just saying that to—to encourage me.' replied Ken, hopelessly. 'I can't play ball. I thought I could, but I know now. I'll never go out on the field again.'

'Peg, you are goin' to throw me down too?'

'Mr Arthurs! I—I—'

'Listen Peg. Cut out the dumps. Get over 'em. You made the varsity today. Understand? You earned your big W. You needn't mention it, but I've picked you to play somewhere. You weren't a natural infielder, and you didn't make much of a showin' in the outfield. But it's the spirit I want. Today was a bad day for a youngster. There's always lots of feelin' about college athletics, but here at Wayne this year the strain's awful. And you fought yourself and stagefright and the ridicule of 'em quitter students. You *tried*, Peg! I never saw a gamer try. You didn't fail me. And after you made that desperate run and tried to smash the bleachers with your face the students shut up their guying. It made a difference, Peg. Even the varsity was a little ashamed. Cheer up, now!'

Ken was almost speechless; he managed to mumble something, at which the coach smiled in reply and then walked rapidly away. Ken limped to his room and took off his baseball suit. The skin had been peeled from his elbow, and his body showed several dark spots that Ken knew would soon be black-and-blue bruises. His legs from his knees down bore huge lumps so sore to the touch that Ken winced even at gentle rubbing. But he did not mind the pain. All the darkness seemed to have blown away from his mind.

'What a fine fellow Worry is!' said Ken 'How I'll work for him! I must write to brother Hal and Dick Leslie, to tell them I've made the varsity ... No, not yet; Worry said not to mention it ... And now to plug. I'll have to take my exams before the first college game, April 8th, and that's not long.'

In the succeeding days Ken was very busy with attendance at college in the mornings, baseball practice in the afternoons, and study at night.

If Worry had picked any more players for the varsity. Ken could not tell who they were. Of course Graves would make the team, and Weir and Raymond were pretty sure of places. There were sixteen players for the other five positions, and picking them was only guesswork. It seemed to Ken that some of the players showed streaks of fast playing at times, and then as soon as they were opposed to one another in the practice game they became erratic. His own progress was slow. One thing he could do that brought warm praise from the coach—he could line the ball home from deep outfield with wonderful speed and accuracy.

After the varsity had annihilated Worry's 'Kids', as they had come to be known, the students showed no further interest. When they ceased to appear on the field the new players were able to go at their practice without being ridiculed. Already an improvement had been noticeable. But rivalry was so keen for places, and the coach's choice so deep a mystery, that the contestants played under too great a tension, and schoolboys could have done better.

It was on the first of April that Arthurs took Ken up into College Hall to get permission for him to present himself to the different professors for the early examinations. While Ken sat waiting in the office he heard Arthurs talking to men he instantly took to be the heads of the Athletic Association. They were in an adjoining room with the door open, and their voices were very distinct, so that Ken could not help hearing.

'Gentlemen, I want my answer to-day' said the coach.

'Is there so great a hurry? Wait a little,' was the rejoinder.

'I'm sorry, but this is April 1st and I'll wait no longer. I'm ready to send some of my boys up for early exams, and I want to know where I stand.'

'Arthurs, what is it exactly that you want? Things have been in an awful mess, we know. State your case and we'll try to give you a definite answer.'

'I want full charge of the coachin'—the handlin' of the team, as I always had before. I don't want any grad coaches. The directors seem divided, one half want this, the other half that. They've cut out the trainin' quarters. I've had no help from Murray; no baths or rub-downs or trainin' for my candidates. Here's openin' day a week off and I haven't picked my team. I want to take them to the trainin' table and have them under my eye all the time. If I can't have what I want I'll resign. If I can I'll take the whole responsibility of the team on my shoulders.'

'Very well Arthurs, we'll let you go ahead and have full charge. There has been talk this year of abolishing a private training house and table for this green varsity. But rather than have you resign we'll waive that. You can rest assured from now on you will not be interfered with. Give us the best team you can under the circumstances. There has been much dissension among the directors and faculty because of our new elegibility rules. It has stirred everybody up, and the students are sore. There has been talk of not having a professional coach this year, but we over-ruled that in last night's meeting. We're going to see what you can do. I may add, Arthurs, if you shape up a varsity this year that makes any kind of showing against Place and Herne you will win the eternal gratitude of the directors who have fostered this change in athletics. Otherwise I'm afraid the balance of opinion will favour the idea of dispensing with professional coaches in the future.

Ken saw that Arthurs was white in the face when he left the room. They went out together, and Worry handed Ken a card that read for him to take his examinations at once.

'Are you up on 'em?' asked the coach anxiously.

'I—I think so,' replied Ken.

'Well, Peg, good luck to you! Go at 'em like you went at Dreer's hit.'

Much to his amazement it was for Ken to discover that, now the time had come for him to face his examinations, he was not at all sanguine. He began to worry. He forgot about the textbooks he had mastered in his room during the long winter when he feared to venture out because of the sophomores. It was not very long till he had worked himslf into a state somewhat akin to his trepidation in the varsity ball game. Then he decided to go up at once and have it done with. His whole freshman year had been one long agony. What a relief to have it ended!

Ken passed four examinations in one morning, passed them swimmingly, smilingly, splendidly, and left College Hall in an ecstasy. Things were working out fine. But he had another examination, and it was in a subject he had voluntarily included in his course. Whatever on earth he had done it for he could not now tell. The old doctor who held the chair in that department had thirty years before earned the name of Crab. And slowly in the succeeding years he had grown crabbier, crustier, so student rumor had it. Ken had rather liked the dry old fellow, and had been much absorbed in his complex lectures, but he had never been near him and now the prospect changed color. Foolishly Ken asked a sophomore in what light old crab might regard a student who was ambitious to pass his exams early. The picture painted by that sophomore would have made a flaming-mouthed dragon appear tame. Nerving himself to the ordeal, Ken took his card and presented himself one evening at the doctor's house.

A maid ushered him into the presence of a venerable old man who did not look at all, even to Ken's distorted sight, like a crab or a dragon. His ponderous brow seemed as if it had all the thought in the world behind it. He looked over huge spectacles at Ken's card and then spoke in a dry, quavering voice.

'Um-m, Sit down, Mr Ward.'

Ken found his breath and strangely lost his fear and trembling. The doctor dryly asked him why he thought he knew more than other students, who were satisfied to wait months longer before examination. Ken hastened to explain that it was no desire of his; that although he had studied hard and had not missed many lectures, he knew he was unprepared. Then he went on to tell about the baseball situation and why he had been sent up.

'Um-m.' The professor held a glass paperweight up before Ken and asked a question about it. Next he held out a ruler and asked something about that, and also a bottle of ink. Following this he put a few queries about specific gravity, atomic weight, and the like. Then he sat thrumming his desk and appeared far away in thought. After a while he turned to Ken with a smile that made his withered, parchment-like face vastly different.

'Where do you play?' he asked.

'S-sir?' stammered Ken.

'In baseball, I mean. What place do you play? Catch? Thrower? I don't know the names much.'

Ken replied eagerly, and then it seemed he was telling this stern old man all about baseball. He wanted to know what fouls were, and how to steal bases, and he was nonplussed by such terms as 'hit-and-run.' Ken discoursed eloquently on his favorite sport, and it was like a kind of dream to be there. Strange things were always happening to him.

'I've never seen a game.' said the professor. 'I used to play myself long ago when we had a yarn ball and pitched under hand. I'll have to come out to the field some day. President Halstead, why he likes baseball, he's a—a—what do you call it?'

'A fan—a rooter?' replied Ken, smiling?

'Um-m. I guess that's it. Well, Mr Ward I'm glad to meet you. You may go now.'

Ken got up blushing like a girl. 'But Doctor you were to—I was to be examined.'

'I've examined you,' he drawled, with a dry chuckle, and he looked over his huge spectacles at Ken. 'I'll give you a passing mark. But,

Mr Ward, you know a heap more about baseball than you know about physics.'

As Ken went out he trod upon air. What a splendid old fellow! The sophomore had lied. For that matter, when had a sophomore ever been known to tell the truth? But, he suddenly exclaimed, he himself was no longer a freshman. He pondered happily on the rosy lining to his old cloud of gloom. How different things appeared after a little time. That old doctor's smile would linger long in Ken's memory. He felt deep remorse that he had ever misjudged him. He hurried on to Worry Arthurs's house to tell him the good news. And as he walked his mind was full with the wonder of it all—his lonely, wretched freshman days, now forever past; the slow change from hatred; the dawning of some strange feeling for the college and his teachers; and, last, the freedom, the delight, the quickening stir in the present.

Giants vs Baltimore Orioles

NEW YORK TIMES

NEW YORK, Oct. 7, 1894—New York's baseball team added to the discomfort of the Baltimore Orioles yesterday and the chances are that the Temple Cup, offered by a Pittsburgh enthusiast for a contest between the first and second clubs in the league race, will be captured this year by the New York Giants. Only one more victory is necessary in order to bring about this result. The New Yorks have captured all three of the games played thus far and have handled the champions as though the team was composed of an aggregation of castoff minor leaguers. Yesterday's score was 4 to 1.

Since the opening of the season the Baltimores have gained a reputation for their skillful fielding, daring base running, heavy hitting, and marvelous team work, but, strange to say, in the present series they have failed to put up even an ordinary game. Their batting is weak, their field work commonplace, their base running slow, and the team work was missing altogether.

The game yesterday was a repetition of the contests in Baltimore. Rusie was the stumbling block, and when men were on bases he sent the ball over the plate with the speed of a rifle shot. After a few innings it was easily to be seen that the Baltimores would lower their colors again. They could not do any batting, and judging from their feeble efforts both in the field and at the bat, they appeared to regard defeat as a certainty, and when it finally came along they accepted it with rare grace. Instead of the lively Orioles who met and defeated the Giants this Summer, the team played like a lot of cripples.

With the Giants it was different. Early in the season their work was suggestive of the good old 'has beens', but as the contests wore on, they appeared to improve and today they are playing a wonderfully strong game of ball, and could defeat any club in the country as easily as they have the Baltimores. They had just warmed up to their work, and if the league season opened next week, they would be big favorites for first honors. The strong point in the work of the Giants is the great pitching of both Rusie and Meekin. Both are in the best possible condition and are today head and shoulders above any pair of pitchers in the profession.

The poor Baltimores are handicapped by the absence of McMahon, their best pitcher. He is suffering from a sore arm.

Every baseball enthusiast in town was at the Polo Grounds yesterday afternoon and watched the slaughter of the Orioles with feelings of pleasure. It was estimated that 20,000 persons saw the game.

'Who's going to pitch?'

The query was put to the scorecard boys a thousand times, and when it was learned that the great and only Amos Rusie would occupy the box, there was a grin of satisfaction and inward chuckle, and the average crank waited to witness the big fellow's hypnotic influence over the Baltimore batters. The wait was not a long one. Big Dan Brouthers was the only man to make two hits, and one of these was a scratch of the most pronounced order. Rusie did a good afternoon's work. Only one run was charged against him, and he retired six men on strikes.

The game was replete with incidents. The wild shouts of the onlookers, the strains of the Catholic Protectory Band, the discordant toots of hundreds of fish horns, and the general outbreak that follows the gathering of thousands of cranks caused a stampede in the horseshed. There were two runaways. One horse upset his carriage, broke the harness, and for a few moments was master of the field. He stopped the game, but was finally captured in left field.

One of the side rails of the free seats gave way, and a dozen persons fell to the ground below, but luckily none was injured. Umpire Emslie and Third Baseman McGraw had a tilt, and for a time a fight was imminent. Just when the umpire was about to show what he knows about Marquis of Queensberry rules, Catcher Farrell prevented them from spoiling each other's appearance.

Throughout the contest the spectators kept jeering at McGraw, whose rowdyism in the games played at Baltimore was the topic of conversation among the spectators. But McGraw was apparently undisturbed and appeared to rather like the distinction given him. Umpire Hurst was knocked unconscious by a foul tip. After he recovered he rubbed a lump as big as a walnut on his forehead, and, remarking that Rusie had his speed with him, resumed his duties.

The Giants began to score in the opening inning. After Burke had gone out on a grounder to Jennings, Tiernan hit to Brouthers, who tossed the ball to Hemming. The latter dropped it, and the batter was safe. Then Davis hit to left field. Kelley failed to check the ball and before Brodie returned it Tiernan had scored. Davis, however, was put out while trying to make third on the play. Doyle followed with a hit, but he was disposed of trying to steal to second.

In the fourth inning Brouthers tallied the single run that saved Baltimore from the stigma of a 'Chicago'. Brouthers made his scratch hit, got to second on a passed ball, was advanced to third on a base on balls and a batter being hit, and came home when Ward fumbled Jennings' grounder.

Fuller, in the fifth, started by getting his base on balls, but he was forced out on Farrell's grounder to Jennings. While trying to execute a double play, Reitz threw past Brouthers, and Farrell got to third. He came in on Rusie's sacrifice and the Giants once more were in front. McGraw failed to stop Davis' grounder in the sixth, and Doyle made a two-base hit, sending in a run. Ward's sacrifice advanced Doyle, and he tallied on Robinson's poor throw to third.

In every inning but the first the Baltimores had men on bases, but sharp field work and the clever pitching of Rusie could not be overcome, nine men being left on bases. As the Baltimores left the field with measured tread, the picture of gloom and despair, a mighty shout went up from the assemblage, cheer after cheer, was given for the victors, and the band played 'Carry the News to Mary.'

'Best' Team Won, Even If It Wasn't Most Talented

THOMAS BOSWELL

THANKS, WE NEEDED THAT.

After drug trials, a stupid strike following on the tedium of 1984, baseball was ready for the Kansas City Royals.

We needed the most preposterous postseason in history to end in the crowning of the wonderful, ridiculous, awful, spunky, lucky Royals as winners of the I-70 World Series.

Are they the worst team ever to win the World Series? Well, let's hope so. These guys deserve to be remembered. If they aren't the worst, let's say they were, anyway.

This is a club that merits more than, 'Well, sure, they were pretty mediocre, but somebody sometime probably had even less talent and more luck.' No, no, no. That won't do.

Was this the greatest never-say-die comeback performance in the history of baseball? Well, by all means, let's pretend it was. It's a fact that no Series winner ever before survived six sudden-death, win-or-go-home games.

Stop that whispering out there, you spoiled sports. We're trying to forget the '81 Dodgers. They survived five must-win games before the Series ever began, *then* lost the first two to New York.

Let's not let the facts get in the way of a fairy-tale ending. Just for today, let's ignore about 10 teams that accomplished comebacks so outlandish that it's almost impossible to compare degrees of difficulty. (In recent times, give me the '78 Yankees any day.)

Let's make sure we give K.C. its due. No baseball team ever did more with less, or had to dig out of deeper holes to accomplish it, than these Royals.

Let's hear if for a loaf of Brett, a slice of Biancalana and a pound of Balboni. Darryl Motley and Dane Iorg, we don't even know you, but when it comes to heroes, you're our kind of guys.

Whoever thought that the nation's sixth-graders would be able to pass a spelling bee on Saberhagen, Gubicza, Quisenberry, Leibrandt and Concercion?

Let's be honest. Can we talk here?

Could the Royals have won the World Series if The Tarp That Ate St Louis hadn't broken an itsy-bitsy teeny-weeny bone on Vince Coleman's knee.

Of course not. Don't be silly. Tito Landrum (.360) produced only three runs in the whole Series. Coleman can create that many in one havoc-riddled game.

Could the Royals have won without the fine work of Joaquin Andujar? No way. K.C. should vote the Cardinals' astronaut a full share.

Could the Royals have won without Don Denkinger? Maybe so. But maybe not, too. The Cardinals looked like they never recovered from the American League ump's bad call in Game 6 which let the leadoff Royal reach base in the ninth inning of a 1–0 game.

Given a break, K.C. hardly kicked down the door. Let the record show that while the Royals took a title on Sunday, the Cardinals gave it away Saturday.

Kansas City started the last inning of Game 6 with a grounder to first, a popup near the dugout and a terrible sacrifice bunt back to the mound. Before the Royals could figure out what happened, they had the bases loaded with one out.

Kansas City won 91 games and had to squeeze blood from stones to do that. They had the sixth-best record in baseball and that's about right.

The reason we like the Royals, the reason their triumph will warm baseball fans so much more through the winter than a Cardinal victory is the nature of the people who won. Who really cares about talent? Who cares that the Blue Jays, Cardinals, Yankees, Mets and maybe even the Dodgers could beat the Royals over a long fair season.

Sometimes it's better when the best team *doesn't* win.

The Royals' owner does not have himself drawn around his ball park on a chariot of beer kegs, nor does he have an odious commercial jingle blaring over the public address system between pitches. Royals stadium is not a tacky testimonial to the glories of peddling beer. It's a beautiful park full of water fountains.

The Royals manager does not denigrate teams before he plays them, then deny his cheap-shot quotes until they're played back to him on a tape recorder. He does not abuse Pulitzer Prize-winning journalists for asking a polite professional question. He does not push blame toward his players and away from himself. After he wins the pennant, he doesn't use four-letter words to rub his foes' noses in their loss.

'The K.C. manager does not accuse umpires of deliberate prejudice when there is no evidence of it. He does not throw tantrums on the field when he loses. He doesn't lay on the charm for the national TV cameras, then bad mouth the team that just beat him once he gets back to his office.

When Dick Howser of the Royals makes a hard decision and gets second-guessed nationwide, he stands like a little soldier in one spot for an hour and, politely, humorously, tells anyone who asks just why he did what he did and why he'd do it again.

The Royals are easy to like. Make that easy to love. George Brett, Frank White and Hal McRae—the soul of the team since 1973—are hard-nosed, honest and smart. They play hurt. And they've swallowed post-season losses in '76, '77, '78, '80, '81 and '84 without losing their confidence, drive or leadership.

Dan Quisenberry not only is the best relief pitcher of his time, but a gentleman who minimizes his importance, mourns whenever he lets down his mates (whom he considers 'real' players) and is a very funny fellow.

Some Royals have won tougher contests than a baseball game. Willie Wilson went to jail behind a drug rap and came back a stronger man. Lonnie Smith has beaten a bad cocaine habit.

You'd need a miner's helmet to find Royals General Manager John Schuerholz, he's so busy hiding from the credit for the team he's built. Nonetheless, he knows why his club is so special.

When the Royals trailed early in this Series, Schuerholz said, 'I think the interaction of your players among themselves is more important now than it ever was. You can't say what makes good chemistry within a group of people. But you better pay attention to getting it, and then to keeping it.'

For at least the last 10 years, the Royals have concentrated as much on building a team with character as they have on amasssing talent or signing free agents. Many times, like the '77-to-'83 Baltimore Orioles whom they resemble, they have narrowly failed and been told they would never be world champions until they had more swagger, more muscle and less good humor.

Too soon the Royals will have to begin replacing some of the 35-and-over crowd that has given this club its tone: John Wathan, Greg Pryor, White, Iorg, McRae, Jorge Orta. Then, like the now inert Orioles, they may find how mysteriously difficult it is to build a team that is significantly better than any objective analysis would indicate.

Whether the Kansas City Royals are the 'best' team in baseball at the moment is a quesion of definition.

That they represent what is best in baseball is beyond doubt.

And that's more important.

Sixth-Century Baseball

MARK TWAIN

AT THE END of a month I sent the vessel home for fresh supplies, and for news. We expected her back in three or four days. She would bring me, along with other news, the results of a certain experiment which I had been starting. It was a project of mine to replace the tournament with something which might furnish an escape for the extra steam of the chivalry, keep those bucks entertained and out of mischief, and at the same time preserve the best thing in them, which was their hardy spirit of emulation. I had had a choice band of them in private training for some time, and the date was now arriving for their first public effort.

This experiment was baseball. In order to give the thing vogue from the start, and place it out of the reach of criticism, I chose my nines by rank, not capacity. There wasn't a knight in either team who wasn't a sceptered sovereign. As for material of this sort, there was a glut of it always around Arthur. You couldn't throw a brick in any direction and not cripple a king. Of course, I couldn't get these people to leave off their armor; they wouldn't do that when they bathed. They consented to differentiate the armor so that a body could tell one team from the other, but that was the most they would do. So, one of the teams wore chainmail ulsters, and the other wore plate armor made of my new Bessemer steel. Their practice in the field was the most fantastic thing I ever saw. Being ball-proof, they never skipped out of the way, but stood still and took the result; when a Bessemer was at the bat and a ball hit him, it would bound a hundred and fifty yards sometimes. And when a man was running, and threw himself on his stomach to slide to his base, it was like an ironclad coming into port. At first I appointed men of no rank to act as umpires, but I had to discontinue that. These people were no easier to please than other nines. The umpire's first decision was usually his last; they broke him in two with a bat, and his friends toted him home on a shutter. When it was noticed that no umpire ever survived a game, umpiring got to be unpopular. So I was obliged to appoint somebody whose rank and lofty position under the government would protect him.

Here are the names of the nines:

BESSEMERS	ULSTERS
KING ARTHUR	EMPEROR LUCIUS
KING LOT OF LOTHIAN	KING LOGRIS
KING OF NORTHGALIS	KING MARHALT OF IRELAND
KING MARSIL	KING MORGANORE
KING OF LITTLE BRITAIN	KING MARK OF CORNWALL
KING LABOR	KING NENTRES OF GARLOT
KING PELLAM OF LISTENGESE	KING MELIODAS OF LIONES
KING BAGDEMAGUS	KING OF THE LAKE
KING TOLLEME LA FEINTES	THE SOWDAN OF SYRIA

Umpire—CLARENCE

The first public game would certainly draw fifty thousand people; and for solid fun would be worth going around the world to see. Everything would be favorable; it was balmy and beautiful spring weather now, and Nature was all tailored out in her new clothes.

Line-up For Yesterday
An ABC of Baseball Immortals

OGDEN NASH

A is for Alex
The great Alexander;
More goose eggs he pitched
Than a popular gander.

B is for Bresnahan
Back of the plate;
The Cubs were his love
And McGraw was his hate.

C is for Cobb
Who grew spikes and not corn;
And made all the basemen
Wish they weren't born.

D is for Dean,
The grammatical Diz,
When they asked, Who's the tops?
Said correctly, I is.

E is for Evers
His jaw in advance;
Never afraid
To Tinker with Chance.

F is for Fordham
And Frankie and Frisch;
I wish he were back
With the Giants, I wish.

G is for Gehrig,
The pride of the Stadium;
His record pure gold,
His courage, pure radium.

H is for Hornsby;
When pitching to Rog;
The pitcher would pitch,
Then the pitcher would dodge.

I is for Me,
Not a hard-sitting man;
But an outstanding all-time
Incurable fan.

J is for Johnson
The Big Train in his prime
Was so fast he could throw
Three strikes at a time.

K is for Keeler,
As fresh as green paint,
The fustest and mostest
To hit where they ain't.

L is Lajoie
Whom Clevelanders love;
Napoleon himself
With glue in his glove.

M is for Matly,
Who carried a charm
In the form of an extra
Brain in his arm.

N is for Newsom,
Bobo's favorite kin.
If you ask how he's here,
He talked himself in.

O is for Ott
Of the restless right foot.
When he leaned on the pellet,
The pellet stayed put.

P is for Plank,
The arm of the A's;
When he tangled with Matty
Games lasted for days.

Q is Don Quixote
Cornelius Mack;
Neither Yankees nor years
Can halt his attack.

R is for Ruth
To tell you the truth,
There's no more to be said,
Just R is for Ruth.

S is for Speaker,
Swift center field tender;
When the ball saw him coming,
It yelled, 'I surrender.'

T is for Terry
The Giant from Memphis
Whose 400 average
You can't overemphis.

U would be Ubbell
If Carl were a cockney;
We say Hubbell and baseball
Like football and Rockne.

V is for Vance
The Dodgers' own Dazzy;
None of his rivals
Could throw as fast as he.

W, Wagner,
The bowlegged beauty;
Short was closed to all traffic
With Honus on duty.

X is the first
Of two x's in Foxx
Who was right behind Ruth
With his powerful soxx.

Y is for Young
The magnificent Cy;
People batted against him,
But I never knew why.

Z is for Zenith,
The summit of fame.
These men are up there,
These men are the game.

The Barbarians

PATRICIA HIGHSMITH

STANLEY HUBBELL PAINTED on Sundays, the only day he had to paint. Saturdays he helped his father in the hardware store in Brooklyn. Weekdays he worked as a researcher for a publishing house specializing in trade journals. Stanley did not take his painting very seriously: it was a kind of occupational therapy for his nerves recommended by his doctor. After six months, he was painting fairly well.

One Sunday in early June, Stanley was completing a portrait of himself in a white shirt with a green background. It was larger than his first self-portrait, and it was much better. He had caught the troubled frown of his left eyebrow. The eyes were finished—light brown, a little sad, intense, hopeful. Hopeful of what? Stanley didn't know. But the eyes on the canvas were so much his own eyes they made him smile with pleasure when he looked at them. There remained the highlight to put down the long, somewhat crooked nose, and then to darken the background.

He had been working perhaps twenty minutes, hardly long enough to moisten his brushes or limber up the colors on his palette, when he heard them stomping through the narrow alley at the side of the building. He hesitated, while half his mind still imagined the unpainted highlight down the nose and the other half listened to find out how many there were going to be this afternoon.

Do it now, he told himself, and quickly bent toward the canvas, his left hand clutching the canvas frame, his right hand braced against his left forearm. The point of his brush touched the bridge of his nose.

'Let's *have* it, Franky!'

'Yee-hoooo!'

'Ah, g'wan! What dyuh think I wanna do? Fight the whole goddam . . .'

'Ah-ha-*haaaaaaaah!*'
'Put it *here*, Franky!'
Thud!
They always warmed up for fifteen minutes or so with a hard ball and catchers' mitts.

Stanley's brush stopped after half an inch. He paused, hoping for a lull, knowing there wouldn't be any. The braying voices went on, twenty feet below his window, bantering, directing one another, explaining, exhorting.

'*Get the goddam bush outa the way! Pull it up!*' a voice yelled. Stanley flinched as if it had been said to him.

Two Sundays ago they had had quite an exchange about the bushes. One of the men had tumbled over them in reaching for the ball, and Stanley, seeing it, had shouted down: 'Would you please not go against the hedge?' It burst out of him involuntarily—he was sorry he had not made the remark a lot stronger—and they had all joined in yelling back at him: 'What d'yah think this is, your lot?' and 'Who're you, the gardener?—Hedges! Hah!'

Stanley edged closer to the window, close enough to see the bottom of the brick wall that bounded the far side of the lot. There were still five little bushes standing in front of the wall, forlorn and scraggly, but still standing, still growing—at this minute. Stanley had put them there. He had found them growing, or rather struggling for survival, in cindery corners of the lot and by the ash-cans at the end of the alley. None of the bushes was more than two feet tall, but they were unmistakably hedge bushes. He had transplanted them for two reasons; to hide the ugly wall somewhat and to put the plants in a spot where they could get some sunshine. It has been a tiny gesture toward beautifying something that was, essentially, unbeautifiable, but he had made the effort and it had given him satisfaction. And the men seemed to know he had planted them, perhaps because he had shouted down to watch out for them, and also because the superintendent, who was never around and barely took care of the garbage cans, would never have done anything like set out hedge bushes by a brick wall.

Moving nearer the window, Stanley could see the men. There were five of them today, deployed around the narrow rectangular lot, throwing the ball to one another in no particular order, which meant that four were at all times yelling for the ball to be thrown to them.

'Here y'are, Joey, *here!*'

Thud!

They were all men of thirty or more, and two had the beginnings of paunches. One of the paunchy men was red-headed and he had the loudest, most unpleasant voice, though it was the dark-haired man in blue jeans who yelled the most, really never stopped yelling, even when he caught and threw the ball, and by the same token none of his companions seemed to pay any attention to what he said. The red-headed man's name was Franky, Stanley had learned, and the dark-haired man was Bob. Two of the others had cleated shoes, and pranced and yelled between catches, lifting their knees high and pumping their arms.

'*Wanna see me break a window?*' yelled Franky, winding up. He slammed the ball at one of the cleat-shod men, who let out a wail as he caught it as if it had killed him.

Why was he watching it, Stanley asked himself. He looked at his clock. Only twenty past two. They would play until five, at least. Stanley was aware of a nervous trembling inside him, and he looked at his hands. They seemed absolutely steady. He walked to his canvas. The portrait looked like paint and canvas now, nothing more. The voices might have been in the same room with him. He went to one window and closed it. It was really too hot to close both windows.

Then, from somewhere above him, Stanley heard a window go up, and as if it were a signal for battle, he stiffened: the window-opener was on his side. Stanley stood a little back from the window and looked down at the lot.

'Hey!' the voice from upstairs cried. 'Don't you know you're not supposed to play ball there? People're trying to sleep!'

'*Go ahead 'n sleep!*' yelled the blue jeans, spitting on the ground between his spread knees.

An obscenity from the redhead, and then, 'Let's go, Joey, let's *have* it!'

'Hey!—I'm going to get the law on you if you don't clear out!' from the upstairs window.

The old man was really angry—it was Mr Collins, the nightwatchman—but the threat of the law was empty and everybody knew it. Stanley had spoken to a policeman a month ago, told him about the Sunday ballplayers, but the policeman had only smiled at him—a smile of indulgence for the ballplayers—and had mumbled something about nobody's being able to do anything about people who wanted to play ball on

Sundays. Why couldn't you, Stanley wondered. What about the NO BALLPLAYING written on the side of his own building and signed by the Police Department? What about the right of law-abiding citizens to spend a quiet Sunday at home if they cared to? What about the anti-noise campaign in New York? But he hadn't asked the policeman these questions, because he had seen that the policeman was the same kind of man the ballplayers were, only in uniform.

They were still yelling, Mr Collins and the quintet below. Stanley put his palms on the brick ledge of the windowsill and leaned out to add the support of his visible presence to Mr Collins.

'We ain't breakin' any law! Go to hell!'

'I mean what I say!' shouted Mr Collins. 'I'm a working man!'

'Go back to bed, grampa!'

Then the redheaded man picked up a stone or a large cinder and made as if to throw it at Mr Collins, whose voice shut off in the middle of a sentence. *'Shut up or we'll bust yuh windows!'* the redheaded man bellowed, then managed to catch the ball that was coming his way.

Another window went up, and Stanley was suddenly inspired to yell: 'Isn't there another place to play ball around here? Can't you give us a break one Sunday?'

'Ah, the hell with 'em!' said one of the men.

The batted ball made a sick sound and spun up behind the batter, stopping in mid-air hardly four feet in front of Stanley's nose, before it started its descent. They were playing two-base baseball now with a stick bat and a soft ball.

The blond woman who lived on the floor above Stanley and to the left was having a sympathetic discussion with Mr Collins: 'Wouldn't you think that grown men—'

Mr Collins, loudly: 'Ah, they're worse than children! Hoodlums, that's what they are! Ought to get the police after them!'

'And the language they use! I've told my husband about 'em but he works Sundays and he just can't *realize!*'

'So her husband ain't home, huh?' said the redheaded man, and the others guffawed.

Stanley looked down on the bent, freckled back of the redheaded man who had removed his shirt now and whose hands were braced on his knees. It was a revolting sight—the white back mottled with brown freckles, rounded with fatty muscle and faintly shiny with sweat. I wish I had a BB gun, Stanley thought as he had often thought before. I'd shoot them, not enough to hurt them, just enough to annoy them. Annoy them the hell out of here!

A roar from five throats shocked him, shattered his thoughts and left him shaking.

He went into the bathroom and wet his face at the basin. Then he came back and closed his other window. The closed windows made very little difference in the sound. He bent toward his easel again, touching the brushtip to the partly drawn highlight on the nose. The tip of his brush had dried and stiffened. He moistened it in the turpentine cup.

'Franky!'

'Run, boy run!'

Stanley put the brush down. He had made a wide white mark on the nose. He wiped at it with a rag, trembling.

Now there was an uproar from below, as if all five were fighting. Stanley looked out. Frank and the other pot-bellied man were wrestling for the ball by the hedges. With a wild, almost feminine laugh, the redhead toppled onto the hedges, yelping as the bushes scratched him.

Stanley flung the window up. 'Would you please watch out for the hedge?' he shouted.

'Ah, f'Chris' sake!' yelled the redhead, getting up from one knee, at the same time yanking up a bush from the ground and hurling it in Stanley's direction.

The others laughed.

'You're not allowed to destroy public property!' Stanley retorted with a quick, bitter smile, as if he had them. His heart was racing.

'What d'yuh mean we're not allowed?' asked the blue jeans, crashing a foot into another bush.

'Cut that out!' Stanley yelled.

'Oh, pipe down!'

'I'm gettin' thirsty! Who's goin' for drinks?'

Now the redheaded man swung a foot and kicked another bush up into the air.

'Pick that hedge up again! Put it back!' Stanley shouted, clenching his fists.

'Pick up yer ass!'

Stanley crossed his room and yanked the door open, ran down the steps and out. Suddenly, he was standing in the middle of the lot in the bright sunshine. 'You'd better put that hedge back!' Stanley yelled.

'One of you'd better put all those bushes back!'

'Look who's here!'

'Oh, dry up! Come on, Joey!'

The ball hit Stanley on the shoulder, but he barely felt it, barely wondered if it had been directed at him. He was no match for any of the men physically, certainly not for all of them together, but this fact barely brushed the surface of his mind, either. He was mad enough to have attacked any or all of them, and it was only their scattered number that kept him from moving. He didn't know where to begin.

'Isn't any of you going to put those back?' he demanded.

'No!'

'Outa the way, Mac! You're gonna get hurt!'

While reaching for the ball near Stanley, the blue jeans put out an arm and shoved him. Stanley's neck made a snapping sound and he just managed to recover his balance without pitching on his face. No one was paying the least attention to him now. They were like a scattered, mobile army, confident of their ground. Stanley walked quickly toward the alley, oblivious of the ball that bounced off his head, oblivious of the laughter that followed.

The next thing he knew, he was in the cool, darkish hall of his building. His eye fell on the flat stone that was used now and then to prop the front door open. He picked it up and began to climb the stairs with it. He thought of hurling it out his window, down into the midst of them. The barbarians!

He rested the stone on his windowsill, still holding it between his hands. The man in blue jeans was walking along by the brick wall, kicking at the remaining bushes. They had stopped playing for some reason.

'Got the stuff, fellows! Come 'n get it!' One of the pot-bellied men had arrived with his fists full of soft drink bottles.

Heads tipped back as they drank. There were animal murmurs and grunts of satisfaction. Stanley leaned farther out.

The redheaded man was sitting right below his window on a board propped up on a couple of rocks to make a bench. He couldn't miss if he dropped it, Stanley thought, and almost at the same time, he held the stone a few inches out from his sill and dropped it. Ducking back, Stanley heard a deep-pitched, lethal-sounding crack, then a startled curse.

'Who did that?'

'Hey, Franky! *Franky!* Are you okay?'

Stanley heard a groan.

'We gotta get a doctor! Gimme a hand, somebody!'

'That bastard upstairs!' It came clearly.

Stanley jumped as something crashed through his other window, hit the shade and slid to the floor—a stone the size of a large egg.

Now he could hear their voices moving up the alley. Stanley expected them to come up the stairs for him. He clenched his fists and listened for feet on the stairs.

But nothing happened. Suddenly there was silence.

'Thank—*God*,' Stanley heard the blond woman say, wearily.

The telephone would ring, he thought. That would be next. The police.

Stanley sat down in a chair, sat rigidly for several minutes. The rock had weighed eight or ten pounds, he thought. The very least that could have happened was that the man had suffered a concussion. But Stanley imagined the skull fractured, the brain partly crushed. Perhaps he had lived only a few moments after the impact.

He got up and went to his canvas. Boldly, he mixed a color for the entire nose, painted over the messy highlight, then attacked the background, making it a darker green. By the time he had finished the background, the nose was dry enough for him to put the highlight in, which he did quickly and surely. There was no sound anywhere except that of his rather accelerated breathing. He painted as if he had only five minutes more to paint, five minutes more to live before they came for him.

But by six o'clock, nobody had come. The telephone had not rung, and the picture was done. It was good, better than he had dared hope it would be. Stanley felt exhausted. He remembered that there was no coffee in the house. No milk, either. He'd have to have a little coffee. He'd have to go out.

Fear was sneaking up on him again. Were they waiting for him downstairs in front of the house? Or were they still at the hospital, watching their friend die? What if he were dead? You wouldn't kill a man for playing ball below your window on Sunday—even though you might like to.

He tried to pull himself together, went into the bathroom and took a quick, cool shower, because he had been perspiring quite a bit. He put on a clean blue shirt and combed his hair. Then he pushed his wallet and keys into his pocket and went out. He saw no sign of the ballplayers on the sidewalk, or of anyone who seemed interested in him. He bought milk and coffee at the delicatessen around the corner, and on the way back he ran into the blonde woman of about forty who lived on the floor above him.

'Wasn't that awful this afternoon!' she said to Stanley. 'I saw you down there arguing with them. Good for you! You certainly scared them off.' She shook her head despairingly. 'But I suppose they'll be back next Sunday.'

'Do they play Saturdays?' Stanley asked suddenly, and entirely out of nervousness, since he didn't care whether they played Saturdays or not.

'No,' she said dubiously. 'Well, they once did, but mostly it's Sundays. I swear to God I'm going to make Al stay home one Sunday so he can hear 'em. You must have it a little worse than me, being lower down.' She shook her head again. She looked thin and tired, and there was a complicated meshwork of wrinkles under her lower lids. 'Well, you've got my thanks for breakin' 'em up a little earlier today.'

'Thank you,' Stanley said, really saying it almost involuntarily to thank her for not mentioning, for not having seen what he had done.

They climbed the stairs together.

'Trust this super not to be around whenever somebody needs him,' she said, loud enough to carry into the superintendent's second-floor apartment, which they were then passing. 'And to think we all give him big tips on Christmas!'

'It's pretty bad,' Stanley said with a smile as he unlocked his door. 'Well, let's hope next week's a little better.'

'You said it. I hope it's pouring rain,' she said, and went on up the stairs.

Stanley was in the habit of breakfasting at a small café between his house and the subway, and on Monday morning one of the ballplayers— the one who usually wore blue jeans—was in the café. He was having coffee and doughnuts when Stanley walked in, and he gave Stanley such an unpleasant look, continued for several minutes to give him such an unpleasant look, that a few other people in the café noticed it and began to watch them. Stanley stammeringly ordered coffee. The redheaded man wasn't dead, he decided. He was probably hovering between life and death. If Franky was dead, or if he were perfectly all right now, the dark-haired man's expression would have been differ-ent. Stanley finished his coffee and passed the man on the way to pay his check. He expected the man to try to trip him, or at least say something to him as he passed him, but he didn't.

That evening, when Stanley came home from work at a little after six, he saw two of the ballplayers—the dark-haired man again and one of the paunchy men who looked like a wrestler in his ordinary clothes—standing across the street. They stared at him as he went into his building. Upstairs in his apartment, Stanley pondered the possible significance of their standing across the street from where he lived. Had their friend died, or was he nearer death? Had they just come from the funeral, perhaps? Both of them had been wearing dark suits, suits that might have been their best. Stanley listened for feet on the stairs. There was only the plodding tread of the old woman who lived with her dog on the top floor. She aired her dog at about this time every evening.

All at once Stanley noticed that his windows were shattered. Now he saw three or four stones and fragments of glass on the carpet. There was a stone on his bed, too. The window that had been broken Sunday had almost no glass in it now, and of the upper halves of the windows, which were panelled, only two or three panels remained, he saw when he raised the shades.

He set about methodically picking up the stones and the larger pieces of glass and putting them into a paper bag. Then he got his broom and swept. He was wondering when he would have the time to put the glass back—no use asking the super to do it—and he thought probably not before next weekend, unless he ordered the pieces during his lunch hour tomorrow. He got his yardstick and measured the larger panes, which were of slightly different sizes because it was an old house, and then the panels, and recorded the numbers on a paper which he put into his wallet. He'd have to buy putty, too.

He stiffened, hearing a faint click at his doorlock. 'Who's there?' he called.

Silence.

He had a impulse to yank the door open, then realized he was afraid to. He listened for a few moments. There was no other sound, so he decided to forget the click. Maybe he had only imagined it.

When he came home the next evening, he couldn't get his door open. The key went in, but it wouldn't turn, not a fraction of an inch. Had they put something in it to jam it? Had that been the click he had heard last night? On the other hand, the lock had given him some trouble about six months ago, he remembered. For several days it had been difficult to open, and then it had got all right again. Or had that been the lock on his father's store door? He couldn't quite remember.

He leaned against the stair rail, staring at the key in the lock and wondering what to do.

The blonde woman was coming up the stairs.

Stanley smiled and said, 'Good evening.'

'Hello, there. What happened? Forget your key?'

'No, I—The lock's a little stiff,' he said.

'Oh. Always something wrong in this house, ain't there?' she said, moving on down the hall. 'Did you ever see anything like it?'

'No,' he agreed, smiling. But he looked after her anxiously. Usually, she stopped and chatted a little longer. Had she heard something about his dropping the rock? And she hadn't mentioned his broken windows, though she was home all day and had probably heard the noise.

Stanley turned and attacked the lock, turning the key with all his strength. The lock suddenly yielded. The door was open.

It took him until after midnight to get the panes in. And all the time he worked, he was conscious of the fact that the windows might be broken again when he got home tomorrow.

The following evening the same two men, the paunchy one and the dark-haired one who was in blue jeans and a shirt now, were standing across the street, and to Stanley's horror they crossed the street so as to meet him in front of his door. The paunchy one reached out and took a handful of Stanley's jacket and shirtfront.

'Listen, Mac,' he said in Stanley's face, 'you can go to jail for what you did Sunday. You know that, doncha?'

'I don't know what you're talking about!' Stanley said quickly.

'Oh, you *don't*?'

'No!' Stanley yelled.

The man let him go with a shove. Stanley straightened his jacket, and went on into his house. The lock was again difficult, but he flung himself against it with the energy of desperation. It yielded slowly, and when Stanley removed his key, a rubbery string came with it: they had stuffed his lock with chewing gum. Stanley wiped his key, with disgust, on the floor. He did not begin to shake until he had closed the door of his apartment. Then even as he shook, he thought: I've beaten them. They weren't coming after him. Broken windows, chewing gum? So what? They hadn't sought out the police. He had lied, of course, in saying he didn't know what they were talking about, but that had been the right reply, after all. He wouldn't have lied to a policeman, naturally, but they hadn't brought the police in yet.

Stanley began to feel better. Moreover, his windows were intact, he saw. He decided that the redheaded man was probably going through a prolonged crisis. There was something subdued about the men's behavior, he thought. Or were they planning some worse attack? He wished he knew if the redheaded man were in a hospital or walking around. It was just possible, too, that the man had died, Stanley thought. Maybe the men weren't quite sure that it was he who had dropped the rock—Mr Collins lived above Stanley and might have dropped it, for instance—and perhaps an investigation by the police was yet to come.

On Thursday evening, he passed Mr Collins on the stairs as he was coming home. Mr Collins ws on his way to work. It struck Stanley that Mr Collins' 'Good evening' was cool. He wondered if Mr Collins had heard about the rock and considered him a murderer, or at least some kind of psychopath, to have dropped a ten-pound rock on somebody's head?

Saturday came, and Stanley worked all day in his father's hardware store, went to a movie, and came home at about eleven. Two of the small panes in the upper part of one window were broken. Stanley thought them not important enough to fix until the weather grew cooler. He wouldn't have noticed it, if he hadn't deliberately checked the state of the windows.

He slept late Sunday morning, for he had been extremely tired the night before. It was nearly one o'clock when he set up his easel to paint. He had in mind to paint the aperture between two buildings, which contained a tree, that he could see straight out his window above the lot. He thought this Sunday might be a good Sunday to paint, because the ballplayers probably wouldn't come. Stanley pictured them dampened this Sunday, at least to the extent that they would find another vacant lot to play in.

He had not quite finished his sketch of the scene in charcoal on his canvas, when he heard them. For a moment, he thought he was imagining it, that he was having an auditory hallucination. But no. He heard them ever more clearly in the alley—their particular sullen bravado coming through the murmuring, a collective murmur as recognizable to Stanley as a single familiar voice. Stanley waited, a little way back from his window.

'Okay, boys, let's *go-o-o!*'

'*Yeeeee-hooooooooo!*' Sheer defiance, a challenge to any who might contest their right to play there.

Stanley went closer to the window, looking, wide eyed, for the red-headed man. And there he was! A patch of bandage on the top of his head, but otherwise as brutishly energetic as ever. As Stanley watched, he hurled a catcher's mitt at a companion who was then bending over, hitting him in the buttocks.

Raucous, hooting laughter.

Then from above: 'F'gosh sakes, why don't you guys grow up? Why don't you beat it? We've had enough of you around here!' It was the blonde woman, and Stanley knew that Mr Collins would not be far behind.

'*Ah, save yer throat!*'

'C'mon down 'n get in the game, sister!'

There was a new defiance in their voices today. They were louder. They were determined to win. They had won. They were back.

Stanley sat down on his bed, dazed, frustrated, and suddenly tired. He was glad the redheaded fellow wasn't dead. He really was glad. And yet with his relief something fighting and bitter rose up in him, something borne on a wave of unshed tears.

'Let's have it, Joey, let's *have* it!'

Thud!

'Hey, Franky! Franky, look! Ah-ha-*haaaaaa!*'

Stanley put his hands over his ears, lifted his feet onto the bed, and shut his eyes. He lay in a Z position, his legs drawn up, and tried to be perfectly calm and quiet. No use fighting, he thought. No use fighting, no use crying.

Then he thought of something and sat up abruptly. He wished he had put the hedge bushes back. Now it was too late, he supposed, because they had been lying out on the ground for a week. But how he wished he had! Just that gesture of defiance, just that bit of beauty launched again in their faces.

The Big Black and White Game

RAY BRADBURY

THE PEOPLE FILLED the stands behind the wire screen, waiting. Us kids, dripping from the lake, ran between the white cottages, past the resort hotels, screaming, and sat on the bleachers, making wet bottom marks. The hot sun beat down through the tall oak trees around the baseball diamond. Our fathers and mothers, in golf pants and light summer dresses, scolded us and made us sit still.

We looked toward the hotel and the back door of the vast kitchen, expectantly. A few colored women began walking across the shade-freckled area between, and in ten minutes the far left section of the bleachers was mellow with the color of their fresh-washed faces and arms. After all these years, whenever I think back on it, I can still hear the sounds they made. The sound on the warm air was like a soft moving of dove voices each time they talked among themselves.

Everybody quickened into amusement, laughter rose right up into the clear blue Wisconsin sky, as the kitchen door flung wide and out ran the big and little, the dark and high-yellar uniformed Negro waiters, janitors, bus boys, boatmen, cooks, bottle washers, soda jerks, gardeners, and golf-links tenders. They came capering, showing their fine white teeth, proud of their new red-striped uniforms, their shiny shoes rising and coming down on the green grass as they skirted the bleachers and drifted with lazy speed out on the field, calling to everybody and everything.

Us kids squealed. There was Long Johnson, the lawn-cutting man, and Cavanaugh, the soda-fountain man, and Shorty Smith and Pete Brown and Jiff Miller!

And *there* was Big Poe! Us kids shouted, applauded!

Big Poe was the one who stood so tall by the popcorn machine every night in the million-dollar dance pavilion farther down beyond the hotel on the lake rim. Every night I bought popcorn from Big Poe and he poured lots of butter all over it for me.

I stomped and yelled, 'Big Poe! Big Poe!'

And he looked over at me and stretched his lips to bring out his teeth, waved, and shouted a laugh.

And Mama looked to the right, to the left, and back of us with worried eyes and nudged my elbow. 'Hush,' she said. 'Hush.'

'Land, land,' said the lady next to my mother, fanning herself with a folded paper. 'This is quite a day for the colored servants, ain't it? Only time of year they break loose. They look forward all summer to the big Black and White game. But this ain't nothing. You seen their Cakewalk Jamboree?'

'We got tickets for it,' said Mother. 'For tonight at the pavilion. Cost us a dollar each. That's pretty expensive, I'd say.'

'But I always figure,' said the woman, 'once a year you got to spend. And it's really something to watch them dance. They just naturally got . . .'

'Rhythm,' said Mother.

'That's the word,' said the lady. 'Rhythm. That's what they got. Land, you should see the colored maids up at the hotel. They been buying satin yardage in at the big store in Madison for a month now. And every spare minute they sit sewing and laughing. And I seen some of the feathers they bought for their hats. Mustard and wine ones and blue ones and violet ones. Oh, it'll be a sight!'

'They been airing out their tuxedos,' I said. 'I saw them hanging on lines behind the hotel all week!'

'Look at them prance,' said Mother. 'You'd think they thought they were going to win the game from our men.'

The colored men ran back and forth and yelled with their high, fluting voices and their low, lazy interminable voices. Way out in center field you could see the flash of teeth, their upraised naked black arms swinging and beating their sides as they hopped up and down and ran like rabbits, exuberantly.

Big Poe took a double fistful of bats, bundled them on his huge bull shoulder, and strutted along the first base line, head back, mouth smiling wide open, his tongue moving, singing:

'—gonna dance out both of my shoes,
When they play those Jelly Roll Blues;
Tomorrow night at the Dark Town Strutters' Ball.'

Up went his knees and down and out, swinging the bats like musical batons. A burst of applause and soft laughter came from the lefthand grandstands, where all the young, ripply colored girls with shiny brown eyes sat eager and easy. They made quick motions that were graceful and mellow because, maybe, of their rich coloring. Their laughter was like shy birds; they waved at Big Poe, and one of them with a high voice cried, 'Oh, Big Poe! Oh, Big Poe!'

The white section joined politely in the applause as Big Poe finished his cakewalk. 'Hey, Big Poe!' I yelled again.

'Stop that, Douglas!' said Mother, straight at me.

Now the white men came running between the trees with their uniforms on. There was a great thunder and shouting and rising up in our grandstand. The white men ran across the green diamond, flashing white.

'Oh, there's Uncle George!' said Mother. 'My, doesn't he look nice?' And there was my Uncle George toddling along in his outfit which didn't quite fit because Uncle has a potbelly, and jowls that sit out over any collar he puts on. He was hurrying along, trying to breathe and smile at the same time, lifting up his pudgy little legs. 'My, they look *so* nice,' enthused Mother.

I sat there, watching their movements. Mother sat beside me, and I think she was comparing and thinking, too, and what she saw amazed and disconcerted her. How easily the dark people had come running first, like those slow-motion deer and buck antelopes in those African moving pictures, like things in dreams. They came like beautiful brown, shiny animals that didn't know they were alive, but lived. And when they ran and put their easy, lazy, timeless legs out and followed them with their big, sprawling arms and loose fingers and smiled in the blowing wind, their expressions didn't say. 'Look at *me* run, look at *me* run!' No, not at all. Their faces dreamily said, 'Lord, but it's sure nice to run. See the ground swell soft under me? Gosh, I feel good. My muscles are moving like oil on my bones and it's the best pleasure in the world to run.' And they ran. There was no purpose to their running but exhilaration and living.

The white men worked at their running as they worked at everyhing. You felt embarrassed for them because they were alive too much in the wrong way. Always looking from the corners of their eyes to see if you were watching. The Negroes didn't care if you watched or not; they went on living, moving. They were so sure of playing that they didn't have to think about it any more.

'My, but our men look so nice,' said my mother, repeating herself rather flatly. She had seen, compared the teams. Inside, she realized how laxly the colored men hung swaying in their uniforms, and how tensely, nervously, the white men were crammed, shoved and belted into *their* outfits.

I guess the tenseness began then.

I guess everybody saw what was happening. They saw how the white men looked like senators in sun suits. And they admired the graceful unawareness of the colored men. And, as is always the case, that admiration turned to envy, to jealousy, to irritation. It turned to conversation like:

'That's my husband, Tom, on third base. Why doesn't he pick up his feet? He just *stands* there.'

'Never you mind, never you mind. He'll pick 'em up when the time comes!'

'That's what *I* say! Now, take my Henry, for instance. Henry mightn't be active all the time, but when there's a crisis—just you *watch* him. Uh—I do wish he'd wave or something,though. Oh, *there*! Hello, Henry!'

'Look at that Jimmie Cosnor playing around out there!'

I looked. A medium-sized white man with a freckled face and red hair was clowning on the diamond. He was balancing a bat on his forehead. There was laughter from the white grandstand. But it sounded like the kind of laughter you laugh when you're embarrassed for someone.

'Play ball!' said the umpire.

A coin was flipped. The colored men batted first.

'Darn it,' said my mother.

The colored men ran in from the field happily.

Big Poe was first to bat. I cheered. He picked up the bat in one hand like a toothpick and idled over to the plate and laid the bat on his thick shoulder, smiling along its polished surface toward the stands where the colored women sat with their fresh flowery cream dresses stirring over their legs, which hung down between the seat intervals like crisp new sticks of ginger; their hair was all fancily spun and hung over their ears. Big Poe looked in particular at the little, dainty-as-a-chicken-bone shape of his girl friend Katherine. She was the one who made the beds at the hotel and cottages every morning, who tapped on your door like a bird and politely asked if you was done dreaming, 'cause if you was she'd clean away all them old nightmares and bring in a fresh batch— please use them *one* at a time, thank yoah. Big Poe shook his head, looking at her, as if he couldn't believe she was there. Then he turned, one hand balancing the bat, his left hand dangling free at his side, to await the trial pitches. They hissed past, spatted into the open mouth of the catcher's mitt, were hurled back. The umpire grunted. The next pitch was the starter.

Big Poe let the first ball go by him.

'Stee-rike!' announced the umpire. Big Poe winked good-naturedly at the white folks. Bang! 'Stee-rike two!' cried the umpire.

The ball came for the third time.

Big Poe was suddenly a greased machine pivoting; the dangling hand swept up to the butt end of the bat, the bat swiveled, connected with the ball—*Whack!* The ball shot up into the sky, away down toward the wavering line of oak trees, down toward the lake, where a white sailboat slid silently by. The crowd yelled, me loudest! There went Uncle George, running on his stubby, wool-stockinged legs, getting smaller with distance.

Big Poe stood for a moment watching the ball go. Then he began to run. He went around the bases, loping, and on the way home from third base he waved to the colored girls naturally and happily and they waved back, standing on their seats and shrilling.

Ten minutes later, with the bases loaded and run after run being driven in, and Big Poe coming to bat again, my mother turned to me. 'They're the most inconsiderate people,' she said.

'But that's the game,' I said. 'They've only got two outs.'

'But the score's seven to nothing,' my mother protested.

'Well, just you wait until *our* men come to bat,' said the lady next to my mother, waving away a fly with a pale blue-veined hand. 'Those Negroes are too big for their britches.'

'Stee-rike two!' said the umpire as Big Poe swung.

'All the past week at the hotel,' said the woman next to my mother, staring out at Big Poe steadily, 'the hotel service has been simply terrible. Those maids don't talk about a thing save the Cakewalk Jamboree, and whenever you want ice water it takes them half an hour to fetch it, they're so busy sewing.'

'Ball One!' said the umpire.

The woman fussed. 'I'll be glad when this week's over, that's what I got to say,' she said.

'Ball two!' said the umpire to Big Poe.

'Are they going to *walk* him?' asked my mother of me. 'Are they *crazy*?' To the woman next to her: 'That's right, They been acting funny all week. Last night I had to tell Big Poe twice to put extra butter on my popcorn. I guess he was trying to save money or something.'

'Ball three!' said the umpire.

The lady next to my mother cried out suddenly and fanned herself furiously with her newspaper. 'Land, I just *thought*! Wouldn't it be awful if they *won* the game? They *might*, you know. They might do it.'

My mother looked at the lake, at the trees, at her hands. 'I don't know why Uncle George had to play. Make a fool of himself. Douglas, you run tell him to quit right now. It's bad on his heart.'

'You're out!' cried the umpire to Big Poe.

'Ah,' sighed the grandstand.

The side was retired. Big Poe laid down his bat gently and walked along the base line. The white men pattered in from the field looking red and irritable, with big islands of sweat under their armpits. Big Poe looked over at me. I winked at him. He winked back. Then I knew he wasn't so dumb.

He'd struck out on purpose.

Long Johnson was going to pitch for the colored team.

He ambled out to the rubber, worked his fingers around in his fists to limber them up.

First white man to bat was a man named Kodimer, who sold suits in Chicago all year round.

Long Johnson fed them over the plate with tired, unassuming, controlled accuracy.

Mr Kodimer chopped, Mr Kodimer swatted. Finally Mr Kodimer bunted the ball down the third-base line.

'Out at first base,' said the umpire, an Irishman named Mahoney.

Second man up was a young Swede named Moberg. He hit a high fly to center field which was taken by a little plump Negro who didn't look fat because he moved around like a smooth, round glob of mercury.

Third man up was a Milwaukee truck driver. He whammed a line drive to center field. It was good. Except that he tried to stretch it into a two-bagger. When he pulled up at second base, there was Emancipated Smith with a white pellet in his dark, dark hand, waiting.

My mother sank back in her seat, exhaling. 'Well, I *never!*'

'It's getting hotter,' said the lady elbow-next. 'Think I'll go for a stroll by the lake soon. It's too hot to sit and watch a silly game today. Mightn't you come along with me, missus?' she asked Mother.

It went on that way for five innings.

It was eleven to nothing and Big Poe had struck out three times on purpose, and in the last half of the fifth was when Jimmy Cosner came to bat for our side again. He'd been trying all afternoon, clowning, giving directions, telling everybody just where he was going to blast that pill once he got hold of it. He swaggered up toward the plate now, confident and bugle-voiced. He swung six bats in his thin hands, eyeing them critically with his shiny green little eyes. He chose one, dropped the others, ran to the plate, chopping out little islands of green fresh lawn with his cleated heels. He pushed his cap back on his dusty red hair. 'Watch this!' he called out loud to the ladies. 'You watch me show these dark boys! Ya-hah!'

Long Johnson on the mound did a slow serpentine windup. It was like a snake on a limb of a tree, uncoiling, suddenly darting at you. Instantly Johnson's hand was in front of him, open, like black fangs, empty. And the white pill slashed across the plate with a sound like a razor.

'Stee-rike!'

Jimmie Cosner put his bat down and stood glaring at the umpire. He said nothing for a long time. Then he spat deliberately near the catcher's foot, took up the yellow maple bat again, and swung it so the sun glinted the rim of it in a nervous halo. He twitched and sidled it on his thin-boned shoulder, and his mouth opened and shut over his long nicotined teeth.

Clap! went the catcher's mitt.

Cosner turned, stared.

The catcher, like a black magician, his white teeth gleaming, opened up his oily glove. There, like a white flower glowing, was the baseball.

'Stee-rike two!' said the umpire, far away in the heat.

Jimmie Cosner laid his bat across the plate and hunched his freckled hands on his hips. 'You mean to tell me that was a strike?'

'That's what I said,' said the umpire,'Pick up the bat.'

'To hit you on the head with,' said Cosner sharply.

'Play ball or hit the showers!'

Jimmie Cosner worked his mouth to collect enough saliva to spit, then angrily swallowed it, swore a bitter oath instead. Reaching down, he raised the bat, poised it like a musket on his shoulder.

And here came the ball! It started out small and wound up big in front of him. Powie! An explosion off the yellow bat. The ball spiraled up and up. Jimmie lit out for first base. The ball paused, as if thinking about gravity up there in the sky. A wave came in on the shore of the lake and fell down. The crowd yelled. Jimmie ran. The ball made its decision, came down. A lithe high-yellar was under it, fumbled it. The ball spilled to the turf, was plucked up, hurled to first base.

Jimmie saw he was going to be out. So he jumped feet first at the base.

Everybody saw his cleats go into Big Poe's ankle. Everybody saw the red blood. Everybody heard the shout, the shriek, saw the heavy clouds of dust rising.

'I'm safe!' protested Jimmie two minutes later.

Big Poe sat on the ground. The entire dark team stood around him. The doctor bent down, probed Big Poe's ankle, saying, 'Mmmm,' and 'Pretty bad. Here.' And he swabbed medicine on it and put a white bandage on it.

The umpire gave Cosner the cold-water eye. 'Hit the showers!'

'Like hell!' said Cosner. And he stood on that first base, blowing his cheeks out and in, his freckled hands swaying at his side. 'I'm safe. I'm staying right here, by God! No nigger put *me* out.'

'No,' said the umpire. 'A white man did. *Me. Get!*'

'He dropped the ball! Look up the rules! I'm safe!'

The umpire and Cosner stood glaring at each other.

Big Poe looked up from having his swollen ankle tended. His voice was thick and gentle and his eyes examined Jimmie Cosner gently.

'Yes, he's safe, Mr Umpire. Leave him stay. He's safe.'

I was standing right there. I heard the whole thing. Me and some other kids had run out on the field to see. My mother kept calling me to come back to the stands.

'Yes, he's safe,' said Big Poe again.

All the colored men let out a yell.

'What'sa matter with you, black boy? You get hit in the head?'

'You heard me,' replied Big Poe quietly. He looked at the doctor bandaging him. 'He's safe. Leave him stay.'

The umpire swore.

'Okay, okay. So he's safe!'

The umpire stalked off, his back stiff, his neck red.

Big Poe was helped up, 'Better not walk on that,' cautioned the doctor.

'I can walk,' whispered Big Poe carefully.

'Better not play.'

'I can play,' said Big Poe gently, certainly, shaking his head, wet steaks drying under his white eyes. 'I'll play *good*.' He looked no place at all. 'I'll play plenty good.'

'Oh,' said the second-base colored man. It was a funny sound.

All the colored men looked at each other, a Big Poe, then at Jimmie Cosner, at the sky, at the lake, the crowd. They walked off quietly to take their places. Big Poe stood with his bad foot hardly touching the ground, balanced. The doctor argued. But Big Poe waved him away.

'Batter up!' cried the umpire.

We got settled in the stands again. My mother pinched my leg and asked me why I couldn't sit still. It got warmer. Three or four more waves fell on the shore line. Behind the wire screen the ladies fanned their wet faces and the men inched their rumps forward on the wooden planks, held papers over their scowling brows to see Big Poe standing like a redwood tree out there on first base. Jimmie Cosner standing in the immense shade of that dark tree.

Young Moberg came up to bat for our side.

'Come on, Swede, come on, Swede!' was the cry, a lonely cry, like a dry bird, from out on the blazing green turf. It was Jimmie Cosner calling. The grandstand stared at him. The dark heads turned on their moist pivots in the outfield; the black faces came in his direction, looking him over, seeing his thin, nervously arched back. He was the center of the universe.

'Come on, Swede! Let's show these black boys!' laughed Cosner.

He tailed off. There was a complete silence. Only the wind came through the high, glittering trees.

'Come on, Swede, hang one on that old pill . . .'

Long Johnson, on the pitcher's mound, cocked his head. Slowly, deliberately, he eyed Cosner. A look passed between him and Big Poe, and Jimmie Cosner saw the look and shut up and swallowed hard.

Long Johnson took his time with his windup.

Cosner took a lead off base.

Long Johnson stopped loading his pitch.

Cosner skipped back to the bag, kissed his hand, and patted the kiss dead center on the plate. Then he looked up and smiled around.

Again the pitcher coiled up his long, hinged arm, curled loving dark fingers on the leather pellet, drew it back and—Cosner danced off first base. Cosner jumped up and down like a monkey. The pitcher did not look at him. The pitcher's eyes watched him secretively, slyly, amusedly, sidewise. Then, snapping his head, the pitcher scared Cosner back to the plate. Cosner stood and jeered.

The third time Long Johnson made as if to pitch, Cosner was far off the plate and running toward second.

Snap went the pitcher's hand. *Bom* went the ball in Big Poe's glove at first base.

Everything was sort of frozen. Just for a second.

There was the sun in the sky, the lake and the boats on it, the grandstands, the pitcher on his mound standing with his hand out and down after tossing the ball; there was Big Poe with the ball in his mighty black hand; there was the infield staring, crouching in at the scene, and there was Jimmie Cosner running, kicking up dirt, the only moving thing in the entire summer world.

Big Poe leaned forward, sighted toward second base, drew back his mighty right hand, and hurled that white baseball straight down along the line until it reached Jimmie Cosner's head.

Next instant, the spell was broken.

Jimmie Cosner lay flat on the burning grass. People boiled out of the grandstands. There was swearing, and women screaming, a clattering of wood as the men rushed down the wooden boards of the bleachers. The colored team ran in from the field. Jimmie Cosner lay there. Big Poe, no expression on his face, limped off the field, pushing white men away from him like clothespins when they tried stopping him. He just picked them up and threw them away.

'Come on, Douglas!' shrieked Mother, grabbing me. 'Let's get home! They might have razors! Oh!'

That night, after the near riot of the afternoon, my folks stayed home reading magazines. All the cottages around us were lighted. Everybody was home. Distantly I heard music. I slipped out the back door into the ripe summer-night darkness and ran toward the dance pavilion. All the lights were on, and music played.

But there were no white people at the tables. Nobody had come to the Jamboree.

There were only colored folks. Women in bright red and blue satin gowns and net stockings and soft gloves, with wine-plume hats, and men in glossy tuxedos. The music crashed out, up, down, and around the floor. And laughing and stepping high, flinging their polished shoes out and up in the cakewalk, were Long Johnson and Cavanaugh and Jiff Miller and Pete Brown, and—limping—Big Poe and Katherine, his girl, and all the other lawn-cutters and boatmen and janitors and chambermaids, all on the floor at one time.

It was so dark all around the pavilion; the stars shone in the black sky, and I stood outside, my nose against the window, looking in for a long, long time, silently.

I went to bed without telling anyone what I'd seen.

I just lay in the dark smelling the ripe apples in the dimness and hearing the lake at night and listening to that distant, faint and wonderful music. Just before I slept I heard those last strains again:

'—*gonna dance out both of my shoes,*
When they play those Jelly Roll Blues;
Tomorrow night at the Dark Town Strutters' Ball!'

'Matty' Blanks A's for 3d Time

NEW YORK TIMES

NEW YORK OCT. 15, 1905—Two neatly dressed athletic-looking young men, one a giant in contrast to the squattiness of the other, walked along the veranda of the clubhouse at the Polo Grounds about 5 o'clock yesterday afernoon grinning broadly. Below them was a sea of 10,000 faces, wildly emitting a thunderous eruption of enthusiasm. The young men looked down upon the reverberating ocean of humanity for a moment and then walked to a point directly in front of the plaza, where they were in view of all. The ten thousand throats bellowed a tribute that would have almost drowned a broadside of twelve-inch guns.

The two smiling athletes stopped; one of them drew forth a roll of yellow paper from under his arm. As the crowd pushed and fought and cheered he unrolled the impromptu banner and let it flutter on the breeze. The multitude pressed forward like a wave to read this inscription:

The Giants
World's Champions 1905.

Geological records show that Vesuvius disturbs the earth and that seismic demonstrations are felt by the greater number. But if that doctrine had been promulgated in the vicinity of the Polo Grounds yesterday, as Christy Mathewson and Roger Bresnahan of the New York Baseball Club unfurled their victorious banner, it would have been minimized. For, as volcanoes assert themselves upon the earth's surface, surely must that deafening reverberating roar have lifted Manhattan's soil from its base.

The Giants, the most intelligent, the quickest, strongest, and grittiest combination of baseball players that ever represented this city in any

league, demonstrated beyond quibble paramount superiority over anything extant in diamond life today by winning the fifth and deciding
game of the world championship series with the Athletics by the score
of 2 to 0.

The victory meant an honor which has not hitherto fallen to the lot
of New York through any other team, and the Giants may hold up
their heads, in the athletic world as being the one collection of peerless
ball tossers.

The crowd, in the neighborhood of 27,000 people, saw a battle to cheer
the baseball heart and satisfy the rooter's innermost cravings. At no
time during the contest were the Giants in danger, and at all times
were they masters. It settled the question whether the National or the
American League offered the better brand of baseball. The championship
decree of yesterday, to be accepted as final, lays at rest all doubt and
demonstrates the transcendent superiority of the National brand and
the indisputable invulnerability of the Giants.

And be it recorded right here that New York possesses the pitching
marvel of the century. Christy Mathewson, the giant slabman who made
the world championship possible for his team, may be legitimately designated as the premier pitching wonder of all baseball records. The diamond has known its Clarkson, its Keefe and its Caruthers. Their
records radiate. But to Mathewson belongs the palm. His almost superhuman accomplishments during the series which closed yesterday will
stand as a mark for all pitchers of the future.

Figures show best just what Mathewson accomplished. In the three
victories over which he presided he twirled twenty-seven innings. During that series he allowed not a single run, not an Athletic even reached
third base. He was touched for a total of only fifteen hits, and by men
who are reckoned as the American League's strongest batters. He
allowed only one pass to first, hit only a single batsman, and struck
out sixteen men. The record is a classic. Baseball New York appreciates
this work. That fact was amply demonstrated yesterday, when it gave
Mathewson a marvelous vocal panegyric that evoked a half-suppressed
smile and bow.

The game yesterday was one of giants—clean, fast, and decisive. Both
teams were keyed high, for to the Giants it meant rosy conquest and
to the Athletics a saving chance to redeem themselves. But the Giants
were not to be repulsed. They went at the ball in the first inning with
a we-never-can-lose determination, and there was not a minute during

play in which that spirit did not manifest itself. Philadelphia tried its best, but, strive as hard as it did, it was only a shadow reflecting the masterful Mathewson's will. He bestrode the field like a mighty Colossus, and the Athletics peeped about the diamond like pigmies who struggled gallantly for their lives, but in vain.

Bender, the much feared brave from the Carlisle reservation, sought to repeat his scalping bee of Tuesday, but the Spartan McGraw laconically expressed the situation when at the beginning of the game he remarked good-naturedly to the Athletics' pitcher:

'It will be off the warpath for you today, Chief.' The phlegmatic copper-colored man only smiled grimly.

'It's uncertain,' he replied, 'but I did it once, and I'm going to do my best to do it again.'

Analyzed to the statistical point, the twirling feature of the game shows little advantage to either side, but when weighed in parts Mathewson had by far the advantage. Five hits were all that the Giants could register off Bender, while the Athletics rang up for a total of six against Mathewson. Mathewson fanned only three to Bender's five, but the Indian gave three passes. Mathewson proved a surprise to his admirers by poorly fielding his position. He made two errors, but they luckily resulted in nothing harmful.

The Giants were well rewarded for their hard work in defeating the Athletics. Each man today has a check in his wallet for $1,141.41. That is the share of each of the eighteen Giants for the series. The receipts of the first four games, from which the players derive their profit, were $50,750.50.

The crowd which saw yesterday's game was immense. All the stands were filled, while men and women stood in a line ten deep back of the ropes from the right to the left field bleachers. Men hung on the fence and sat on the grandstand roof, and some peered through glasses from distant poles and housetops.

The New York management had a band on the field to enliven things. As McGraw appeared on the diamond he was met with a volley of applause and was obliged to lift his hat in response.

'Clinch it today, Mac,' yelled the crowd. 'Nothing but the championship will suit us now.'

'That's what you'll get,' he responded smilingly.

While McGraw was walking across the field the Athletics appeared from the clubhouse with Bender in the lead.

'Back to the tepee for yours,' hooted a rooter. 'Giants grab heap much wampum,' yelled another, giving an imitation Indian yell. Bender looked at his foes in stolid silence but smiled widely as the running fire of comments continued. James J. Corbett walked into the field with the Giants and helped the players to warm up.

Mathewson got a magnificent reception, and the crowd yelled for him to doff his cap. Instead of doing so, however, he walked over to McGinnity, the conqueror yesterday, and ostentatiously removed Joe's headgear. McGinnity returned the compliment.

'Shake 'em up Matty. Go after 'em,' screamed the bleachers. As McGraw went to the plate to bat out in practice the band began to play:

> We'll all get stone blind,
> Johnnie go fill up the bowl.

Time and again during the game Bender was yelled at, to rattle him, but the noise might as well have been directed as a steamboat, for he was impassive and cool at all stages. In one inning he gave two bases on balls in succession and the crowed jumped to its feet in glee. Bender was thunderously informed that he was booked for the soap factory. At another time two bunts were made in succession. Again the crowd rose and expressed the opinion that the chief would surely go to the happy hunting grounds, but he refused to die and stood gamely and quietly to the end.

As the game proceeded the crowd saw that it was to be a magnificent pitching struggle, and both twirlers were cheered. After the fourth, when Bender retired the Giants in one, two, three order, he was heartily applauded. Bender lifted his cap in acknowledgement. Philadelphia had men on bases in the first, second, third, fifth and sixth innings but couldn't get one past the second sack.

New York made its runs in the fifth, and eighth. In the fifth inning Mertes got a pass and Dahlen followed suit. With two on bases the crowd roared for Devlin to drive in a run. Devlin, however, had his orders and bunted. He sacrificed the runners to third and second and the crowd nearly yelled itself hoarse.

'Come on, Gilbert, you can do it' roared the stands. Then came a volley of taunts to Bender, who viewed the situation with absolute imperturbability. Gilbert caught one of Bender's twists on the end of his bat and sent the ball to deep left. Hartzel caught it, but Mertes on third raced home with the first tally of the game, The crowd went wild.

In the eighth after Gilbert had flied to Lord, Mathewson went to bat amid a storm of yells and walked. Bresnahan stalked to the plate and carefully inspected the business end of his bat.

'Put it in a balloon, Roger, and send it away for good!' screamed the fans. Roger did the next best thing by driving the ball on a straight line to the left field bleachers. Ordinarily it would have counted for a home run, but under the ground rules he was allowed only two bases. Even Matty was enamored of the coup, for as he trotted around to third he paused, under the ground rule allowance, and clapped his hands with satisfaction. Browne, the next up, swung viciously at one of Bender's curves. It went like a shot straight for the Indian. Bender grabbed at the leather, and it struck his right hand, caroming off to Murphy who retired Browne. Matty, however, jumped across the rubber and registered a second tally.

When the game ended the crowd broke through the police and rushed for the players. The Giants got into the clubhouse before being intercepted. Ten thousand fans surrounded the clubhouse and demanded to see their heroes. One by one the Giants appeared and were cheered. McGraw made a brief speech, in which he said:

'Ladies and Gentlemen: I appreciate the great victory as well as you. I thank you for your patronage, and hope to see you all next Spring.'

The First Kiss

JOHN UPDIKE

THE MANY-HEADED monster called the Fenway Faithful yesterday resumed its romance with twenty-five youngish men in red socks who last year broke its monstrous heart. Just showing up on so dank an Opening Day* was an act of faith. But the wet sky dried to a mottled pewter, tarpaulin was rolled off the infield and stuffed into a mailing tube, and we Faithful braced for the first kiss of another prolonged entanglement.

Who can forget the ups and downs of last year's fling? First, the Supersox, then, the unravelling. Our eyeballs grew calluses, watching Boomer swing from the heels and Hobson throw to the stars. Dismal nights watching the Royals play pinball with our heroes on that plastic prairie in Kansas City. Dreadful days losing count of Yankee singles in the four-game massacre. Fisk standing ever more erect and stoic at the plate, looking more like a Civil War memorial financed with Confederate dollars. The Noble Lost Cause.

In September, the mini-resurrection, Zimmer's last stand, the miraculous last week of no losses, waiting for the Yankees to drop one. Which they did. And then, the cruellest tease, the playoff game surrendered to a shoestring catch and a shortstop's cheap home run. Enough. You'll never get us to care again, Red Sox.

But monsters have short memories, elastic hearts, and very foolable faculties, as many an epic attests. From natty-looking to nasty-looking, the fans turned out. 'We Miss Louis and Bill', one large cardboard complained. 'Windsor Locks Loves the Sox!' a bed sheet benignly rhymed.

---

* An account of the baseball season's Opening Day in Fenway Park, on April 5, 1979, for the Boston *Globe*.

Some fellow behind us exhaled a sweetish small, but the dragon's breath was primarily flavored with malt.

Governor King was booed royally. Power may or may not corrupt, but it does not win friends. A lady from Dedham not only sang all the high notes in 'The Star-Spangled Banner' but put in an extra one of her own, taking 'free' up and out of the ballpark. We loved it. Monsters love high notes and hoards of gold.

The two teams squared off against each other in a state of statistical virginity. Every man in both lineups was batting .000. On the other hand, both pitchers had earned-run averages of 0.00 And every fielder there had thus far played errorless ball.

Eckersley looked quick. A moment of sun made some of the windows of the Prudential Center sparkle. The new Red Sox uniforms appeared tight as outfits for trapeze artists but otherwise struck the proper conservative note, for a team of millionaires: buttons on the shirt and a single red pinstripe. Eckersley yielded a double and then struck out two. The first nicks in statistical virginity had been taken. The season had begun.

Rick Wise didn't look so quick. Jim Rice began to earn his money immediately, singling. Next time up, he looked even more intense than usual and homered to center field, scoring Remy and Burleson ahead of him, and we were back in Sox heaven, where extra bases flow like milk and honey and whence the ghosts of Jimmy Foxx and Johnny Mize, Jackie Jensen and Theodore Williams, Walt Dropo and Clyde Vollmer look smiling down. Before the gray day's long work was over, Lynn had launched a rocket high over right field, Evans had artfully found the corner of the left field net, and Brohamer and Montgomery had offered specimens of that rarest of base hits, the triple. Seven runs scored while Eckersley, his long hair seeming to grow while we watched, allowed two hits. This first kiss tingled down to the toes.

The last inning seemed designed just to remind us that bad things can happen. A walk, an error, a wild pitch. Still, no harm done, and the monster went home happy.

It's a long season. Even an individual game seems long enough. By the sixth inning, that capillary action had begun in the stands that shows the crowd is leaving. What auguries did the Faithful take away, to mull in the gloomy bars of the Back Bay or contemplate among the burgeoning daffodils of suburbia?

Well, we learned that umpires recruited from Buzzards Bay, North

Andover, and Hyannis can maintain law and order in the major leagues.*

We learned that Bob Montgomery and Jack Brohamer, filling in momentarily for the legendary Fisk and doughty Hobson, don't look like spare parts at all.

We saw that Freddy Lynn may this year remind us of his former super self. Stay well, Freddy.**

We saw that Jim Rice can strike out (twice) as well as get hits (two). Still this is the heart of the club. Other players shine; Rich glitters, as if faceted. Only a Mercedes looks as nicely tooled.

We witnessed a little by-play at the beginning that may tell it all. After the Cleveland lineup had been called out, the Red Sox roll began with Zimmer. Out he trotted, last year's anti-hero, the manager who watched ninety-nine victories be not quite enough, with his lopsided cheeks and squint, like a Popeye who has let the spinach settle to his middle. The many-headed monster booed furiously, and Zimmer laughed, shaking hands with his opposite manager, Torborg.

That laugh said a strange thing. It said, *This is fun.* Baseball is meant to be fun, and not all the solemn money men in fur-collared greatcoats, not all the scruffy media cameramen and sour-faced reporters that crowd around the dugouts can quite smother the exhilarating spaciousness and grace of this impudently relaxed sport, a game of innumerable potential redemptions and curious disappointments. This is fun.

A hard lesson for a hungry monster to master, but he has six months to work on it. So let's play ball.

---

* This was the spring of the major-league umpires' strike.

** He did, and enjoyed his best season—the league batting title at .333 and thirty-nine home runs matching Rice. But the club finished eleven and a half games behind Baltimore, taking what satisfaction it could in nosing out the hated Yankees by two games. Zimmer was fired at season's end, and a year later Fisk, Lynn, Burleson, and Hobson were all traded away; thus was dismantled one more of those highly talented Red Sox teams that deserved better luck, or better pitching than they got.

A Female Baseball Club

JAMES A. BAILEY

THE ONLY ATTEMPT on record of Danbury trying to organize a female baseball club occurred last week. It was a rather incipient affair, but it demonstrated everything necessary, and in that particular answered every purpose. The idea was cogitated and carried out by six young ladies. It was merely designed for an experiment on which to base future action. The young ladies were at the house of one of their number when the subject was brought up. The premises are capacious, and include quite a piece of turf, hidden from the street by several drooping, luxuriant, old-fashioned apple-trees. The young lady of the house has a brother who is fond of baseball, and has the necessary machinery for the game. This was taken out on the turf under the trees. The ladies assembled, and divided themselves into two nines of three each. The first three took the bat, and the second three went to the bases, one as catcher, one as pitcher, and the other as chaser, or more technically, fielder. The pitcher was a lively brunette, with eyes full of dead earnestness. The catcher and batter were blondes, with faces aflame with expectation. The pitcher took the ball, braced herself, put her arm straight out from her shoulder, then moved it around to her back without modifying in the least its delightful rigidity, and then threw it. The batter did not catch it. This was owing to the pitcher looking directly at the batter when she aimed it. The fielder got a long pole and soon succeeded in poking the ball from an apple-tree back to the pitcher, where it had lodged. Business was then resumed again, although with a faint semblance of uneasiness generally visible.

The pitcher was very red in the face, and said 'I declare!' several times. This time she took a more careful aim, but still neglected to look in some other direction than toward the batter, and the ball was presently poked out of another tree.

'Why, this is dreadful!' said the batter, whose nerves had been kept at a pretty stiff tension.

'Perfectly dreadful!' chimed in the catcher, with a long sigh.

'I think you had better get up in one of the trees,' mildly suggested the fielder to the batter.

The observation somewhat nettled the pitcher, and she declared she would not try again, whereupon a change was made with the fielder. She was certainly more sensible. Just as soon as she was ready to let drive, she shut her eyes so tight as to loosen two of her puffs and pull out her back comb, and madly fled away. The ball flew directly at the batter, which so startled that lady, who had the bat clinched in both hands with desperate grip, that she involuntarily cried 'Oh, my!' and let it drop and ran. This movement uncovered the catcher, who had both hands extended about three feet apart, in readiness for the catch, but, being intently absorbed in studying the coil on the back of the batter's head, she was not able to recover in time, and the ball caught her in the bodice with sufficient force to deprive her of all her breath, which left her lips with ear-piercing shrillness. There was a lull in the proceedings for ten minutes, to enable the other members of the club to arrange their hair.

The batter again took position, when one of the party, discovering that she was holding the bat very much as a woman carries a broom when she is after a cow in the garden, showed her that the tip must rest on the ground and at her side, with her body a trifle inclined in that direction. The suggester took the bat and showed just how it was done, and brought around the bat with such vehemence as to almost carry her from her feet, and to nearly brain the catcher. That party shivered, and moved back some fifteen feet.

The batter took her place, and laid the tip of the bat on the ground, and the pitcher shut her eyes again as tightly as before, and let drive. The fielder had taken the precaution to get back of a tree, or otherwise she might have been disfigured for life. The ball was recovered. The pitcher looked heated and vexed. She didn't throw it this time. She just gave it a pitching motion, but not letting go of it in time it went over her head, and caused her to sit down with considerable unexpectedness.

Thereupon she declared she would never throw another ball as long as she lived, and changed off with the catcher. This young lady was somewhat determined, which augured success. Then she looked in an altogether different direction for that to the batter.

And this did the business. The batter was ready. She had a tight hold on the bat. Just as soon as she saw the ball start, she made a tremendous lunge with the bat, let go it, and turned around in time to catch the ball in the small of her back, while the bat being on its own hook, and seeing a stone figure holding a vase of flowers, nearly clipped off its arm at the elbow and let the flowers fall to the ground.

There was a chorus of screams, and some confusion of skirts, and then the following dialogue took place;

No 1. 'Let's give up the nasty thing.'

No 2. 'Let's.'

No 3. 'So I say.'

No 4. 'It's just horrid.'

This being a majority, the adjournment was made.

The game was merely an experiment. And it is just as well it was. Had it been a real game, it is likely that some one would have been killed outright.

Man Bites Dog

ELLERY QUEEN

ELLERY QUEEN SOLVES A WORLD SERIES BASEBALL MYSTERY

ANYONE OBSERVING THE tigerish pacings, the gnawings of lip, the contortions of brow, and the fierce melancholy which characterized the conduct of Mr Ellery Queen, the noted sleuth, during those early October days in Hollywood, would have said reverently that the great man's intellect was once more locked in titanic struggles with the forces of evil.

'Paula,' Mr Queen said to Paula Paris, 'I am going mad.'

'I hope,' said Miss Paris tenderly, 'it's love.'

Mr Queen paced, swathed in yards of thought. Queenly Miss Paris observed him with melting eyes. When he had first encountered her, Miss Paris had been in the grip of a morbid psychology. She had been in deathly terror of crowds. 'Crowd phobia,' the doctors called it. Mr Queen had cured her by the curious method of making love to her. And now she was infected by the cure.

'Is it?' asked Miss Paris, her heart in her eyes.'

'Eh?' said Mr Queen. 'What? Oh, no. I mean—it's the World Series.' He looked savage. 'Don't you realize what's happening? The New York Giants and the New York Yankees are waging mortal combat to determine the baseball championship of the world, and I'm three thousand miles away!'

'Oh,' said Miss Paris. Then she said cleverly: 'You poor darling.'

'Never missed a New York series before' wailed Mr Queen. 'Driving me cuckoo. And what a battle! Greatest series ever played. Moore and DiMaggio have done miracles in the outfield. Giants have pulled a triple play. Goofy Gomez struck out fourteen men to win the first game.

Hubbell's pitched a one-hit shutout. And today Dickey came up in the ninth innings with the bases loaded, two out, and the Yanks three runs behind, and slammed a homer over the rightfield stands!'

'Is that good?' asked Miss Paris.

'Good!' howled Mr Queen. 'It *merely* sent the series into a seventh game.'

'Poor darling,' said Miss Paris again, and she picked up her telephone. When she set it down she said: 'Weather's threatening in the East. To-morrow the New York Weather Bureau expects heavy rains.'

Mr Queen stared wildly. 'You mean—'

'I mean that you're taking tonight's plane for the East. And you'll see your beloved seventh game day after tomorrow.'

'Paula, you're a genius!' Then Mr Queen's face fell. 'But the studio, tickets ... *Bigre* ! I'll tell the studio I'm down with elephantiasis, and I'll wire Dad to snare a box. With his pull at City Hall, he ought to—Paula, I don't know what I'd do ...'

'You might,' suggested Miss Paris, 'kiss me ... goodbye.'

Mr Queen did so, absently. Then he started. 'Not at all! You're coming with me!'

'That's what I had in mind,' said Miss Paris contentedly.

And so Wednesday found Miss Paris and Mr Queen at the Polo Grounds, ensconced in a field box behind the Yankees' dugout.

Mr Queen glowed, he revelled, he was radiant. While Inspector Queen, with the suspiciousness of all fathers, engaged Paula in exploratory conversation, Ellery filled his lap and Paula's with peanut hulls, consumed frankfurters and soda pop immoderately, made hypercritical comments on the appearance of the various athletes, derided the Yankees, extolled the Giants, evolved complicated fifty-cent bets with Detective Sergeant Velie, of the Inspector's staff, and leaped to his fee screaming with fifty thousand other maniacs as the news came that Carl Hubbell, the beloved Meal Ticket of the Giants, would oppose Señor El Goofy Gomez, the ace of the Yankee staff, on the mound.

'Will the Yanks murder that apple today!' predicted the Sergeant, who was an incurable Yankee worshipper. 'And will Goofy mow 'em down!'

'Four bits,' said Mr Queen coldly, 'say the Yanks don't score three earned runs off Carl.'

'It's a pleasure!'

'I'll take a piece of that, Sergeant,' chuckled a handsome man to the front of them, in a rail seat. 'Hi, Inspector. Swell day for it, eh?'

'Jimmy Connor!' exclaimed Inspector Queen. 'The old Song-and-Dance Man in person. Say, Jimmy, you never met my son Ellery, did you? Excuse me, Miss Paris, this is the famous Jimmy Connor, God's gift to Broadway.'

'Glad to meet you, Miss Paris,' smiled the Song-and-Dance Man, sniffing at his orchidaceous lapel. 'Read your 'Seeing Stars' column, every day. Meet Judy Starr.'

Miss Paris smiled, and the woman beside Jimmy Connor smiled back, and just then three Yankee players strolled over to the box and began to jeer at Connor for having had to take seats behind the hated Yankee dugout.

Judy Starr was sitting oddly still. She was the famous Judy Starr who had been discovered by Florenz Ziegfeld—a second Marilyn Miller, the critics called her; dainty and pretty, with a perky profile and great honey-coloured eyes, who had sung and danced her way into the heart of New York. Her day of fame was almost over now. Perhaps thought Paula, staring at Judy's profile, that explained the pinch of her little mouth, the fine lines about her tragic eyes, the singing tension of her figure.

Perhaps. But Paula was not sure. There was immediacy, a defence against a palpable and present danger, in Judy Starr's tautness. Paula looked about. And at once her eyes narrowed.

Across the rail of the box, in the box at their left, sat a very tall, leather-skinned, silent and intent man. The man, too, was staring out at the field, in an attitude curiously like that of Judy Starr, whom he could have touched by extending his big, ropy, muscular hand across the rail. And on the man's other side there sat a woman whom Paula recognized instantly. Lotus Verne, the motion-picture actress!

Lotus Verne was a gorgeous, full-blown redhead with deep mercury-colored eyes who had come out of Northern Italy Ludovica Vernicchi, changed her name, and flashed across the Hollywood skies in a picture called *Woman of Bali*, a color film in which loving care had been lavished on the display possibilities of her dark, full, dangerous body. With fame, she had developed a passion for press-agentry, borzois in pairs, and tall brown men with muscles. She was arrayed in sun yellow, and she stood out among the women in the field boxes like a butterfly in a mass of grubs. By contrast little Judy Starr, in her flame-colored outfit, looked almost old and dowdy.

Paula nudged Ellery, who was critically watching the Yankees at batting practice. 'Ellery,' she said softly, 'who is that big, brown, attractive man in the next box?'

Lotus Verne said something to the brown man, and suddenly Judy Starr said something to the Song-and-Dance Man; and then the two women exchanged the kind of glance women use when there is no knife handy.

Ellery said absently: 'Who? Oh! That's Big Bill Tree.'

'Tree?' repeated Paula. 'Big Bill Tree?'

'Greatest left-handed pitcher major league baseball ever saw,' said Mr Queen, staring reverently at the brown man. 'Six feet three inches of bull whip and muscle, with a temper as sudden as the hook on his curve ball and a change of pace that fooled the greatest sluggers of baseball for fifteen years. What a man!'

'Yes, isn't he?' smiled Miss Paris.

'Now what does that mean?' demanded Mr Queen.

'It takes greatness to escort a lady like Lotus Verne to a ball game,' said Paula, 'to find your wife sitting within spitting distance in the next box, and to carry it off as well as your muscular friend Mr Tree is doing.'

'That's right,' said Mr Queen softly, 'Judy Starr *is* Mrs Bill Tree.'

He groaned as Joe DiMaggio hit a ball to the clubhouse clock.

'Funny,' said Miss Paris, her clever eyes inspecting in turn the four people before her: Lotus Verne, the Hollywood siren; Big Bill Tree, the ex-baseball pitcher; Judy Starr, Tree's wife; and Jimmy Connor, the Song-and-Dance Man, Mrs Tree's escort. Two couples, two boxes . . . and not sign of recognition. 'Funny,' murmured Miss Paris, 'From the way Tree courted Judy you'd have thought the marriage would outlast eternity. He snatched her from under Jimmy Connor's nose one night at the Winter Garden, drove her up to Greenwich at eighty miles an hour, and married her before she could catch her breath.'

'Yes,' said Mr Queen politely. 'Come on, you Giants!' he yelled, as the Giants trotted out for batting practice.

'And then something happened,' continued Miss Paris reflectively. 'Tree went to Hollywood to make a baseball picture, met Lotus Verne, and the wench took the overgrown country boy the way the overgrown country boy had taken Judy Starr. What a fall was there, my baseball-minded friend.'

'What a wallop!' cried Mr Queen enthusiastically, as Mel Ott hit one that bounced off the right field fence.

'And Big Bill yammered for a divorce, and Judy refused to give it to him because she loved him, I suppose,' said Paula softly—'and now this. How interesting.'

Big Bill Tree twisted in his seat a little; and Judy Starr was still and pale, staring out of her tragic, honey-colored eyes at the Yankee bat boy and giving him unwarranted delusions of grandeur. Jimmy Connor continued to exchange sarcastic greetings with Yankee players, but his eyes kept shifting back to Judy's face. And beautiful Lotus Verne's arm crept about Tree's shoulders.

'I don't like it,' murmured Miss Paris a little later.

'You don't like it?' said Mr Queen. 'Why, the game hasn't even started.'

'I don't mean your game, silly. I mean the quadrangular situation in front of us.'

'Look, darling,' said Mr Queen. 'I flew three thousand miles to see a ball game. There's only one angle that interests me—the view from this box of the greatest li'l ol' baseball tussle within the memory of gaffers. I yearn, I strain, I hunger to see it. Play with your quadrangle, but leave me to my baseball.'

'I've always been psychic,' said Miss Paris, paying no attention. 'This is—bad. Something's going to happen.'

Mr Queen grinned. 'I know what. The deluge. See what's coming.'

Someone in the grandstand had recognized the celebrities, and a sea of people was rushing down on the two boxes. They swamped the aisle behind the boxes, bobbing pencils and papers, and pleading. Big Bill Tree and Lotus Verne ignored their pleas for autographs; but Judy Starr with a curious eagerness signed paper after paper with the yellow pencils thrust at her by people leaning over the rail. Good-naturedly Jimmy Connor scrawled his signature, too.

'Little Judy,' sighed Miss Paris, setting her natural straw straight as an autograph hunter knocked it over her eyes, 'is flustered and unhappy. Moistening the tip of your pencil with your tongue is scarcely a mark of poise. Seated next to her Lotus-bound husband, she hardly knows what she's doing, poor thing.'

'Neither do I,' growled Mr Queen, fending off an octopus which turned out to be eight pleading arms offering scorecards.

Big Bill sneezed, groped for a handkerchief, and held it to his nose, which was red and swollen. 'Hey, Mac,' he called irritably to a red-coated usher. 'Do somethin' about this mob, huh?' He sneezed again. 'Damn this hay-fever!'

'The touch of earth,' said Miss Paris. 'But definitely attractive.'

'Should 'a' seen Big Bill the day he pitched that World Series final against the Tigers,' chuckled Sergeant Velie. 'He was sure attractive that day. Pitched a no-hit shutout!'

Inspector Queen said: 'Ever hear the story behind that final game, Miss Paris? The night before, a gambler named Sure Shot McCoy, who represented a betting syndicate, called on Big Bill and laid down fifty grand in spot cash in return for Bill's promise to throw the next day's game. Bill took the money, told his manager the whole story, donated the bribe to a fund for sick ball players, and the next day shut out the Tigers without a hit.'

'Byronic, too,' murmured Miss Paris.

'So then Sure Shot, badly bent,' grinned the Inspector, 'called on Bill for the payoff. Bill knocked him down two flights of stairs.'

'Wasn't that dangerous?'

'I guess,' smiled the Inspector, 'you could say so. That's why you see that plug-ugly with the smashed nose sitting over there right behind Tree's box. He's Mr Terrible Turk, late of Cicero, and since that night Big Bill's shadow. You don't see Mr Turk's right hand, because Mr Turk's right hand is holding on to an automatic under his jacket. You'll notice, too, that Mr Turk hasn't for a second taken his eyes of that pasty-cheeked customer eight rows up, whose name is Sure Shot McCoy.'

Paula stared. 'But what a silly thing for Tree to do!'

'Well, yes,' drawled Inspector Queen, 'seeing that when he popped Mr McCoy Big Bill snapped two of the carpal bones of his pitching wrist and wrote finis to his baseball career.'

Big Bill Tree hauled himself to his feet, whispered something to the Verne woman, who smiled coyly, and left his box. His bodyguard, Turk, jumped up; but the big man shook his head, waved aside a crowd of people, and vaulted up the concrete steps towards the rear of the grandstand.

And then Judy Starr said something bitter and hot and desperate across the rail to the woman her husband had brought to the Polo Grounds. Lotus Verne's mercurial eyes glittered, and she replied in a careless, insulting voice that made Bill Tree's wife sit up stiffly. Jimmy Connor began to tell the one about Walter Winchell and the Seven Dwarfs . . . loudly and fast.

The Verne woman began to paint her rich lips with short, vicious strokes of her orange lipstick; and Judy Starr's flame kid glove tightened on the rail between them.

And after a while Big Bill returned and sat down again. Judy said something to Jimmy Connor, and the Song-and-Dance man slid over one seat to his right, and Judy slipped into Connor's seat; so that between her and her husband there was now not only the box rail but an empty chair as well.

Lotus Verne put her arm about Tree's shoulders again.

Tree's wife fumbled inside her flame suède bag. She said suddenly: 'Jimmy, buy me a frankfurter.'

Connor ordered a dozen. Big Bill scowled. He jumped up and ordered some, too, Connor tossed the vendor two one-dollar bills and waved him away.

A new sea deluged the two boxes, and Tree turned round, annoyed. 'All right, all right, Mac,' he growled at the red coat struggling with the pressing mob. 'We don't want a riot here. I'll take six. Just six. Let's have 'em.'

There was a rush that almost upset the attendant. The rail behind the boxes was a solid line of fluttering hands, arms, and scorecards.

'Mr Tree—said—six!' panted the usher; and he grabbed a pencil and card from one of the outstretched hands and gave them to Tree. The overflow of pleaders spread to the next box. Judy Starr smiled her best professional smile and reached for a pencil and card. A group of players on the field, seeing what was happening, ran over to the field rail and handed her scorecards, too, so that she had to set her half-consumed frankfurter down on the empty seat beside her. Big Bill set his frankfurter down on the same empty sea; he licked the pencil long and absently and began to inscribe his name in the stiff, laborious hand of a man unused to writing.

The attendant howled: 'That's six, now! Mr Tree said just six, so that's all!' as if God Himself had said six; and the crowd groaned, and Big Bill waved his immense paw and reached over to the empty seat in the other box to lay hold of his half-eaten frankfurter. But his wife's hand got there first and fumbled around; and it came up with Tree's frankfurter. The big brown man almost spoke to her then; but he did not, and he picked up the remaining frankfurter, stuffed it into his mouth, and chewed anyway, but not as if he enjoyed its taste.

Mr Ellery Queen was looking at the four people before him with a puzzled, worried expression. Then he caught Miss Paula Paris's amused glance and blushed angrily.

The groundkeepers had just left the field and the senior umpire was dusting off the plate to the roar of the crowd when Lotus Verne, who thought a double play was something by Eugene O'Neill, flashed a strange look at Big Bill Tree.

'Bill! Don't you feel well?'

The big ex-pitcher, a sickly blue beneath his tanned skin, put his hand to his eyes and shook his head as if to clear it.

'It's that hot dog,' snapped Lotus. 'No more for you!'

Tree blinked and began to say something, but just then Carl Hubbell completed his warming-up, Crosetti marched to the plate, Harry Danning tossed the ball to his second-baseman, who flipped it to Hubbell and trotted back to his position yipping like a terrier.

The voice of the crowd exploded in one ear-splitting burst. And then silence.

And Crosetti swung at the first ball Hubbell pitched and smashed it far over Joe Moore's head for a triple.

Jimmy Connor gasped as if someone had thrust a knife into his heart. But Detective-Sergeant Velie was bellowing: 'What'd I tell you? It's gonna be a massacree!'

'What is everyone shouting for?' asked Paula.

Mr Queen nibbled his nails as Danning strolled halfway to the pitcher's box. But Hubbell pulled his long pants up, grinning. Red Rolfe was waving a huge bat at the plate. Danning trotted back. Manager Bill Terry had one foot up on the edge of the Giant dugout, his chin on his fist, looking anxious. The infield came in to cut off the run.

Again fifty thousand people made no single little sound.

And Hubbell struck out Rolfe, DiMaggio, and Gehrig.

Mr Queen shrieked his joy with the thousands as the Giants came whooping in. Jimmy Connor did an Indian war dance in the box. Sergeant Velie looked aggrieved. Señor Gomez took his warm-up pitches, the umpire used his whiskbroom on the plate again, and Jo-Jo Moore, the Thin Man, ambled up with his war club.

He walked. Bartell fanned. But Jeep Ripple singled off Flash Gordon's shins on the first pitch; and there were Moore on third and Ripple on first, one out, and Little Mel Ott at bat.

Big Bill Tree got half out of his seat, looking surprised, and then dropped to the concrete floor of the box as if somebody had slammed him behind the ear with a fast ball.

Lotus screamed. Judy, Bill's wife, turned like a shot, shaking. People in the vicinity jumped up. The red-coated attendants hurried down, preceded by the hard-looking Mr Turk. The bench-warmers stuck their heads over the edge of the Yankee dugout to stare.

'Fainted,' growled Turk, on his knees beside the prostrate athlete.

'Loosen his collar,' moaned Lotus Verne. 'He's so p-pale!'

'Have to git him outa here.'

'Yes, Oh, yes!'

The attendants and Turk lugged the big man off, long arms dangling in the oddest way. Lotus stumbled along beside him, biting her lips nervously.

'I think . . .' began Judy in a quivering voice, rising.

But Jimmy Connor put his hand on her arm, and she sank back.

And in the next box Mr Ellery Queen, on his feet from the instant Tree collapsed, kept looking after the forlorn procession, puzzled, mad about something; until somebody in the stands squawked: 'SIDDOWN!' and he sat down.

'Oh, I knew something would happen,' whispered Paula.

'Nonsense!' said Mr Queen shortly. 'Fainted, that's all.'

Inspector Queen said: 'There's Sure Shot McCoy not far off. I wonder if—'

'Too many hot dogs,' snapped his son. 'What's the matter with you people? Can't I see my ball game in peace?' And he howled: 'Come o-o-on, Mel!'

Ott lifted his right leg into the sky and swung. The ball whistled into right field, a long long fly, Selkirk racing madly back after it. He caught it by leaping four feet into the air with his back against the barrier. Moore was off for the plate like a streak and beat the throw to Bill Dickey by inches.

'Yip-ee!' Thus Mr Queen.

The Giants trotted out to their positions at the end of the first innings leading one to nothing.

Up in their press box the working gentlemen of the press tore into their chores, recalling Carl Hubbell's similar feat in the All-Star game when he struck out the five greatest batters of the American League in succession; praising Twinkletoe Selkirk, for his circus catch; and incidentally noting that Big Bill Tree, famous ex-hurler of the National League, had fainted in a field box during the first innings. Joe Williams of the *World-Telegram* said it was excitement, Hype Igoe opined that it was a touch of sun—Big Bill never wore a hat—and Frank Graham of the *Sun* guessed it was too many frankfurters.

Paula Paris said quietly: 'I should think, with your detective instincts, Mr Queen, you would seriously question the 'fainting' of Mr Tree.'

Mr Queen squirmed and finally mumbled: 'It's coming to a pretty pass when a man's instincts aren't his own. Velie, go see what really happened to him.'

'I wanna watch the game,' howled Velie. 'Why don't you go yourself, Maestro?'

'And possibly,' said Mr Queen, 'you ought to go too, Dad. I have a hunch it may lie in your jurisdiction.'

Inspector Queen regarded his son for some time. Then he rose and sighed: 'Come along, Thomas.'

Sergeant Velie growled something about some people always spoiling other people's fun and why the hell did he ever have to become a cop; but he got up and obediently followed the Inspector.

Mr Queen nibbled his fingernails and avoided Miss Paris's accusing eyes.

The second innings was uneventful. Neither side scored.

As the Giants took the field again, an usher came running down the concrete steps and whispered into Jim Connor's ear. The Song-and-Dance Man blinked. He rose slowly. 'Excuse me, Judy.'

Judy grasped the rail. 'It's Bill, Jimmy, tell me.'

'Now, Judy—'

'Something's happened to Bill!' Her voice shrilled, and then broke. She jumped up. 'I'm going with you.'

Connor smiled as if he had just lost a bet, and then he took Judy's arm and hurried her away.

Paula Paris stared after them, breathing hard.

Mr Queen beckoned the redcoat. 'What's the trouble?' he demanded.

'Mr Tree passed out. Some young doc in the crowd tried to pull him out of it up at the office, but he couldn't and he's startin' to look worried—'

'I knew it!' cried Paula as the man darted away. 'Ellery Queen, are you going to sit here and do *nothing?*
But Mr Queen defiantly set his jaw. Nobody was going to jockey him out of seeing this battle of giants; no, ma'am!'

There were two men out when Frank Crosetti stepped up to the plate for his second time at bat, and, with the count two all, plastered a wicked single over Ott's head.

And, of course, Sergeant Velie took just that moment to amble down and say, his eyes on the field: 'Better come along, Master Mind. The old man wouldst have a word with thou. Ah, I see Frankie's on first, Smack it, Red!'

Mr Queen watched Rolfe take a ball. 'Well?' he said shortly. Paula's lips were parted.

'Big Bill's just kicked the bucket. What happened in the second innings?'

'He's . . . *dead?*' gasped Paula.

Mr Queen rose involuntarily. Then he sat down again.

'Damn it,' he roared, 'it isn't fair, I won't go!'

'Suit yourself. Attaboy, Rolfe!' bellowed the Sergeant as Rolfe singled sharply past Bartell and Crosetti pulled up at second base. 'Far's I'm concerned, it's open and shut. The little woman did it with her own little hands.'

'Judy *Starr?*' said Miss Paris.

'Bill's wife?' said Mr Queen. 'What are you talking about?'

'That's right, little Judy. She poisoned his hot dog.' Velie chuckled. 'Man bites dog, and—zowie.'

'Has she confessed?' snapped Mr Queen.

'Naw. But you know dames. She gave Bill the business, all right. C'mon Joe! And I gotta go. What a life.'

Mr Queen did not look at Miss Paris. He bit his lip. 'Here Velie, wait a minute.'

DiMaggio hit a long fly that Leiber caught without moving in his tracks, and the Yankees were retired without a score.

'Ah,' said Mr Queen. 'Good old Hubbell.' And as the Giants trotted in, he took a fat roll of bills from his pocket, climbed on to his seat, and began waving greenbacks at the spectators in the reserved seats behind the box. Sergeant Velie and Miss Paris stared at him in amazement.

'I'll give five bucks,' yelled Mr Queen, waving the money, 'for every autograph Bill Tree signed before the game! In this box right here! Five bucks, gentlemen! Come and get it!'

'You nuts?' gasped the Sergeant.

The mob gaped, and then began to laugh, and after a few moments a pair of sheepish-looking men came down, and then two more, and finally a fifth. An attendant ran over the find out what was the matter.

'Are you the usher who handled the crowd around Bill Tree's box before the game, when he was giving autographs?' demanded Mr Queen.

'Yes, sir. But, look, we can't allow—'

'Take a gander at these five men ... You, bud? Yes, that's Tree's handwriting. Here's your fin. Next!' and Mr Queen went down the line, handing out five-dollar bills with abandon in return for five dirty scorecards with Tree's scrawl on them.

'Anybody else?' he called out, waving his roll of bills.

But nobody else appeared, although there was ungentle badinage from the stands, Sergeant Velie stood there shaking his big head. Miss Paris looked intensely curious.

'Who didn't come down?' rapped Mr Queen.

'Huh?' said the usher, his mouth open.

'There were six autographs. Only five people turned up. Who was the sixth man? Speak up!'

'Oh.' The redcoat scratched his ear. 'Say, it wasn't a man. It was a kid.'

'A *boy?*'

'Yeah, a little squirt in knee-pants.'

Mr Queen looked unhappy, Velie growled: 'Sometimes I think society's takin' an awful chance lettin' you run around loose,' and the two men left the box. Miss Paris, bright-eyed, followed.

'Have to clear this mess up in a hurry,' muttered Mr Queen. 'Maybe we'll still be able to catch the late innings.'

Sergeant Velie led the way to an office, before which a policeman was lounging. He opened the door, and inside they found the Inspector pacing. Turk, the thug, was standing with a scowl over a long still thing on a couch covered with newspapers. Jimmy Connor sat between the two women; and none of the three so much as stirred a foot. They were all pale and breathing heavily.

'This is Dr Fielding,' said Inspector Queen, indicating an elderly white-haired man standing quietly by a window. 'He was Tree's physician. He happened to be in the park watching the game when the rumor reached his ears that Tree had collapsed. So he hurried up here to see what he could do.'

Ellery went to the couch and pulled the newspaper off Bill Tree's still head. Paula crossed swiftly to Judy Starr and said: 'I'm horribly sorry, Mrs Tree,' but the woman, her eyes closed, did not move. After a while Ellery dropped the newspaper back into place and said irritably: 'Well, well let's have it.'

'A young doctor,' said the Inspector, 'got here before Dr Fielding did, and treated Tree for fainting. I guess it was his fault—'

'Not at all,' said Dr Fielding sharply. 'The early picture was compatible with fainting, from what he told me. He tried the usual restorative methods—even injected caffeine and picrotoxin. But there was no convulsion, and he didn't happen to catch the odor of bitter almonds.'

'Prussic!' said Ellery. 'Taken orally?'

'Yes HCN—hydrocyanic acid, or prussic, as you prefer. I suspected it at once because—well,' said Dr Fielding in a grim voice, 'because of something that occurred in my office only the other day.'

'What was that?'

'I had a two-ounce bottle of hydrocyanic acid on my desk—I sometimes use it in minute quantities as a cardiac stimulant. Mrs Tree,' the doctor's glance flickered over the silent woman, 'happened to be in my office, resting in preparation for a metabolism test. I left her alone. By coincidence, Bill Tree dropped in the same morning for a physical check-up. I saw another patient in another room, returned, gave Mrs Tree her test, saw her out, and came back with Tree. It was then I noticed the bottle, which had been plainly marked DANGER—POISON, was missing from my desk. I thought I had mislaid it, but now . . .'

'I didn't take it,' said Judy Starr in a lifeless voice, still not opening her eyes, 'I never even saw it.'

The Song-and-Dance Man took her limp hand and gently stroked it.

'No hypo marks on the body,' said Dr Fielding dryly. 'And I am told that fifteen to thirty minutes before Tree collapsed he ate a frankfurter under . . . peculiar conditions.'

'I didn't!' screamed Judy. 'I didn't do it!' She pressed her face, sobbing, against Connor's orchid.

Lotus Verne quivered. 'She made him pick up her frankfurter. I saw it. They both laid their frankfurters down on that empty seat, and she picked up his. So he had to pick up hers. She poisoned her own frankfurter and then saw to it that he ate it by mistake. Poisoner!' She glared hate at Judy.

'Wench,' said Miss Paris *sotto voce*, glaring hate at Lotus.

'In other words,' put in Ellery impatiently, 'Miss Starr is convicted on the usual two counts, motive and opportunity. Motive—her jealousy of Miss Verne and her hatred—an assumption—of Bill Tree, her husband. And opportunity both to lay hands on the poison in your office, Doctor, and to sprinkle some on her frankfurter, contriving to exchange hers for his while they were both autographing scorecards.'

'She hated him,' snarled Lotus. 'And me for having taken him from her!'

'Be quiet, you,' said Mr Queen. He opened the corridor door and said to the policeman outside. 'Look, McGillicuddy, or whatever your name is, go tell the announcer to make a speech over the loudspeaker system. By the way, what's the score now?'

'Still one to skunk,' said the officer. 'Them boys Hubbell an' Gomez are hot, know what I mean.'

'The announcer is to ask the little boy who got Bill Tree's autograph just before the game to come to this office. If he does, he'll receive a ball, bat, pitcher's glove, and an autographed picture of Tree in uniform to hang over his itsy-bitsy bed. Scram!'

'Yes *sir*,' said the officer.

'King Carl pitching his heart out,' grumbled Mr Queen, shutting the door, 'and me strangulated by this blamed thing. Well Dad, do you think, too, that Judy Starr dosed that frankfurter?'

'What else can I think?' said the Inspector absently. His ears were cocked for the faint crowd shouts from the park.

'Judy Starr,' replied his son, 'didn't poison her husband any more than I did.'

Judy looked up slowly, her mouth muscles twitching. Paula said gladly: 'You wonderful man!'

'She didn't?' said the Inspector, looking alert.

'The frankfurter theory,' snapped Mr Queen, 'is too screwy for words. For Judy to have poisoned her husband, she had to unscrew the cap of a bottle and douse her hot dog on the spot with the hydrocyanic acid. Yet Jimmy Connor was seated by her side, and in the only period in which she could possibly have poisoned the frankfurter a group of

Yankee ball players was *standing before her* across the field rail getting her autograph. Were they all accomplices? And how could she have known Big Bill would lay his hot dog on that empty seat? The whole thing is absurd.'

A roar from the stands made him continue hastily: 'There was one plausible theory that fitted the facts. When I heard that Tree had died of poisoning, I recalled that at the time he was autographing the six scorecards, *he had thoroughly licked the end of a pencil* which had been handed to him with one of the cards. It was possible, then, that the pencil he licked had been poisoned. So I offered to buy the six auto-graphs.'

Paula regarded him tenderly, and Velie said: 'I'll be a so-and-so if he didn't.'

'I didn't expect the poisoner to come forward, but I knew the innocent ones would. Five claimed the money. The sixth, the missing one, the usher informed me, had been a small boy.'

'A kid poisoned Bill?' growled Turk, speaking for the first time. 'You're crazy from the heat.'

'In spades,' added the Inspector.

'Then why didn't the boy come forward?' put in Paula quickly. 'Go on darling!'

'He didn't come forward, not because he was guilty but because he wouldn't sell Bill Tree's autograph for anything. No, obviously a hero-worshipping boy wouldn't try to poison the great Bill Tree. Then, just as obviously, he didn't realize what he was doing. Consequently, he must have been an innocent tool. The question was—and still is—of whom?'

'Sure Shot,' said the Inspector slowly.

Lotus Verne sprang to her feet, her eyes glittering. 'Perhaps Judy Starr didn't poison that frankfurter, but if she didn't then she hired that boy to give Bill—'

Mr Queen said disdainfully: 'Miss Starr didn't leave the box once,' Someone knocked on the corridor door and he opened it. For the first time he smiled. When he shut the door they saw that his arm was about the shoulders of a boy with brown hair and quick clever eyes. The boy was clutching a scorecard tightly. .

'They say over the announcer,' mumbled the boy, 'that I'll get a auto-graphed pi'ture of Big Bill Tree if . . .' He stopped, abashed at their strangely glinting eyes.

'And you'll certainly get it, too,' said Mr Queen heartily. 'What's your name, Sonny?'

'Fenimore Feigenspan,' replied the boy, edging towards the door. 'Gran' Concourse, Bonx. Here's the scorecard. How about the pi'ture?'

'Let's see that, Fenimore,' said Mr Queen. 'When did Bill Tree give you this autograph?'

'Before the game. He said he'd on'y give six—'

'Where's the pencil you handed him, Fenimore?'

The boy looked suspicious, but he dug into a bulging pocket and brought forth one of the ordinary yellow pencils sold at the park with scorecards. Ellery took it from him gingerly, and Dr Fielding took it from Ellery, and sniffed its tip. He nodded, for the first time a look of peace came over Judy Starr's still face and she dropped her head tiredly to Connor's shoulder.

Mr Queen ruffled Fenimore Feigenspan's hair. 'That's swell, Fenimore. Somebody gave you that pencil while the Giants were at batting practice, isn't that so?'

'Yeah.' The boy stared at him.

'Who was it?' asked Mr Queen lightly.

'I dunno. A big guy with a coat an' a turned-down hat an' a moustache, an' big black sunglasses. I couldn't see his face good. Where's my pi'ture? I wanna see the game!'

'Just where was it that this man gave you the pencil?'

'In the—' Fenimore paused, glancing at the ladies with embarrassment. Then he muttered: 'Well, I hadda go, an' this guy says—in there—he's ashamed to ask her for her autograph, so would I do it for him—'

'What? What's that?' exclaimed Mr Queen. 'Did you say "her"?'

'Sure,' said Fenimore. 'The dame, he says, wearin' the red hat an' red dress an' red gloves in the field box near the Yanks' dugout he says. He even took me outside an' pointed down to where she was sittin'. Say!' cried Fenimore, goggling. 'That's her! That's the dame!' and he levelled a grimy forefinger at Judy Starr.

Judy shivered and felt blindly for the Song-and-Dance Man's hand.

'Let me get this straight, Fenimore,' said Mr Queen softly. 'This man with the sunglasses asked you to get this lady's autograph for him, and gave you the pencil and scorecard to get it with?'

'Yeah, an' two bucks too, sayin' he'd meet me after the game to pick up the card, but—'

'But you didn't get the lady's autograph for him, did you? You went down to get it, and hung around waiting for your chance, but then you spied Big Bill Tree, your hero, in the next box and forgot all about the lady, didn't you?'

The boy shrank back. 'I didn't mean to, honest, Mister. I'll give the two bucks back!'

'And seeing Big Bill there, your hero, you went right over to get *his* autograph for *yourself*, didn't you?' Fenimore nodded, frightened. 'You gave the usher the pencil and scorecard this man with the sunglasses had handed you, and the usher turned the pencil and scorecard over to Bill Tree in the box—wasn't that the way it happened?'

'Y-yes sir, an' ...' Fenimore twisted out of Ellery's grasp, 'an' so I—I gotta go.' And before anyone could stop him he was indeed gone, racing down the corridor like the wind.

The policeman outside shouted, but Ellery said: 'Let him go, officer,' and shut the door. Then he opened it again and said: 'How's she stand now?'

'Dunno exactly, sir. Somethin' happened out there just now. I think the Yanks scored.'

'Damn,' groaned Mr Queen, and he shut the door again.

'So it was Mrs Tree who was on the spot, not Bill,' scowled the Inspector. 'I'm sorry, Judy Starr ... Big man with a coat and hat and moustache and sunglasses. Some description!'

'Sounds like a phony to me,' said Sergeant Velie.

'If it was a disguise, he dumped it somewhere,' said the Inspector thoughtfully. 'Thomas, have a look in the Men's Room behind the section where we were sitting. And Thomas,' he added in a whisper, 'find out what the score is.' Velie grinned and hurried out. Inspector Queen frowned. 'Quite a job finding a killer in a crowd of fifty thousand people.'

'Maybe,' said his son suddenly, 'maybe it's not such a job after all ... What was used to kill? Hydrocyanic acid. Who was intended to be killed. Bill Tree's wife. Any connection between anyone in the case and hydrocyanic acid. Yes—Dr Fielding 'lost' a bottle of it under suspicious circumstances. Which were? That Bill Tree's wife could have taken that bottle ... *or Bill Tree himself.*'

'Bill Tree!' gasped Paula.

'Bill?' whispered Judy Starr.

'Quite! Dr Fielding didn't miss the bottle until *after* he had shown you, Miss Starr, out of his office. He then returned to his office with your husband. Bill could have slipped the bottle into his pocket as he stepped into the room.'

'Yes, he could have,' muttered Dr Fielding.

'I don't see,' said Mr Queen, 'how we can arrive at any other conclusion. We know his wife was intended to be the victim to-day, so obviously she didn't steal the poison. The only other person who had opportunity to steal it was Bill himself.'

The Verne woman sprang up. 'I don't believe it! It's a frame up to protect *her,* now that Bill can't defend himself!'

'Ah, but didn't he have motive to kill Judy?' asked Mr Queen. 'Yes indeed: she wouldn't give him the divorce he craved so that he could marry *you.* I think, Miss Verne, you would be wiser to keep the peace ... Bill had opportunity to steal the bottle of poison in Dr Fielding's office. He also had opportunity to hire Fenimore to-day, for he was the *only* one of the whole group who left those two boxes during the period when the poisoner must have searched for someone to offer Judy the poisoned pencil.

'All of which fits for what Bill had to do—get to where he had cached his disguise, probably yesterday; look for a likely tool; find Fenimore, give him his instructions and pencil; get rid of the disguise again; and return to his box. And didn't Bill know better than anyone his wife's habit of moistening a pencil with her tongue—a habit she probably acquired from *him*?'

'Poor Bill,' murmured Judy Starr brokenly.

'Women,' remarked Miss Paris, '*are fools.*'

'There were other striking ironies,' replied Mr Queen. 'For if Bill hadn't been suffering from a hay-fever attack, he would have smelled the odor of bitter almonds when his own poisoned pencil was handed to him and stopped in time to save his worthless life. For that matter, if he hadn't been Fenimore Feigenspan's hero, Fenimore would not have handed him his own poisoned pencil in the first place.'

'No,' said Mr Queen gladly, 'putting it all together, I'm satisfied that Mr Big Bill Tree, in trying to murder his wife, very neatly murdered himself instead.'

'That's all very well for *you*,' said the Inspector disconsolately. 'But *I* need proof.'

'I've told you how it happened,' said his son airily, making for the door. 'Can any man do more? Coming, Paula?'

But Paula was already at a telephone, speaking guardedly to the New

York office of the syndicate for which she worked, and paying no more attention to him than if he had been a worm.

'What's the score? What's been going on?' Ellery demanded of the world at large as he regained his box seat. 'Three to three! What the devil's got into Hubbell, anyway? How'd the Yanks score? What innings is it?'

'Last of the ninth,' shrieked somebody. 'The Yanks got three runs in the eighth on a walk, a double, and DiMag's homer! Danning homered in the sixth with Ott on base! Shut up!'

Bartell singled over Gordon's head. Mr Queen cheered.

Sergeant Velie tumbled into the next seat. 'Well, we got it,' he puffed. 'Found the whole outfit in the Men's Room—coat, hat, fake moustache, glasses and all. What's the score?'

'Three-three. Sacrifice, Jeep!' shouted Mr Queen.

'There was a rain check in the coat pocket from the sixth game, with Big Bill's box number on it. So there's the old man's proof. Chalk up another win for you.'

'Who cares? . . . *Zowie!*'

Jeep Ripple sacrificed Bartell successfully to second.

'Lucky stiff,' howled a Yankee fan near by. 'That's the breaks. See the breaks they get? See?'

'And another thing,' said the Sergeant, watching Mel Ott stride to the plate. 'Seein' as how all Big Bill did was cross himself up, and no harm done except to his own carcass, and seein' as how organized baseball could get along without a murder, and seein' as how thousands of kids like Fenimore Feigenspan worship the ground he walked on—'

'Sew it up, Mel!' bellowed Mr Queen.

'—and seein' as how none of the newspaper guys know what happened, except that Bill passed out of the picture after a faint, and seein' as everybody's only too glad to shut their traps—'

Mr Queen, awoke suddenly to the serious matters of life. 'What's that? What did you say?'

'Strike him out, Goofy!' roared the Sergeant to Señor Gomez, who did not hear. 'As I was sayin', it ain't cricket, and the old man would be broke out of the force if the big cheese heard about it . . .'

Someone puffed up behind them, and they turned to see Inspector Queen, red-faced as if after a hard run, scrambling into the box with the assistance of Miss Paula Paris, who looked cool, serene and star-eyed as ever.

'Dad!' said Mr Queen, staring. 'With a murder on your hands, how can you—'

'Murder?' panted Inspector Queen. 'What murder?' And he winked at Miss Paris, who winked back.

'But Paula was telephoning the story—'

'Didn't you hear?' said Paula in a coo, setting her straw straight and slipping into the seat beside Ellery's. 'I fixed it all up with your Dad. Tonight all the world will know is that Mr Bill Tree died of heart failure.'

They all chuckled then—all but Mr Queen, whose mouth was open.

'So now,' said Paula, 'your Dad can see the finish of your precious game just as well as *you*, you selfish oaf!'

But Mr Queen was already fiercely rapt in contemplation of Mel Ott's bat as it swung back and Señor's Gomez's ball as it left the Señor's hand to streak towards the plate.

Baseball Hattie

DAMON RUNYON

IT COMES ON springtime, and the little birdies are singing in the trees in Central Park, and the grass is green all around and about, and I am at the Polo Grounds on the opening day of the baseball season, when who do I behold but Baseball Hattie. I am somewhat surprised at this spectacle, as it is years since I see Baseball Hattie, and for all I know she long ago passes to a better and happier world.

But there she is, as large as life, and in fact twenty pounds larger, and when I call the attention of Armand Fibleman, the gambler, to her, he gets up and tears right out of the joint as if he sees a ghost, for if there is one thing Armand Fibleman loathes and despises, it is a ghost.

I can see that Baseball Hattie is greatly changed, and to tell the truth, I can see that she is getting to be nothing but an old bag. Her hair that is once as black as a yard up a stove-pipe is grey, and she is wearing gold-rimmed cheaters, although she seems to be pretty well dressed and looks as if she may be in the money a little bit, at that.

But the greatest change in her is the way she sits there very quiet all afternoon, never once opening her yap, even when many of the customers around her are claiming that Umpire William Klem is Public Enemy No. 1 to 16 inclusive, because they think he calls a close one against the Giants. I am wondering if maybe Baseball Hattie is stricken dumb somewhere back down the years, because I can remember when she is usually making speeches in the grandstand in favor of hanging such characters as Umpire William Klem when they call close ones against the Giants. But Hattie just sits there as if she is in a church while the public clamor goes on about her, and she does not as much as cry out robber, or even you big bum at Umpire William Klem.

I see many a baseball bug in my time, male and female, but without doubt the worst bug of them all is Baseball Hattie, and you can say it again. She is most particularly a bug about the Giants, and she never misses a game they play at the Polo Grounds, and in fact she sometimes bobs up watching them play in other cities, which is always very embarrassing to the Giants, as they fear the customers in these cities may get the wrong impression of New York womanhood after listening to Baseball Hattie a while.

The first time I ever see Baseball Hattie to pay any attention to her is in Philadelphia, a matter of twenty-odd years back, when the Giants are playing a series there, and many citizens of New York, including Armand Fibleman and myself, are present, because the Philadelphia customers are great hands for betting on baseball games in those days, and Armand Fibleman figures he may knock a few of them in the creek.

Armand Fibleman is a character who will bet on baseball games from who-laid-the-chunk, and in fact he will bet on anything whatever, because Armand Fibleman is a gambler by trade and has been such since infancy. Personally, I will not bet you four dollars on a baseball game, because in the first place I am not apt to have four dollars, and in the second place I consider horse races a much sounder investment, but I often go around and about with Armand Fibleman, as he is a friend of mine, and sometimes he gives me a little piece of one of his bets for nothing.

Well, what happens in Philadelphia but the umpire forfeits the game in the seventh inning to the Giants by a score of nine to nothing when the Phillies are really leading by five runs, and the reason the umpire takes this action is because he orders several of the Philadelphia players to leave the field for calling him a scoundrel and a rat and a snake in the grass, and also a baboon, and they refuse to take their departure, as they still have more names to call him.

Right away the Philadelphia customers become infuriated in a manner you will scarcely believe, for ordinarily a Philadelphia baseball customer is as quiet as a lamb, no matter what you do to him, and in fact in those days a Philadelphia baseball customer is only considered as somebody to do something to.

But these Philadelphia customers are so infuriated that they not only chase the umpire under the stand, but they wait in the street outside the baseball orchard until the Giants change into their street clothes and come out of the clubhouse. Then the Philadelphia customers begin pegging rocks, and one thing and another, at the Giants, and it is a most exciting and disgraceful scene, that is spoken of for years afterward.

Well, the Giants march along towards the North Philly station to catch a train for home, dodging the rocks and one thing and another the best they can, and wondering why the Philadelphia gendarmes do not come to the rescue, until somebody notices several gendarmes among the customers doing some of the throwing themselves, so the Giants realize that this is a most inhospitable community, to be sure.

Finally all of them get inside the North Philly station and are safe, except a big, tall, left-handed pitcher by the name of Haystack Duggeler, who just reports to the club the day before and who finds himself surrounded by quite a posse of these infuriated Philadelphia customers, and who is unable to make them understand that he is nothing but a rookie, because he has a Missouri accent, and besides, he is half paralysed with fear.

One of the infuriated Philadelphia customers is armed with a brickbat and is just moving forward to maim Haystack Duggeler with this instrument, when who steps into the situation but Baseball Hattie, who is also on her way to the station to catch a train, and who is greatly horrified by the assault on the Giants.

She seizes the brickbat from the infuriated Philadelphia customer's grasp, and then tags the customer smack-dab between the eyes with his own weapon, knocking him so unconscious that I afterward hear he does not recover for two weeks, and that he remains practically an imbecile the rest of his days.

Then Baseball Hattie cuts loose on the other infuriated Philadelphia customers with language that they never before hear in those parts, causing them to disperse without further ado, and after the last customer is beyond the sound of her voice, she takes Haystack Duggeler by the pitching arm and personally escorts him to the station.

Now out of this incident is born a wonderful romance between Baseball Hattie and Haystack Duggeler, and in fact it is no doubt love at first sight, and about this period Haystack Duggeler begins burning up the league with his pitching, and at the same time giving Manager Mac plenty of headaches, including the romance with Baseball Hattie, because anybody will tell you that a left hander is tough enough on a manager without a romance, and especially a romance with Baseball Hattie.

It seems that the trouble with Hattie is she is in business up in Harlem, and this business consists of a boarding- and rooming-house where

ladies and gentlemen board and room, and personally I never see anything out of line in the matter, but the rumor somehow gets around,
as rumors will do, that in the first place it is not a boarding- and rooming-house, and in the second place that the ladies and gentlemen who
room and board there are by no means ladies and gentlemen, and
especially the ladies.

Well, this rumor becomes a terrible knock to Baseball Hattie's social
reputation. Furthermore, I hear Manager Mac sends for her and requests
her to kindly lay off his ballplayers, and especially off a character who
can make a baseball sing high C like Haystack Duggeler. In fact, I hear
Manager Mac gives her such a lecture on her civic duty to New York
and to the Giants that Baseball Hattie sheds tears, and promises she
will never give Haystack another tumble the rest of the season.

'You know me, Mac,' Baseball Hattie says. 'You know I will cut off
my nose rather than do anything to hurt your club. I sometimes figure
I am in love with this big bloke, but,' she says, 'maybe it is only gas
pushing up around my heart. I will take something for it. To hell with
him, Mac!' she says.

So she does not see Haystack Duggeler again, except at a distance,
for a long time, and he goes on to win fourteen games in a row, pitching
a no-hitter and four two-hitters among them, and hanging up a reputation as a great pitcher, and also as a 100-per-cent heel.

Haystack Duggeler is maybe twenty-five at this time, and he comes
to the big league with more bad habits than anybody in the history
of the world is able to acquire in such a short time. He is especially
a great rumpot, and after he gets going good in the league, he is just
as apt to appear for a game all mulled up as not.

He is fond of all forms of gambling, such as playing cards and shooting craps, but after they catch him with a deck of readers in a poker
game and a pair of tops in a crap game, none of the Giants will play
with him any more, except of course when there is nobody else to play
with.

He is ignorant about many little things, such as reading and writing
and geography and mathematics, as Haystack Duggeler himself admits
he never goes to school any more than he can help, but he is so wise
when it comes to larceny that I always figure they must have great
tutors back in Haystack's old home town of Booneville, Mo.

And no smarter jobbie ever breathes than Haystack when he is out
there pitching. He has so much speed that he just naturally throws

the ball past a batter before he can get the old musket off his shoulder, and along with his hard one, Haystack has a curve like the letter Q. With two ounces of brains, Haystack Duggeler will be the greatest pitcher that ever lives.

Well, as far as Baseball Hattie is concerned, she keeps her word about not seeing Haystack, although sometimes when he is mulled up he goes around to her boarding- and rooming-house, and tries to break down the door.

On days when Haystack Duggeler is pitching, she is always in her favorite seat back of third, and while she roots hard for the Giants no matter who is pitching, she puts on extra steam when Haystack is bending them over, and it is quite an experience to hear her crying lay them in there, Haystack, old boy, and strike the big tramp out, Haystack, and other exclamations of a similar nature, which please Haystack quite some, but annoy Baseball Hattie's neighbors back of third base, such as Armand Fibleman, if he happens to be betting on the other club.

A month before the close of his first season in the big league, Haystack Duggeler gets so ornery that Manager Mac suspends him, hoping maybe it will cause Haystack to do a little thinking, but naturally Haystack is unable to do this, because he has nothing to think with. About a week later, Manager Mac gets to noticing how he can use a few ball games, so he starts looking for Haystack Duggeler, and he finds him tending bar on Eighth Avenue with his uniform hung up back of the bar as an advertisement.

The baseball writers speak of Haystack as eccentric which is a polite way of saying he is a screwball, but they consider him a most unique character and are always writing humorous stories about him, though any one of them will lay you plenty of 9 to 5 that Haystack winds up an umbay. The chances are they will raise their price a little, as the season closes and Haystack is again under suspension with cold weather coming on and not a dime in his pants' pockets.

It is some time along in the winter that Baseball Hattie hauls off and marries Haystack Duggeler, which is a great surprise to one and all, but not nearly as much of a surprise as when Hattie closes her boarding- and rooming-house and goes to live in a little apartment with Haystack Duggeler up on Washington Heights.

It seems that she finds Haystack one frosty night sleeping in a hallway, after being around slightly mulled up for several weeks, and she takes him to her home and gets him a bath and a shave and a clean shirt and two boiled eggs and some toast and coffee and a shot or two of rye whisky, all of which is greatly appreciated by Haystack, especially the rye whisky.

Then Haystack proposes marriage to her and takes a paralysed oath that if she becomes his wife he will reform, so what with loving Haystack anyway, and with the fix commencing to request more dough off the boarding-and-rooming-house business than the business will stand, Hattie takes him at his word, and there you are.

The baseball writers are wondering what Manager Mac will say when he hears these tidings, but all Mac says is that Haystack cannot possibly be any worse married than he is single-o, and then Mac has the club office send the happy couple a little paper money to carry them over the winter.

Well, what happens but a great change comes over Haystack Duggeler. He stops bending his elbow and helps Hattie cook and wash the dishes, and holds her hand when they are in the movies, and speaks of his love for her several times a week, and Hattie is as happy as nine dollars' worth of lettuce. Manager Mac is so delighted at the change in Haystack that he has the club office send over more paper money, because Mac knows that with Haystack in shape he is sure of twenty-five games, and maybe the pennant.

In late February, Haystack reports to the training camp down South still as sober as some judges, and the other ballplayers are so impressed by the change in him that they admit him to their poker game again. But of course it is too much to expect a man to alter his entire course of living all at once, and it is not long before Haystack discovers four nines in his hand on his own deal and breaks up the game.

He brings Baseball Hattie with him to the camp and this is undoubtedly a slight mistake, as it seems the old rumor about her boarding-and-rooming-house business gets around among the ever-loving wives of the other players, and they put on a large chill for her. In fact, you will think Hattie has the smallpox.

Naturally, Baseball Hattie feels the frost, but she never lets on, as it seems she runs into many bigger and better frosts than this in her time. Then Haystack Duggeler notices it, and it seems that it makes him a little peevish towards Baseball Hattie, and in fact it is said that he gives her a slight pasting one night in their room, partly because she has no better social standing and partly because he is commencing to cop a few sneaks on the local corn now and then, and Hattie chides him for same.

Well, about this time it appears that Baseball Hattie discovers that she is going to have a baby, and as soon as she recovers from her astonishment, she decides that it is to be a boy who will be a great baseball player, maybe a pitcher, although Hattie admits she is willing to compromise on a good second baseman.

She also decides that his name is to be Derrill Duggeler, after his paw, as it seems Derrill is Haystack's real name, and he is only called Haystack because he claims he once makes a living stacking hay, although the general opinion is that all he ever stacks is cards.

It is really quite remarkable what a belt Hattie gets out of the idea of having this baby, though Haystack is not excited about the matter. He is not paying much attention to Baseball Hattie by now, except to give her a slight pasting now and then, but Hattie is so happy about the baby that she does not mind these pastings.

Haystack Duggeler meets up with Armand Fibleman along in midsummer. By this time, Haystack discovers horse racing and is always making bets on the horses, and naturally he is generally broke, and then I commence running into him in different spots with Armand Fibleman, who is now betting higher than a cat's back on baseball games.

It is late August, and the Giants are fighting for the front end of the league, and an important series with Brooklyn is coming up, and everybody knows that Haystack Duggeler will work in anyway two games of the series, as Haystack can generally beat Brooklyn just by throwing his glove on the mound. There is no doubt but what he has the old Indian sign on Brooklyn, and the night before the first game, which he is sure to work, the gamblers along Broadway are making the Giants 2-to-1 favorites to win the game.

This same night before the game, Baseball Hattie is home in her little apartment on Washington Heights waiting for Haystack to come in and eat a delicious dinner of pigs' knuckles and sauerkraut, which she personally prepares for him. In fact, she hurries home right after the ball game to get this delicacy ready, because Haystack tells her he will surely come home this particular night, although Hattie knows he is never better than even money to keep his word about anything.

But sure enough, in he comes while the pigs' knuckles and sauerkraut are still piping hot, and Baseball Hattie is surprised to see Armand Fibleman with him, as she knows Armand backwards and forwards and does not care much for him, at that. However, she can say the same thing about four million other characters in this town, so she makes Armand welcome, and they sit down and put on the pigs' knuckles and sauerkraut together, and a pleasant time is enjoyed by one and all. In fact, Baseball Hattie puts herself out to entertain Armand Fibleman, because he is the first guest Haystack ever brings home.

Well, Armand Fibleman can be very pleasant when he wishes, and he speaks very nicely to Hattie. Naturally, he sees that Hattie is expecting, and in fact he will have to be blind not to see it, and he seems greatly interested in this matter and asks Hattie many questions, and Hattie is delighted to find somebody to talk to about what is coming off with her, as Haystack will never listen to any of her remarks on the subject.

So Armand Fibleman gets to hear all about Baseball Hattie's son, and how he is to be a great baseball player, and Armand says is that so, and how nice, and all this and that, until Haystack Duggeler speaks up as follows and to wit:

'Oh, daggone her son!' Haystack says. 'It is going to be a girl, anyway, so let us dismiss this topic and get down to business. Hat,' he says, 'you fan yourself into the kitchen and wash the dishes, while Armand and me talk.'

So Hattie goes into the kitchen, leaving Haystack and Armand sitting there talking, and what are they talking about but a proposition for Haystack to let the Brooklyn club beat him the next day so Armand Fibleman can take the odds and clean up a nice little gob of money, which he is to split with Haystack.

Hattie can hear every word they say, as the kitchen is next door to the dining-room where they are sitting, and at first she thinks they are joking, because at this time nobody ever even as much as thinks of skulduggery in baseball, or anyway, not much.

It seems that at first Haystack is not in favour of the idea, but Armand Fibleman keeps mentioning money that Haystack owes him for bets on the horse races, and he asks Haystack how he expects to continue betting on the races without fresh money, and Armand also speaks of the great injustice that is being done Haystack by the Giants in not paying him twice the salary he is getting, and how the loss of one or two games is by no means such a great calamity.

Well, finally Baseball Hattie hears Haystack say all right, but he wishes a thousand dollars then and there as a guarantee, and Armand Fibleman says this is fine, and they will go downtown and he will get the money at once, and now Hattie realizes that maybe they are in earnest, and she pops out the kitchen and speaks as follows:

'Gentlemen,' Hattie says, 'you seem to be sober, but I guess you are drunk. If you are not drunk, you must both be daffy to think of such a thing as phenagling around with a baseball game.'

'Hattie,' Haystack says, 'kindly close your trap and go back in the kitchen, or I will give you a bust in the nose.'

And with this he gets up and reaches for his hat, and Armand Fibleman gets up to, and Hattie says like this:

'Why, Haystack,' she says, 'you are not really serious in this matter, are you?'

'Of course I am serious,' Haystack says. 'I am sick and tired of pitching for starvation wages, and besides, I will win a lot of games later on to make up for the one I lose tomorrow. Say,' he says, 'these Brooklyn bums may get lucky tomorrow and knock me loose from my pants, anyway, no matter what I do, so what difference does it make?'

'Haystack,' Baseball Hattie says, 'I know you are a liar and a drunkard and a cheat and no account generally, but nobody can tell me you will sink so low as to purposely toss off a ball game. Why, Haystack, baseball is always on the level. It is the most honest game in all this world. I guess you are just ribbing me, because you know how much I love it.'

'Dry up!' Haystack says to Hattie. 'Furthermore, do not expect me home again tonight. But anyway, dry up.'

'Look, Haystack,' Hattie says, 'I am going to have a son. He is your son and my son, and he is going to be a great ballplayer when he grows up, maybe a greater pitcher than you are, though I hope and trust he is not left handed. He will have your name. If they find out you toss off a game for money, they will throw you out of baseball and you will be disgraced. My son will be known as the son of a crook, and what chance will he have in baseball? Do you think I am going to allow you to do this to him, and to the game that keeps me from going nutty for marrying you?'

Naturally, Haystack Duggeler is greatly offended by Hattie's crack about her son being maybe a greater pitcher than he is, and he is about to take steps, when Armand Fibleman stops him. Armand Fibleman is commencing to be somewhat alarmed at Baseball Hattie's attitude, and he gets to thinking that he hears that people in her delicate condition are often irresponsible, and he fears that she may blow a whistle on this enterprise without realizing what she is doing. So he undertakes a few soothing remarks to her.

'Why, Hattie,' Armand Fibleman say, 'nobody can possibly find out about this little matter, and Haystack will have enough money to send your son to college, if his markers at the race track do not take it all. Maybe you better lie down and rest a while,' Armand says.

But Baseball Hattie does not as much as look at Armand, though she goes on talking to Haystack. 'They always find out thievery, Haystack,' she says, 'especially when you are dealing with a fink like Fibleman. If you deal with him once, you will have to deal with him again and again, and he will be the first to holler copper on you, because he is a stool pigeon in his heart.'

'Haystack,' Armand Fibleman says, 'I think we better be going.'

'Haystack,' Hattie says, 'you can go out of here and stick up somebody or commit a robbery or murder, and I will still welcome you back and stand by you. But if you are going out to steal my son's future, I advise you not to go.'

'Dry up!' Haystack says. 'I am going.'

'All right, Haystack,' Hattie says, very calm. 'But just step into the kitchen with me and let me say one little word to you by yourself, and then I will say no more.'

Well, Haystack Duggeler does not care for even just one little word more, but Armand Fibleman wishes to get this disagreeable scene over with, so he tells Haystack to let her have her word, and Haystack goes into the kitchen with Hattie, and Armand cannot hear what is said, as she speaks very low, but he hears Haystack laugh heartily and then Haystack comes out of the kitchen, still laughing, and tells Armand he is ready to go.

As they start for the door, Baseball Hattie outs with a long-nosed .38-calibre Colt's revolver, and goes root-a-toot-toot with it, and the next thing anybody knows, Haystack is on the floor yelling bloody murder, and Armand Fibleman is leaving the premises without bothering to open the door. In fact, the landlord afterward talks some of suing Haystack Duggeler because of the damage Armand Fibleman does to the door. Armand himself afterward admits that when he slows down for a breather a couple of miles down Broadway he finds splinters stuck all over him.

Well, the doctors come, and the gendarmes come, and there is great confusion, especially as Baseball Hattie is sobbing so she can scarcely make a statement, and Haystack Duggeler is so sure he is going to die that he cannot think of anything to say except oh-oh-oh, but finally the landlord remembers seeing Armand leave with his door, and everybody starts questioning Hattie about this until she confesses that Armand is there all right, and that he tries to bribe Haystack to toss off a ball game, and that she then suddenly finds herself with a revolver in her hand, and everything goes black before her eyes, and she can remember no more until somebody is sticking a bottle of smelling salts under her nose.

Naturally, the newspaper reporters put two and two together, and what they make of it is that Hattie tries to plug Armand Fibleman for his rascally offer, and that she misses Armand and gets Haystack, and right away Baseball Hattie is a great heroine, and Haystack is a great hero, though nobody thinks to ask Haystack how he stands on the bribe proposition, and he never brings it up himself.

And nobody will ever offer Haystack any more bribes, for after the doctors get through with him he is shy a left arm from the shoulder down, and he will never pitch a baseball again, unless he learns to pitch right handed.

The newspapers make quite a lot of Baseball Hattie protecting the fair name of baseball. The National League plays a benefit game for Haystack Duggeler and presents him with a watch and a purse of twenty-five thousand dollars, which Baseball Hattie grabs away from him, saying it is for her son, while Armand Fibleman is in bad with one and all.

Baseball Hattie and Haystack Duggeler move to the Pacific Coast, and this is all there is to the story, except that one day some years ago, and before he passes away in Los Angeles, a respectable grocer, I run into Haystack when he is in New York on a business trip, and I say to him like this:

'Haystack,' I say, 'it is certainly a sin and a shame that Hattie misses Armand Fibleman that night and puts you on the shelf. The chances are that but for this little accident you will hang up one of the greatest pitching records in the history of baseball. Personally,' I say, 'I never see a better left-handed pitcher.'

'Look,' Haystack says, 'Hattie does not miss Fibleman. It is a great newspaper story and saves my name, but the truth is she hits just where she aims. When she calls me into the kitchen before I start out with Fibleman, she shows me a revolver I never before know she has, and says to me, "Haystack," she says, "if you leave with this weasel on the errand you mention, I am going to fix you so you will never make another wrong move with your pitching arm. I am going to shoot it off for you.''

'I laugh heartily.' Haystack says. 'I think she is kidding me, but I find out different. By the way.' Haystack says, 'I afterward learn that long before I meet her, Hattie works for three years in a shooting gallery at Coney Island. She is really a remarkable broad.' Haystack says.

I guess I forget to state that the day Baseball Hattie is at the Polo Grounds she is watching the new kid sensation of the big leagues, Derrill Duggeler, shut out Brooklyn with three hits.

He is a wonderful young left-hander.

My Roomy

RING LARDNER

NO—I AIN'T signed for next year; but there won't be no trouble about
that. The dough part of it is all fixed up. John and me talked it over
and I'll sign as soon as they send me a contract. All I told him was
that he'd have to let me pick my own roommate after this and not sic
no wild man on to me.

You know I didn't hit much the last two months o' the season. Some
o' the boys, I notice, wrote some stuff about me gettin' old and losin'
my battin' eye. That's all bunk! The reason I didn't hit was because
I wasn't gettin' enough sleep. And the reason for that was Mr Elliott.

He wasn't with us after the last part o' May, but I roomed with him
long enough to get the insomny. I was the only guy in the club game
enough to stand for him; but I was sorry afterward that I done it, because
it sure did put a crimp in my little old average.

And do you know where he is now? I got a letter today and I'll read
it to you. No—I guess I better tell you somethin' about him first. You
fellers never got acquainted with him and you ought to hear the dope
to understand the letter. I'll make it as short as I can.

He didn't play in no league last year. He was with some semi-pros
over in Michigan and somebody writes John about him. So John sends
Needham over to look at him. Tom stayed there Saturday and Sunday,
and seen him work twice. He was playin' the outfield, but as luck would
have it they wasn't a fly ball hit in his direction in both games. A base
hit was made out his way and he booted it, and that's the only report
Tom could get on his fieldin'. But he wallops two over the wall in one
day and they catch two line drives off him. The next day he gets four
blows and two o' them is triples.

So Tom comes back and tells John the guy is a whale of a hitter and

fast as Cobb, but he don't know nothin' about his fieldin'. Then John
signs him to a contract—twelve hundred or somethin' like that. We'd
been in Tampa a week before he showed up. Then he comes to the
hotel and just sits round all day, without tellin' nobody who he was.
Finally the bellhops was going to chase him out and he says he's one
o' the ballplayers. Then the clerk gets John to go over and talk to him.
He tells John his name and says he hasn't had nothin' to eat for three
days, because he was broke. John told me afterward that he'd drew
about three hundred in advance—last winter sometime. Well, they took
him in the dinin' room and they tell me he inhaled about four meals
at once. That night they roomed him with Heine.

Next mornin' Heine and me walks out to the grounds together and
Heine tells me about him. He says:

'Don't never call me a bug again. They got me roomin' with the
champion o' the world.'

'Who is he?' I says.

'I don't know and I don't want to know,' says Heine; 'but if they
stick him in there with me again I'll jump to the Federals. To start with,
he ain't got no baggage. I ask him where his trunk was and he says
he didn't have none. Then I ask him if he didn't have no suitcase,
and he says: 'No. What do you care?' I was goin' to lend him some
pajamas, but he put on the shirt o' the uniform John gave him last
night and slept in that. He was asleep when I got up this mornin'.'
I seen his collar layin' on the dresser and it looked like he had wore
it in Pittsburgh every day for a year. So I throwed it out the window
and he comes down to breakfast with no collar. I ask him what size
collar he wore and he says he didn't want none, because he wasn't
goin' out nowheres. After breakfast he beat it up to the room again
and put on his uniform. When I got up there he was lookin' in the
glass at himself, and he done it all the time I was dressin'.

When we got out to the park I got my first look at him. Pretty good-
lookin' guy, too, in his unie—big shoulders and well put together; built
somethin' like Heine himself. He was talkin' to John when I come up.

'What position do you play?' John was askin' him.

'I play anywheres,' says Elliott.

'You're the kind I'm lookin' for,' says John. Then he says: 'You was
an outfielder up there in Michigan, wasn't you?'

'I don't care where I play,' says Elliott.

John sends him to the outfield and forgets all about him for a while.

Pretty soon Miller comes in and says:

'I ain't goin' to shag for no bush outfielder.'

John ast him what was the matter, and Miller tells him that Elliott ain't' doin' nothin' but just standin' out there; that he ain't makin' no attemp' to catch the fungoes, and that he won't even chase 'em. Then John starts watchin' him, and it was just like Miller said. Larry hit one pretty near in his lap and he stepped out o' the way. John calls him in and ast him:

'Why don't you go after them fly balls?'

'Because I don't want 'em,' says Elliott.

John gets sarcastic and says:

'What do you want? Of course we'll see that you get anythin' you want!'

'Give me a ticket back home,' says Elliott.

'Don't you want to stick with the club?' says John, and the busher tells him, no, he certainly did not. Then John tells him he'll have to pay his own fare home and Elliott don't get sore at all. He just says:

'Well, I'll have to stick, then—because I'm broke.'

We was havin' battin' practice and John tells him to go up and hit a few. And you ought to of seen him bust 'em!

Lavender was in there workin' and he'd been pitchin' a little all winter, so he was in pretty good shape. He lobbed one up to Elliott, and he hit it 'way up in some trees outside the fence—about a mile, I guess. Then John tells Jimmy to put somethin' on the ball. Jim comes through with one of his fast ones and the kid slams it agin the right-field wall on a line.

'Give him your spitter!' yells John, and Jim handed him one. He pulled it over first base so fast that Bert, who was standin' down there, couldn't hardly duck in time. If it'd hit him it'd killed him.

Well, he kep' on hittin' everythin' Jim give him—and Jim had somethin' too. Finally John gets Pierce warmed up and sends him out to pitch, tellin' him to hand Elliott a flock o' curve balls. He wanted to see if left-handers was goin' to bother him. But he slammed 'em right along, and I don't b'lieve he hit more'n two the whole mornin' that wouldn't of been base hits in a game.

They sent him out to the outfield again in the afternoon, and after a lot o' coaxin' Leach got him to go after fly balls; but that's all he did—just go after 'em. One hit him on the bean and another on the shoulder. He run back after the short ones and 'way in after the ones that went over his head. He catched just one—a line drive that he couldn't get out o' the way of; and then he acted like it hurt his hands.

I come back to the hotel with John. He ast me what I thought of Elliott.

'Well,' I says, 'he'd be the greatest ballplayer in the world if he could just play ball. He sure can bust 'em.'

John says he was afraid he couldn't never make an outfielder out o' him. He says:

'I'll try him on the infield to-morrow. They must be some place he can play. I never seen a left-hand hitter that looked so good agin left-hand pitchin'—and he's got a great arm; but he acts like he'd never saw a fly ball.'

Well, he was just as bad on the infield. They put him at short and he was like a sieve. You could of drove a hearse between him and second base without him gettin' near it. He'd stoop over for a ground ball about the time it was bouncin' up agin the fence; and when he'd try to cover the bag on a peg he'd trip over it.

They tried him at first base and sometimes he'd run 'way over in the coachers' box and sometimes out in right field lookin' for the bag. Once Heine shot one acrost at him on a line and he never touched it with his hands. It went bam! right in the pit of his stomach—and the lunch he'd ate didn't do him no good.

Finally John just give up and says he'd have to keep him on the bench and let him earn his pay by bustin' 'em a couple 'o times a week or so. We all agreed with John that this bird would be a whale of a pinch hitter—and we was right too. He was hittin' 'way over five hundred when the blowoff come, along about the last o' May.

II

Before the trainin' trip was over, Elliott had roomed with pretty near everybody in the club. Heine raised an awful holler after the second night down there and John put the bug in with Needham. Tom stood him for three nights. Then he doubled up with Archer, and Schulte, and Miller, and Leach, and Saier—and the whole bunch in turn, averagin' about two nights with each one before they put up a kick. Then John tried him with some o' the youngsters, but they wouldn't stand for him no more'n the others. They all said he was crazy and they was afraid he'd get violent some night and stick a knife in 'em.

He always insisted on havin' the water run in the bathtub all night, because he said it reminded him of the sound of the dam near his home. The fellers might get up four or five times a night and shut off the faucet, but he'd get right up after 'em and turn it on again. Carter, a big bush pitcher from Georgia, started a fight with him about it one night, and Elliott pretty near killed him. So the rest o' the bunch, when they'd saw Carter's map next mornin', didn't have the nerve to do nothin' when it come their turn.

Another o' his habits was the thing that scared 'em though. He'd brought a razor with him—in his pocket. I guess—and he used to do his shavin' in the middle o' the night. Instead o' doin' it in the bathroom he'd lather his face and then come out and stand in front o' the lookin' glass on the dresser. Of course he'd have all the lights turned on, and that was bad enough when a feller wanted to sleep; but the worst of it was that he'd stop shavin' every little while and turn round and stare at the guy who was makin' a failure o' tryin' to sleep. Then he'd wave his razor round in the air and laugh, and begin shavin' agin. You can imagine how comf'table his roomies felt!

John had bought him a suitcase and some clothes and things, and charged 'em up to him. He'd drew so much dough in advance that he didn't have nothin' comin' till about June. He never thanked John and he'd wear one shirt and one collar till some one throwed 'em away.

Well, we finally gets to Indianapolis, and we was goin' from there to Cincy to open. The last day in Indianapolis John come and ast me how I'd like to change roomies. I says I was perfectly satisfied with Larry. Then John says:

'I wisht you'd try Elliott. The other boys all kicks on him, but he seems to hang round you a lot and I b'lieve you could get along all right.'

'Why don't you room him alone?' I ast.

'The boss or the hotels won't stand for us roomin' alone,' says John. 'You go ahead and try it, and see how you make out. If he's too much for you let me know; but he likes you and I think he'll be diff'rent with a guy who can talk to him like you can.'

So I says I'd tackle it, because I didn't want to throw John down. When we got to Cincy they stuck Elliott and me in one room, and we was together till he quit us.

III

I went to the room early that night, because we was goin' to open next day and I wanted to feel like somethin'. First thing I done when I got undressed was turn on both faucets in the bathtub. They was makin' an awful racket when Elliott finally come in about midnight. I was layin' awake and I opened right up on him. I says:

'Don't shut off that water, because I like to hear it run.'

Then I turned over and pretended to be asleep. The bug got his clothes off, and then what did he do but go in the bathroom and shut off the water! Then he come back in the room and says:

'I guess no one's goin' to tell me what to do in here.'

But I kep' right on pretendin' to sleep and didn't pay no attention. When he'd got into his bed I jumped out o' mine and turned on all the lights and begun stroppin' my razor. He says:

'What's comin' off?'

'Some o' my whiskers,' I says, 'I always shave along about this time.'

'No, you don't!' he says. 'I was in your room one mornin' down in Louisville and I seen you shavin' then.'

'Well,' I says, 'the boys tell me you shave in the middle o' the night; and I thought if I done all the things you do mebbe I'd get so's I could hit like you.'

'You must be superstitious!' he says. And I told him I was. 'I'm a good hitter,' he says, 'and I'd be a good hitter if I never shaved at all. That don't make no diff'rence.'

'Yes it does,' I says. 'You prob'ly hit good because you shave at night; but you'd be a better fielder if you shaved in the mornin'.'

You see, I was tryin' to be just as crazy as him—though that wasn't hardly possible.

'If that's right,' says he, 'I'll do my shavin' in the mornin'—because I seen in the papers where the boys says that if I could play the outfield like I can hit I'd be as good as Cobb. They tell me Cobb gets twenty thousand a year.'

'No,' I says; 'he don't get that much—but he gets about ten times as much as you do.'

'Well,' he says, 'I'm goin' to be as good as him, because I need the money.'

'What do you want with money?' I says.

He just laughed and didn't say nothin'; but from that time on the water didn't run in the bathtub at nights and he done his shavin' after breakfast. I didn't notice, though, that he looked any better in fieldin' practice.

IV

It rained one day in Cincy and they trimmed us two out o' the other three; but it wasn't Elliott's fault.

They had Larry beat four to one in the ninth innin' o' the first game. Archer gets on with two out, and John sends my roomy up to hit—though Benton, a left-hander, is workin' for them. The first thing Benton serves up there Elliott cracks it a mile over Hobby's head. It would of been good for three easy—only Archer—playin' safe, o' course—pulls up at third base. Tommy couldn't do nothin' and we was licked.

The next day he hits one out o' the park off the Indian; but we was 'way behind and they was nobody on at the time. We copped the last one without usin' no pinch hitters.

I didn't have no trouble with him nights durin' the whole series. He come to bed pretty late while we was there and I told him he'd better not let John catch him at it.

'What would he do?' he says.

'Fine you fifty,' I says.

'He can't fine me a dime,' he says, 'because I ain't got it.'

Then I told him he'd be fined all he had comin' if he didn't get in the hotel before midnight; but he just laughed and says he didn't think John had a kick comin' so long as he kep' bustin' the ball.

'Some day you'll go up there and you won't bust it,' I says.

'That'll be an accident,' he says.

That stopped me and I didn't say nothin'. What could you say to a guy who hated himself like that?'

The 'accident' happened in St Louis the first day. We needed two runs in the eighth and Saier and Brid was on, with two out. John tells Elliott to go up in Pierce's place. The bug goes up and Griner gives him two bad balls—'way outside. I thought they was goin' to walk him— and it looked like good judgement, because they'd heard what he done in Cincy. But no! Griner comes back with a fast one right over and Elliott pulls it down the right foul line, about two foot foul. He hit it so hard you'd of thought they'd sure walk him then; but Griner gives him another fast one. He slammed it again just as hard, but foul. Then Griner gives him one 'way outside and it's two and three. John says, on the bench:

'If they don't walk him now he'll bust that fence down.'

I thought the same and I was sure Griner wouldn't give him nothin to hit; but he come with a curve and Rigler calls Elliott out. From where we sat the last one looked low, and I thought Elliott'd make a kick. He come back to the bench smilin'.

John starts for his position, but stopped and ast the bug what was the matter with that one. Any busher I ever knowed would of said 'It was too low,' or 'It was outside,' or 'It was inside.' Elliott says:

'Nothin' at all. It was right over the middle.'

'Why didn't you bust it, then?' says John.

'I was afraid I'd kill somebody,' says Elliott, and laughed like a big boob.

John was pretty near chokin'.

'What are you laughin' at?' he says.

'I was thinkin' of a nickel show I seen in Cincinnati,' says the bug.

'Well,' says John, so mad he couldn't hardly see, 'that show and that laugh'll cost you fifty.'

We got beat, and I wouldn't of blamed John if he'd fined him his whole season's pay.

Up 'n the room that night I told him he'd better cut out that laughin' stuff when we was gettin' trimmed or he never would have no pay day. Then he got confidential.

'Pay day wouldn't do me no good,' he says. 'When I'm all squared up with the club and begin to have a pay day, I'll only get a hundred bucks at a time, and I'll owe that to some o' you fellers. I wisht we could win the pennant and get in on that World's Series dough. Then I'd get a bunch at once.'

'What would you do with a bunch o' dough?' I ast him.

'Don't tell nobody, sport,' he says; 'but if I ever get five hundred at once I'm goin' get married.'

'Oh!' I says. 'And who's the lucky girl?'

'She's a girl up in Muskegon,' says Elliott; 'and you're right when you call her lucky.'

'You don't like yourself much, do you?' I says.

'I got reason to like myself,' says he. 'You'd like yourself, too, if you could hit 'em like me.'

'Well,' I says, 'you didn't show me no hittin' to-day.'

'I couldn't hit because I was laughin' too hard,' says Elliott.

'What was it you was laughin' at?' I says.

'I was laughin' at that pitcher.' he says. 'He thought he had somethin' and he didn't have nothin.'

'He had enough to whiff you with,' I says.

'He didn't have nothin'!' says he again. 'I was afraid if I busted one off him they'd can him, and then I couldn't never hit agin him no more.'

Naturally I didn't have no comeback to that. I just sort o' gasped and got ready to go to sleep; but he wasn't through.

'I wisht you could see this bird!' he says.

'What bird?' I says.

'This dame that's nuts about me,' he says.

'Good looker?' I ast.

'No,' he says, 'she ain't no bear for looks. They ain't nothin' about her for a guy to rave over till you hear her sing. She sure can holler some.'

'What kind o' voice has she got?' I ast.

'A bear,' says he.

'No,' I says; 'I mean is she a barytone or an air?'

'I don't know,' he says; 'but she's got the loudest voice I ever hear on a woman. She's pretty near got me beat.'

'Can you sing?' I says; and I was sorry right afterward that I ast him that question.

I guess it must of been bad enough to have the water runnin' night after night and to have him wavin' that razor round; but that couldn't of been nothin' to his singin'. Just as soon as I'd pulled that boner he says, 'Listen to me!' and starts in on 'Silver Threads Among the Gold.' Mind you, it was after midnight and they was guests all round us tryin' to sleep!

They used to be noise enough in our club when we had Hofman and Sheckard and Richie harmonizin'; but this bug's voice was louder'n all o' theirn combined. We once had a pitcher named Martin Walsh—brother o' Big Ed's—and I thought he could drownd out the Subway; but this guy made a boiler factory sound like Dummy Taylor. If the whole hotel wasn't awake when he'd howled the first line it's a pipe they was when he cut loose, which he done when he come to 'Always young and fair to me.' Them words could of been heard easy in East St Louis.

He didn't get no encore from me, but he goes right through it again—or starts to. I knowed somethin' was goin' to happen before he finished— and somethin' did. The night clerk and the house detective come bangin' at the door. I let 'em in and they had plenty to say. If we made another sound the whole club'd be canned out o' the hotel. I tried to salve 'em, and I says:

'He won't sing no more.'

But Elliott swelled up like a poisoned pup.

'Won't I?' he says. 'I'll sing all I want to.'

'You won't sing in here,' says the clerk.

'They ain't room for my voice in here anyways,' he says. 'I'll go outdoors and sing.'

And he puts his clothes on and ducks out. I didn't make no attemp' to stop him. I heard him bellowin' 'Silver Threads' down the corridor and down the stairs, with the clerk and the dick chasin' him all the way and tellin' him to shut up.

Well, the guests make a holler the next mornin'; and the hotel tells Charlie Williams that he'll either have to let Elliott stay somewheres else or the whole club'll have to move. Charlie tells John, and John was thinkin' o' settlin' the question by releasin' Elliott.

I guess he'd about made up his mind to do it; but that afternoon they had us three to one in the ninth, and we got the bases full, with two down and Larry's turn to hit. Elliott had been sittin' on the bench sayin' nothin'.

'Do you think you can hit one today?' says John.

'I can hit one any day,' says Elliott.

'Go up and hit that left-hander, then,' says John, 'and remember there's nothin' to laugh at.'

Sallee was workin'—and workin' good; but that didn't bother the bug. He cut into one, and it went between Oakes and Whitted like a shot. He come into third standin' up and we was a run to the good. Sallee was so sore he kind o' forgot himself and took pretty near his full windup pitchin' to Tommy. And what did Elliott do but steal home and get away with it clean!

Well, you couldn't can him after that, could you? Charlie gets him a room somewheres and I was relieved of his company that night. The next evenin' we beat it for Chi to play about two weeks at home. He didn't tell nobody where he roomed there and I didn't see nothin' of him, 'cep' out to the park. I ast him what he did with himself nights and he says:

'Same as I do on the road—borrow some dough some place and go to the nickel shows.'

'You must be stuck on 'em,' I says.

'Yes,' he says; 'I like the ones where they kill people—because I want to learn how to do it. I may have that job some day.'

'Don't pick on me,' I says.

'Oh,' says the bug, 'you never can tell who I'll pick on.'

It seemed as if he just couldn't learn nothin' about fieldin', and finally John told him to keep out o' the practice.

'A ball might hit him in the temple and croak him,' says John.

But he busted up a couple o' games for us at home, beaten' Pittsburgh once and Cincy once.

V

They gave me a great big room at the hotel in Pittsburgh; so the fellers picked it out for the poker game. We was playin' along about ten o'clock one night when in come Elliott—the earliest he'd showed up since we'd been roomin' together. They was only five of us playin' and Tom ast him to sit in.

'I'm busted,' he says.

'Can you play poker?' I ast him.

'They's nothin' I can't do!' he says. 'Slip me a couple o' bucks and I'll show you.'

So I slipped him a couple o' bucks and honestly hoped he'd win, because I knowed he never had no dough. Well, Tom dealt him a hand and he picks it up and says:

'I only got five cards.'

'How many do you want?' I says.

'Oh,' he says, 'if that's all I get I'll try to make 'em do.'

The pot was cracked and raised, and he stood the raise. I says to myself: 'There goes my two bucks!' But no—he comes out with three queens and won the dough. It was only about seven bucks; but you'd of thought it was a million to see him grab it. He laughed like a kid.

'Guess I can't play this game!' he says; and he had me fooled for a minute—I thought he must of been kiddin' when he complained of only havin' five cards.

He copped another pot right afterward and was sittin' there with about eleven bucks in front of him when Jim opens a roodle pot for a buck. I stays and so does Elliott. Him and Jim both drawed one card and I took three. I had kings or queens—I forget which. I didn't help 'em none; so when Jim bets a buck I throws my hand away.

'How much can I bet?' says the bug.

'You can raise Jim a buck if you want to,' I says.

So he bets two dollars. Jim comes back at him. He comes right back at Jim. Jim raises him again and he tilts Jim right back. Well, when he'd boosted Jim with the last buck he had, Jim says:

'I'm ready to call. I guess you got me beat. What have you got?'

'I know what I've got, all right,' says Elliott. 'I've got a straight.' And he throws his hand down. Sure enough, it was a straight, eight high. Jim pretty near fainted and so did I.

The bug had started pullin' in the dough when Jim stops him.

'Here! Wait a minute!' says Jim. 'I thought you had somethin'. I filled up.' Then Jim lays down his nine full.

'You beat me, I guess,' says Elliott, and he looked like he'd lost his last friend.

'Beat you?' says Jim. 'Of course I beat you! What did you think I had.'

'Well,' says the bug. 'I thought you might have a small flush or somethin'.'

When I regained consciousness he was beggin' for two more bucks.

'What for?' I says. 'To play poker with? You're barred from the game for life!'

'Well,' he says, 'if I can't play no more I want to go to sleep, and you fellers will have to get out o' this room.'

Did you ever hear o' nerve like that? This was the first night he'd came in before twelve and he orders the bunch out so's he can sleep! We politely suggested to him to go to Brooklyn.

Without sayin' a word he starts in on his 'Silver Threads'; and it wasn't two minutes till the game was busted up and the bunch—all but me—was out o' there. I'd of beat it too, only he stopped yellin' as soon as they'd went.

'You're some buster!' I says. 'You bust up ball games in the afternoon and poker games at night.'

'Yes,' he says; 'that's my business—bustin' things.'

And before I knowed what he was about he picked up the pitcher of ice water that was on the floor and throwed it out the window—through the glass and all.

Right then I give him a plain talkin' to. I tells him how near he come to gettin' canned down in St Louis because he raised so much Cain singin' in the hotel.

'But I had to keep my voice in shape,' he says. 'If I ever get dough enough to get married the girl and me'll go out singin' together.'

'Out where?' I ast.

'Out on the vaudeville circuit,' says Elliott.

'Well,' I says, 'if her voice is like yours you'll be wastin' money if you travel round. Just stay up in Muskegon and we'll hear you, all right!'

I told him he wouldn't never get no dough if he didn't behave himself. That, even if we got in the World's Series, he wouldn't be with us—unless he cut out the foolishness.

'We ain't goin' to get in no World's Series,' he says, 'and I won't never get a bunch o' money at once; so it looks like I couldn't get married this fall.'

Then I told him we played a city series every fall. He'd never thought o' that and it tickled him to death. I told him the losers always got about five hundred apiece and that we were about due to win it and get about eight hundred. 'But,' I says, 'we still got a good chance for the old pennant; and if I was you I wouldn't give up hope o' that yet —not where John can hear you, anyway.'

'No,' he says, 'we won't win no pennant, because he won't let me play reg'lar, but I don't care so long as we're sure o' that city-series dough.'

'You ain't sure of it if you don't behave,' I says.

'Well,' says he, very serious, 'I guess I'll behave.' And he did—till we made our first Eastern trip.

VI

We went to Boston first, and that crazy bunch goes out and piles up a three-run lead on us in seven innin's the first day. It was the pitcher's turn to lead off in the eighth, so up goes Elliott to bat for him. He kisses the first thing they hands him for three bases; and we says, on the bench: 'Now we'll get 'em!'—because, you know, a three-run lead wasn't nothin' in Boston.

'Stay right on that bag!' John hollers to Elliott.

Mebbe if John hadn't said nothin' to him everythin' would of been all right; but when Perdue starts to pitch the first ball to Tommy, Elliott starts to steal home. He's out as far as from here to Seattle.

If I'd been carryin' a gun I'd of shot him right through the heart. As it was, I thought John'd kill him with a bat, because he was standin' there with a couple of 'em, waitin' for his turn; but I guess John was too stunned to move. He didn't even seem to see Elliott when he went to the bench. After I'd cooled off a little I says:

'Beat it and get into your clothes before John comes in. Then go to the hotel and keep out o' sight.'

When I got up in the room afterward, there was Elliott, lookin' as innocent and happy as though he'd won fifty bucks with a pair o' treys.

'I thought you might of killed yourself,' I says.

'What for?' he says.

'For that swell play you made,' says I.

'What was the matter with the play?' ast Elliott, surprised. 'It was all right when I done it in St Louis.'

'Yes,' I says; 'but they was two out in St Louis and we wasn't no three runs behind.'

'Well,' he says, 'if it was all right in St Louis I don't see why it was wrong here.'

'It's a diff'rent climate here,' I says, too disgusted to argue with him.

'I wonder if they'd let me sing in this climate?' says Elliott.

'No,' I says. 'Don't sing in this hotel, because we don't want to get fired out o' here—the eats is too good.'

'All right,' he says, 'I won't sing. 'But when I starts down to supper he says: 'I'm li'ble to do somethin' worse'n sing.'

He didn't show up in the dinin' room and John went to the boxin' show after supper; so it looked like him and Elliott wouldn't run into each other till the murder had left John's heart. I was glad o' that— because a Mass'chusetts jury might not consider it justifiable hommer- cide if one guy croaked another for givin' the Boston club a game.

I went down to the corner and had a couple o' beers; and then I come straight back, intendin' to hit the hay. The elevator boy had went for a drink or somethin', and they was two old ladies already waitin' in the car when I stepped in. Right along after me comes Elliott.

'Where's the boy that's supposed to run this car?' he says, I told him the boy'd be right back; but he says: 'I can't wait. I'm much too sleepy.'

And before I could stop him he'd slammed the door and him and I and the poor old ladies was shootin' up.

'Let us off at the third floor, please!' says one o' the ladies, her voice kind o' shakin'.

'Sorry, madam,' says the bug; 'but this is a express and we don't stop at no third floor.'

I grabbed his arm and tried to get him away from the machinery; but he was as strong as a ox and he throwed me agin the side o' the car like I was a baby. We went to the top faster'n I ever rode in an elevator before. And then we shot down to the bottom, hittin' the bumper down there so hard I thought we'd be smashed to splinters.

The ladies was too scared to make a sound durin' the first trip; but while we was goin' up and down the second time—even faster'n the first—they begun to scream. I was hollerin' my head off at him to quit and he was makin' more noise than the three of us—pretendin' he was the locomotive and the whole crew o' the train.

Don't never ask me how many times we went up and down! The women fainted on the third trip and I guess I was about as near it as I'll ever get. The elevator boy and the bellhops and the waiters and the night clerk and everybody was jumpin' round the lobby screamin'; but no one seemed to know how to stop us.

Finally—on about the tenth trip, I guess—he slowed down and stopped at the fifth floor, where we was roomin'. He opened the door and beat it for the room, while I, though I was tremblin' like a leaf, run the car down to the bottom.

The night clerk knowed me pretty well and knowed I wouldn't do nothin' like that; so him and I didn't argue, but just got to work together to bring the old women to. While we was doin' that Elliott must of run down the stairs and slipped out o' the hotel, because when they sent the officers up to the room after him he'd blowed.

They was goin' to fire the club out; but Charlie had a good stand-in with Amos, the proprietor, and he fixed it up to let us stay—providin' Elliott kep' away. The bug didn't show up at the ball park next day and we didn't see no more of him till we got on the rattler for New York. Charlie and John both bawled him, but they give him a berth—an upper—and we pulled into the Grand Central Station without him havin' made no effort to wreck the train.

VII

I'd studied the thing pretty careful, but hadn't come to no conclusion. I was sure he wasn't no stew, because none o' the boys had ever saw him even take a glass o' beer, and I couldn't never detect the odor o' booze on him. And if he'd been a dope I'd of knew about it—roomin' with him.

There wouldn't of been no mystery about it if he'd been a left-hand pitcher—but he wasn't. He wasn't nothin' but a whale of a hitter and he throwed with his right arm. He hit left-handed, o' course, but so did Saier and Brid and Schulte and me, and John himself; and none of us was violent. I guessed he must of been just a plain nut and li'ble to break out any time.

They was a letter waitin' for him at New York, and I took it, intendin' to give it to him at the park, because I didn't think they'd let him room at the hotel; but after breakfast he come up to the room, with his suitcase. It seems he'd promised John and Charlie to be good, and made it so strong they b'lieved him.

I give him his letter, which was addressed in a girl's writin' and come from Muskegon.

'From the girl?' I says.

'Yes,' he says, and, without openin' it, he tore it up and throwed it out the window.

'Had a quarrel,' I ast.

'No, no,' he says; 'but she can't tell me nothin' I don't know already. Girls always writes the same junk. I got one from her in Pittsburgh, but I didn't read it.'

'I guess you ain't so stuck on her,' I says.

He swells up and says:

'Of course I'm stuck on her! If I wasn't, do you think I'd be goin' round with this bunch and gettin' insulted all the time? I'm stickin' here because o' that series dough, so's I can get hooked.'

'Do you think you'd settle down if you was married?' I ast him.

'Settle down?' he says. 'Sure, I'd settle down. I'd be so happy that I wouldn't have to look for no excitement.'

Nothin' special happened that night 'cep' that he come in the room about one o'clock and woke me up by pickin' up the foot o' the bed and dropping it on the floor, sudden-like.

'Give me a key to the room,' he says.

'You must of had a key,' I says, 'or you couldn't of got in.'

'That's right!' he says, and beat it to bed.

One o' the reporters must of told Elliott that John had ast for waivers on him and New York had refused to waive, because next mornin' he come to me with that dope.

'New York's goin' to win this pennant!' he says.

'Well,' I says, 'they will if some one else don't. But what of it?'

'I'm goin' to play with New York, he says, 'so's I can get the World's Series dough.'

'How you goin' to get away from this club?' I ast.

'Just watch me!' he says. 'I'll be with New York before this series is over.'

Well, the way he goes after the job was original, anyway. Rube'd had one of his good days the day before and we'd got a trimmin'; but this second day the score was tied up at two runs apiece in the tenth, and Big Jeff'd been wabblin' for two or three innin's.

Well, he walks Saier and me, with one out, and Mac sends for Matty, who was warmed up and ready. John sticks Elliott in in Brid's place and the bug pulls one into the right-field stand.

It's a cinch McGraw thinks well of him then, and might of went after him if he hadn't went crazy the next afternoon. We're tied up in the ninth and Matty's workin'. John sends Elliott up with the bases choked; but he doesn't go right up on the plate. He walks over to their bench and calls McGraw out. Mac tells us about it afterward.

'I can bust up this game right here!' says Elliott.

'Go ahead,' says Mac, 'but be careful he don't whiff you.'

Then the bug pulls it.

'If I whiff,' he says, 'will you get me on your club?'

'Sure!' says Mac, just as anybody would.

By this time Bill Koem was hollerin' about the delay; so up goes Elliott and gives the worst burlesque on tryin' to hit that you ever see. Matty throws one a mile outside and high, and the bug swings like it was right over the heart. Then Matty throws one at him and he ducks out o' the way—but swings just the same. Matty must of been wise by this time, for he pitches one so far outside that the Chief almost has to go to the coacher's box after it. Elliott takes his third healthy and runs through the field down to the clubhouse.

We got beat in the eleventh; and when we went in to dress he has his street clothes on. Soon as he seen John comin' he says; 'I got to see McGraw!' And he beat it.

John was goin' to the fights that night; but before he leaves the hotel he had waivers on Elliott from everybody and had sold him to Atlanta.

'And,' says John, 'I don't care if they pay for him or not.'

My roomy blows in about nine and got the letter from John out of his box. He was goin' to tear it up, but I told him they was news in it. He opens it and reads where he's sold. I was still sore at him, so I says:

'Thought you was goin' to get on the New York club?'

'No,' he says, 'I got turned down cold. McGraw says he wouldn't have me in his club. He says he'd had Charlie Faust—and that was enough for him.

'What are you goin' to do now?' I says.

'I'm goin' to sell this ticket to Atlanta,' he says, 'and go back to Muskegon, where I belong.'

'I'll help you pack,' I says.

'No,' says the bug. 'I come into this league with this suit o' clothes and a collar. They can have the rest of it.' Then he sits down on the bed and begins to cry like a baby. 'No series dough for me,' he blubbers, 'and no weddin' bells! My girl'll die when she hears about it!'

Of course that made me feel kind o' rotten, and I says:

'Brace up, boy! The best thing you can do is go to Atlanta and try hard. You'll be up here again next year.'

'You can't tell me where to go!' he says, and he wasn't cryin' no more. 'I'll go where I please—and I'm li'ble to take you with me.'

I didn't want no argument, so I kep' still. Pretty soon he goes up to the lookin'-glass and stares at himself for five minutes. Then, all of a sudden, he hauls off and takes a wallop at his reflection in the glass. Naturally he smashed the glass all to pieces and he cut his hand somethin' awful.

Without lookin' at it he come over to me and says: 'Well, goodbye, sport!'—and holds out his other hand to shake. When I starts to shake hands with him he smears his bloody hand all over my map. Then he laughed like a wild man and run out o' the room and out o' the hotel.

VIII

Well, boys, my sleep was broke up for the rest o' the season. It might of been because I was used to sleepin' in all kinds o' racket and excitement, and couldn't stand for the quiet after he'd went—or it might of been because I kep' thinkin' about him and feelin' sorry for him.

I of'en wondered if he'd settle down and be somethin' if he could get married; and finally I got to b'lievin' he would. So when we was dividin' the city series dough I was thinkin' of him and the girl. Our share o' the money—the losers', as usual—was twelve thousand seven hundred sixty bucks or somethin' like that. They was twenty-one of us and that meant six hundred seven bucks apiece. We was just goin' to cut it up that way when I says:

'Why not give a divvy to poor old Elliott?'

About fifteen of 'em at once told me that I was crazy. You see, when he got canned he owed everybody in the club. I guess he'd stuck me for the most—about seventy bucks—but I didn't care nothin' about that. I knowed he hadn't never reported to Atlanta, and I thought he was prob'ly busted and a bunch o' money might make things all right for him and the other songbird.

I made quite a speech to the fellers, tellin' 'em how he'd cried when he left us and how his heart'd been set on gettin' married on the series dough. I made it so strong that they finally fell for it. Our shares was cut to five hundred eighty apiece, and John sent him a check for a full share.

For a while I was kind o' worried about what I'd did. I didn't know if I was doin' right by the girl to give him the chance to marry her.

He'd told me she was stuck on him, and that's the only excuse I had for tryin' to fix it up between 'em; but, b'lieve me, if she was my sister or a friend o' mine I'd just as soon of had her manage the Cincinnati Club as marry that bird. I thought to myself:

'If she's all right she'll take acid in a month—and it'll be my fault; but if she's really stuck on him they must be somethin' wrong with her too, so what's the diff'rence?'

Then along comes this letter that I told you about. It's from some friend of his up there—and they's a note from him. I'll read 'em to you and then I got to beat it for the station:

Dear Sir: They have got poor Elliott locked up and they are goin' to take him to the asylum at Kalamazoo. He thanks you for the check, and we will use the money to see that he is made comf'table.

When the poor boy came back here he found that his girl was married to Joe Bishop, who runs a soda fountain. She had wrote to him about it, but he did not read her letters. The news drove him crazy—poor boy—and he went to the place where they was livin' with a baseball bat and very near killed 'em both. Then he marched down the street singin' 'Silver Threads Among the Gold' at the top of his voice. They was goin' to send him to prison for assault with intent to kill, but the jury decided he was crazy.

He wants to thank you again for the money.

Yours truly.
Jim—

I can't make out his last name—but it don't make no diff'rence. Now I'll read you his note:

Old Roomy:

I was at bat twice and made two hits; but I guess I did not meet 'em square. They tell me they are both alive yet, which I did not mean 'em to be. I hope they got good curve-ball pitchers where I am goin'. I sure can bust them curves—can't I sport?

Yours,
B. Elliott.

P.S.—The B Stands for Buster.

That's all of it, fellers; and you can see I had some excuse for not hittin'. You can also see why I ain't never goin' to room with no bug again—not for John or nobody else!

Joe DiMaggio

RED SMITH

AFTER THE YANKEES chewed up the Dodgers in the second game of the World Series, Joe DiMaggio relaxed in the home club's gleaming tile boudoir and deposed at length in defense of Pete Reiser, the Brooklyn center fielder, who had narrowly escaped being smitten upon the isthmus rhombencephali that day by sundry fly balls.

The moving, mottled background of faces and shirt collars and orchids, Joe said, made a fly almost invisible until it had cleared the top deck. The tricky, slanting shadows of an October afternoon created a problem involving calculus, metaphysics, and social hygiene when it came to judging a line drive. The roar of the crowd disguised the crack of bat against ball. And so on.

Our Mr Robert Cooke, listening respectfully as one should to the greatest living authority on the subject, nevertheless stared curiously at DiMaggio. He was thinking that not only Reiser but also J. DiMaggio had played that same center field on that same afternoon, and there were no knots on Joe's slick coiffure.

'How about you, Joe?' Bob asked. 'Do those same factors handicap you out there?'

DiMaggio permitted himself one of his shy, toothy smiles.

'Don't start worrying about the old boy after all these years,' he said.

He didn't say 'the old master.' That's a phrase for others to use. But it would be difficult to define more aptly than Joe did the difference between this unmitigated pro and all the others, good, bad, and ordinary, who also play in major-league outfields.

There is a line that has been quoted so often the name of its originator has been lost. But whoever said it first was merely reacting impulsively to a particular play and not trying to coin a mot when he ejaculated:

'The sonofagun! Ten years I've been watching him, and he hasn't had a hard chance yet!'

It may be that Joe is not, ranked on his defensive skill alone, the finest center fielder of his time. Possibly Terry Moore was his equal playing the hitter, getting the jump on the ball, judging a fly, covering ground, and squeezing the ball once he touched it.

Joe himself has declared that his kid brother, Dominic, is a better fielder than he. Which always recalls the occasion when the Red Sox were playing the Yanks and Dom fled across the country line to grab a drive by Joe that no one but a DiMaggio could have reached. And the late Sid Mercer, shading his thoughtful eyes under a hard straw hat, remarked to the press box at large: 'Joe should sue his old man on that one.'

Joe hasn't been the greatest hitter that baseball has known, either. He'll not match Ty Cobb's lifetime average, he'll never threaten Babe Ruth's home-run record, nor will he ever grip the imagination of the crowds as the Babe did. Or even as Babe Herman did. That explains why the contract that he signed the other day calls for an estimated $65,000 instead of the $80,000 that Ruth got. If he were not such a matchless craftsman he might be a more spectacular player. And so, perhaps, more colorful. And so more highly rewarded.

But you don't rate a great ballplayer according to his separate, special talents. You must rank him off the sum total of his component parts, and on this basis there has not been, during Joe's big-league existence, a rival close to him. None other in his time has combined such savvy and fielding and hitting and throwing—Tom Laird, who was writing sports in San Francisco when Joe was growing up, always insisted that a sore arm 'ruined' DiMaggio's throwing in his first season with the Yankees—and such temperament and such base running.

Because he does so many other things so well and makes no speciality of stealing. DiMaggio rarely has received full credit for his work on the bases. But travel with a second-division club in the league for a few seasons and count the times when DiMaggio, representing the trying or winning run, whips you by coming home on the unforeseen gamble and either beats the play or knocks the catcher into the dugout.

Ask American League catchers about him, or National Leaguers like Ernie Lombardi, Big Lom will remember who it was who ran home from first base in the last game of the 1939 World Series while Ernie lay threshing in the dust behind the plate and Bucky Walters stood bemused on the mound.

These are the reasons why DiMaggio, excelled by Ted Williams in all offensive statistics and reputedly Ted's inferior in crowd appeal and financial standing, still won the writers' accolade as the American League's most valuable in 1947.

It wasn't the first time Williams earned this award with his bat and lost it with his disposition. As a matter of fact, if all other factors were equal save only the question of character, Joe never would lose out to any player. The guy who came out of San Francisco as a shy lone wolf, suspicious of Easterners and of Eastern writers, today is the top guy in any sports gathering in any town. The real champ.

The Natural

BERNARD MALAMUD

AT THE CLUBHOUSE the next morning the unshaven Knights were glum and redeyed. They moved around listlessly and cursed each step. Angry fist fights broke out among them. They were sore at themselves and the world, yet when Roy came in and headed for his locker they looked up and watched with interest. He opened the door and found his new uniform knotted up dripping wet on a hook. His sanitary socks and woolen stockings were slashed to shreds and all the other things were smeared black with shoe polish. He located his jock, with two red apples in it, swinging from a cord attached to the light globe, and both his shoes were nailed to the ceiling. The boys let out a bellow of laughter. Bump just about doubled up howling but Roy yanked the wet pants off the hook and caught him with it smack in the face. The players let out another yowl.

Bump comically dried himself with a bath towel, digging deep in his ears, wiping under the arms, and shimmying as he rubbed across his fat behind.

'Fast guesswork, buster, and to show you there's no hard feelings, how's about a Camel?'

Roy wanted nothing from the bastard but took the cigarette because everyone was looking on. When he lit it, someone in the rear yelled, 'Fire!' and ducked as it burst in Roy's face. Bump had disappeared. The players fell into each other's arms. Tears streamed down their cheeks. Some of them could not unbend and limped around from laughing so.

Roy flipped the ragged butt away and began to mop up his wet locker.

Allie Stubbs, the second baseman, danced around the room in imitation of a naked nature dancer. He pretended to discover a trombone at the foot of a tree and marched around blowing oompah, oompah, oompah.

Roy then realized the bassoon case was missing. It startled him that he hadn't thought of it before.

'Who's got it, boys?'—but no one answered. Allie now made out like he was flinging handfuls of rose petals into the trainer's office.

Going in there, Roy saw that Bump had broken open the bassoon case and was about to attack Wonderboy with a hacksaw.

'Lay off of that, you goon,'

Bump turned and stepped back with the bat raised. Roy grabbed it and with a quick twist tore it out of his sweaty hands, turning him around as he did and booting him hard with his knee. Bump grunted and swung but Roy ducked. The team crowded into the trainer's office, roaring with delight.

But Doc Casey pushed his way through them and stepped between Roy and Bump. 'That'll do, boys. We want no trouble here. Go on outside or Pop will have your hides.'

Bump was sweaty and sore. 'You're a lousy sport, alfalfa.'

'I don't like the scummy tricks you play on people you have asked for a favor,' Roy said.

'I hear you had a swell time, wonderboy.'

Again they grappled for each other, but Doc, shouting for help, kept them apart until the players pinned Roy's arms and held on to Bump.

'Lemme at him,' Bump roared, 'and I will skin the skunk.'

Held back by the team, they glared at one another over the trainer's head.

'What's going on in there?' Pop's shrill blast came from inside the locker room. Earl Wilson poked his grayhaired, sunburned head in and quickly called, 'All out, men, on the double.' The players scurried past Pop and through the tunnel. They felt better.

Dizzy hustled up a makeshift rig for Roy. He dressed and polished his bat, a little sorry he had lost his temper, because he had wanted to speak quietly to the guy and find out whether he was expecting the redhead in his room last night.

Thinking about her made him uneasy. He reported to Pop in the dugout.

'What was the trouble in there between Bump and you?' Pop asked.

Roy didn't say and Pop got annoyed. 'I won't stand for any ructions between players so cut it out or you will find yourself chopping wood back in the sticks. Now report to Red.'

Roy went over to where Red was catching Chet Schultz, today's pitcher, and Red said to wait his turn at the batting cage.

The field was overrun with droopy players. Half a dozen were bunched near the gate of the cage, waiting to be pitched to by Al Fowler, whom Pop had ordered to throw batting practice for not bearing down in the clutches yesterday. Some of the men were at the sidelines, throwing catch. A few were shagging flies in the field, a group was playing pepper. On the line between home and first Earl Wilson was hacking out grounders to Allie Stubbs, Cal Baker at short, Hank Benz, the third baseman, and Emil Lajong, who played first. At the edge of the outfield, Hinkle and Hill, two of the regular starters, and McGee, the reliefer, were doing a weak walk-run-walk routine. No one seemed to be thoroughly awake, but when Roy went into the batting cage they came to life and observed him.

Fowler, a southpaw, was in a nasty mood. He didn't like having his ears burned by Pop, called a showboat in front of other men, and then shoved into batting practice the day after he had pitched. Fowler was twenty-three but looked thirty. He was built rangy, with very light hair and eyelashes, and small blue eyes. As a pitcher he had the stuff and knew it, but all season long he had been erratic and did a great amount of griping. He was palsy with Bump, who as a rule had no friends.

When Roy came up with Wonderboy, he hugged the plate too close to suit Fowler, who was in there anyway only to help the batters find their timing. In annoyance Fowler pitched the ball at Roy's head. Roy hit the dirt.

Pop shrieked, 'Cut that out, you blasted fool.' Fowler mumbled something about the ball slipping. Yet he wanted to make Roy look silly and burned the next one in. Roy swung and the ball sailed over the right field fence. Red-faced, Fowler tried a hard, sharp-breaking curve. Roy caught it at the end of his bat and pulled it into the left field stands.

'Try this one, grandpa,' Fowler flung a stiff-wrist knuckler that hung in the air without spin before it took a sudden dip, but Roy scooped it up with the stick and lifted it twenty rows up into the center field stands. Then he quit. Fowler was scowling at his feet. Everybody else stared at Roy.

Pop called out, 'Lemme see that bat, son.'

Both he and Red examined it, hefting it and rubbing along the grain with their fingers.

'Where'd you get it?' Pop asked.

Roy cleared his throat. He said he had made it himself.

'Did you brand this name Wonderboy on it?'

'That's right.'

'What's it mean?'

'I made it long ago,' Roy said, 'when I was a kid. I wanted it to be a very good bat and that's why I gave it that name.'

'A bat's cheap to buy,' Red said.

'I know it but this tree near the river where I lived was split by lightning. I liked the wood inside it so I cut me out a bat. Hadn't used it much until I played semipro ball, but I always kept it oiled with sweet oil and boned it so it wouldn't chip.'

'Sure is white. Did you bleach the wood?'

'No, that's the true color.'

'How long ago d'you make it?' Pop asked.

'A long time—I don't remember.'

'Whyn't you get into the game then?'

Roy couldn't answer for a minute. 'I sorta got sidetracked.'

But Pop was all smiles. 'Red'll measure and weigh it. If there's no filler and it meets specifications you'll be allowed to use it.'

'There's nothing in it but wood.'

Red clapped him on the back. 'I feel it in my bones that you will have luck with it.' He said to Pop, 'Maybe we can start Roy in the line up soon?'

Pop said they would see how it worked out.

But he sent Roy out to left field and Earl hit fungoes to him all over the lot. Roy ran them down well. He took one shot over his shoulder and two caroming off the wall below the stands. His throwing was quick, strong, and bull's eye.

When Bump got around to his turn in the cage, though he did not as a rule exert himself in practice, he now whammed five of Fowler's fast pitches into the stands. Then he trotted out to his regular spot in the sun field and Earl hit him some long flies, all of which he ran for and caught with gusto, even those that went close to the wall, which was unusual for him because he didn't like to go too near it.

Practice picked up. The men worked faster and harder than they had in a long time. Pop suddenly felt so good, tears came to his eyes and he had to blow his nose.

*

In the clubhouse about an hour and a half before game time, the boys were sitting around in their underwear after showers.

They were bulling, working crossword puzzles, shaving and writing letters. Two were playing checkers, surrounded by a circle of others, and the rest were drinking soda, looking at the *Sporting News*, or just resting their eyes. Though they tried to hide it they were all nervous, always glancing up whenever someone came into the room. Roy couldn't make sense of it.

Red took him around to meet some of the boys and Roy spoke a few words to Dave Olson, the squat catcher, also to the shy Mexican center fielder, Juan Flores and to Gabby Laslow, who patrolled right field. They sidestepped Bump, sitting in front of his locker with a bath towel around his rump, as he worked a red thread across the yellowed foot of a sanitary sock.

'Changes that thread from sock to sock every day,' Red said in a low voice. 'Claims it keeps him hitting.'

As the players began to get into clean uniforms, Pop, wearing half-moon specs, stepped out of his office. He read aloud the batting order, then flipping through his dog-eared, yellow-paged notebook he read the names of the players opposing them and reminded them how the pitchers were to pitch and the fielders field them. This information was scribbled all over the book and Pop had to thumb around a lot before he had covered everybody. Roy then expected him to lay on with a blistering mustard plaster for all, but he only glanced anxiously at the door and urged them all to be on their toes and for gosh sakes get some runs.

Just as Pop finished his pep talk the door squeaked open and a short and tubby man in a green suit peeked in. Seeing they were ready, he straightened up and entered briskly, carrying a briefcase in his hand. He beamed at the players and without a word from anybody they moved chairs and benches and arranged themselves in rows before him. Roy joined the rest, expecting to hear some kind of talk. Only Pop and the coaches sat behind the man, and Dizzy lounged, half open mouthed, at the door leading to the hall.

'What's the act?' Roy asked Olson.

'It's Doc Knobb.' The catcher looked sleepy.

'What's he do?'

'Pacifies us.'

The players were attentive, sitting as if they were going to have their pictures snapped. The nervousness Roy had sensed among them was all but gone. They looked like men whose worries had been lifted, and even Bump gave forth a soft grunt of contentment.

The doctor removed his coat and rolled up his shirtsleeves. 'Got to hurry today,' he told Pop, 'got a polo team to cheer up in Brooklyn.'

He smiled at the men and then spoke so softly, at first they couldn't hear him. When he raised his voice it exuded calm.

'Now, men,' he purred, 'all of you relax and let me have your complete attention. Don't think of a thing but me.' He laughed, brushed a spot off his pants, and continued. 'You know what my purpose is. You're familiar with that. It's to help you get rid of the fears and personal inferiorities that tie you into knots and keep you from being aces in this game. Who are the Pirates? Not supermen, only mortals. What have they got that you haven't got? I can't think of a thing, absolutely not one. It's the attitude that's licking you—your own, not the Pirates'. What do you mean to yourselves? Are you a flock of bats flying around in a coffin, or the sun shining calmly on a blue lake? Are you sardines being swallowed up in the sea, or the whale that does the swallowing? That's why I'm here, to help you answer that question in the affirmative, to help you by mesmerism and autosuggestion, meaning you do the suggesting, not I. I only assist by making you receptive to your own basic thoughts. If you think you are winners, you will be. If you don't, you won't. That's psychology. That's the way the world works. Give me your whole attention and look straight into my eyes. What do you see there? You see sleep. That's right, sleep. So relax, sleep, relax . . .'

His voice was soft, lulling, peaceful. He had raised his pudgy arms and with stubby fingers was making ripples on a vast calm sea. Already Olson was gently snoring. Flores, with the tip of his tongue protruding, Bump, and some of the other players were fast asleep. Pop looked on, absorbed.

Staring at the light gleaming on Pop's bald bean. Roy felt himself going off . . . way way down, drifting through the tides into golden water as he searched for this lady fish, or mermaid, or whatever you called her. His eyes grew big in the seeking, first fish eyes, then bulbous frog eyes. Sailing lower into the pale green sea, he sought everywhere for the reddish glint of her scales, until the water became dense and dark green and then everything gradually got so black he lost all sight of where he was. When he tried to rise up into the light he couldn't find it. He darted in all directions, and though there were times he saw flashes of her green tail, it was dark everywhere. He threshed up a storm of luminous bubbles but they gave out little light and he did not know where in all the glass to go.

Roy ripped open his lids and sprang up. He shoved his way out from between the benches.

The doctor was startled but made no attempt to stop him. Pop called out, 'Hey, where do you think you're going?'

'Out.'

'Sit down, dammit, you're on the team.'

'I might be on the team but no medicine man is going to hypnotize me.'

'You signed a contract to obey orders,' Pop snapped shrilly.

'Yes, but not to let anybody monkey around in my mind.'

As he headed into the tunnel he heard Pop swear by his eight-foot uncle that nobody by the name of Roy Hobbs would ever play ball for him as long as he lived.

He had waited before . . . and he waited now, on a spike-scruffed bench in the dugout, hidden from sky, wind and weather, from all but the dust that blew up from Knights Field and lodged dry in the throat, as the grass grew browner. And from time ticking off balls and strikes, batters up and out, halves and full innings, games won and (mostly) lost, days and nights, and the endless train miles from Philly, with in-between stops, along the arc to St Louis, and circling back by way of Chi, Boston, Brooklyn . . . still waiting.

'C'mon Roy,' Red had urged, 'apologize to Pop, then the next time Knobb comes around, join the boys and everything will be okay.'

'Nix on that,' said Roy, 'I don't need a shyster quack to shoot me full of confidence juice. I want to go through on my own steam.'

'He only wants everybody to relax and be able to do their best.'

Roy shook his head. 'I been a long time getting here and now that I am, I want to do it by myself, not with that kind of bunk.'

'Do what?' Red asked.

'What I have to do.'

Red shrugged and gave him up as too stubborn. Roy sat around, and though it said on his chest he was one of the team, he sat among them alone; at the train window, gazing at the moving trees, in front of his locker, absorbed in an untied shoe lace, in the dugout, squinting at the great glare of the game. He traveled in their company and dressed where they did but he joined them in nothing, except maybe batting practice, entering the cage with the lumber on his shoulder glistening like a leg bone in the sun and taking his chops at the pill. Almost always he hammered the swift, often murderous throws (the practice pitchers dumped their bag of tricks on him) deep into the stands, as the players watched and muttered at the swift flight of the balls, then forgot him when the game started. But there were days when the waiting got him. He could feel the strength draining from his bones, weakening him so he could hardly lift Wonderboy. He was unwilling to move then, for fear he would fall over on his puss and have to crawl away on all fours. Nobody noticed he did not bat when he felt this way except Pop; and Bump, seeing how white his face was, squirted contemptuous tobacco juice in the dust. Then when Roy's strength ebbed back, he would once again go into the batters' cage and do all sorts of marvelous things that made them watch in wonder.

He watched *them* and bad as he felt he had to laugh. They were a nutty bunch to begin with but when they were losing they were impossible. It was like some kind of sickness. They threw to the wrong bases, bumped heads together in the outfield, passed each other on the baselines, sometimes batted out of order, throwing both Pop and the ump into fits, and cussed everybody else for their mistakes. It was not uncommon to see them pile three men on a bag, or behold a catcher on the opposing team, in a single skip and jump, lay the tag on two of them as they came thundering together into home plate. Or watch Gabby Laslow, in a tight spot, freeze onto the ball, or Allie Stubbs get socked with it in the jaw, thrown by Olson on a steal as Allie admired a lady in the stands. Doc Knobb's hypnotism cut down their jitters but it didn't much help their coordination, yet when they were left unhypnotized for a few days, they were afflicted with more than the usual number of hexes and whammies and practiced all sorts of magic to undo them. To a man they crossed their fingers over spilled salt, or coffee or tea, or at the sight of a hearse. Emil Lajong did a backward flip whenever he located a cross-eyed fan in the stands. Olson hated a woman who wore the same drab brown-feathered hat every time she showed up. He spat through two fingers whenever he spotted her in the crowd. Bump went through his ritual with the colored threads in his socks and shorts. Pop sometimes stroked a rabbit's foot. Red Blow never changed his clothes during a 'winning streak' and Flores secretly touched his genitals whenever a bird flew over his head.

They were not much different from the fans in the patched and peeling stands. On weekdays the stadium usually looked like a haunted house but over the weekend crowds developed. The place often resembled a zoo full of oddballs, including gamblers, bums, drunks, and some ugly crackpots. Many of them came just to get a laugh out of the bonehead plays. Some, when the boys were losing, cursed and jeered, showering them—whenever they came close enough—with rotten cabbages, tomatoes, blackened bananas and occasionally an eggplant. Yet let the umpire call a close play against the Knights and he became a target for pop bottles, beer cans, old shoes or anything that happened to be lying around loose. Surprisingly, however, a few players were chosen for affection and even admiration by their fans. Sadie Sutter, a girl of sixty-plus, who wore large flowered hats, bobby sox, and short skirts, showed her undying love for Dave Olson every time he came up to the plate by banging with all her might on a Chinese gong she dragged into the stadium every day. A Hungarian cook, a hearty man with a hard yellow straw hat jammed tight on his skull, hopped up on his seat and crowed like a rooster whenever Emil Lajong originated a double play. And there was a girl named Gloria from Mississippi, a washed-out flower of the vestibules, who between innings when her eyes were not on the game, lined up a customer or two for a quickie later. She gave her heart to Gabby, yelling 'Get a move on, mo-lasses,' to set him in motion after a fly ball. Besides these, there had appeared early in the present season, a pompous Otto P. Zipp, whose peevish loudspeaker could be heard all over the park, his self-chosen mission to rout the critics of Bump Baily, most of whom razzed the big boy for short legging on the other fielders. The dwarf honked a loud horn at the end of a two-foot walking stick, and it sounded as if a flock of geese had been let loose at the offenders, driving them—his purple curses ringing in their ears—to seek shelter in some hidden hole in the stands or altogether out of the ballpark. Zipp was present at every home game, sitting at the rail in short left field, and Bump made it his much publicized business, as he trotted out to his position at the start of the game, to greet him with a loud kiss on the forehead, leaving Otto in a state of creamy bliss.

Roy got to know them all as he waited, all one if you looked long enough through the haze of cigarette smoke, except one . . . Memo Paris. Pop's redheaded niece, sad, spurned lady, who sat without wifehood in the wives' box behind third base. He could, if she would let him, find her with his eyes shut, with his hands alone as he had in the dark. Always in the act of love she lived in his mind, the only way he knew her, because she would not otherwise suffer his approach. *He* was to blame, she had wept one bitter midnight, so she hated his putrid guts. Since the team's return to the city (the phone banged in his ear and she ripped up his letters when they were delivered) whenever he got up from his seat in the hotel lobby as she stepped out of the elevator, to say how sorry he was for beginning at the wrong end, she tugged at her summer furpiece and breezed past him in greeneyed scorn, withering in the process Bump at the cigar stand, who had laughed aloud at Roy's rout. ('Honeybunch,' he had explained, 'it was out of the pity of my heart that I took that shmo into my room, because they didn't have one for him and I was intending to pass the night at the apartment of my he cousin from Mobile. How'd I know you'd go in there when you said you weren't speaking to me?' He swore it hadn't been a gag—had he ever pulled one on her?—but Memo punished him in silence, punishing herself, and he knew it because she still came every day to see him play.) She walked out of the lobby, with her silver bracelets tinkling, swaying a little on her high heels, as if she had not too long ago learned to walk on them, and went with her beautiful body away, for which Roy everlastingly fried Bump Baily in the deepfat of his abomination.

It was for her he waited.

On the morning of the twenty-first of June Pop told Roy that as of tomorrow he was being shipped to a Class B team in the Great Lakes Association. Roy said he was quitting baseball anyway, but that same day, in answer to an angry question of Pop's as to why the team continued to flop, Doc Knobb said that the manager's hysterical behavior was undoing all the good he had done, and he offered to hypnotize Pop along with the others without hiking his fee. Pop shrilly told the psychologist he was too old for such bamboozlement, and Knobb retorted that his attitude was not only ridiculous but stupid. Pop got redfaced and told him to go to perdition with his hocus pocus and as of right then the doctor was canned.

That afternoon the Knights began a series with the second place Phils. Instead of falling into a swoon when they learned there was to be no further hypnosis, the team played its best ball in weeks. Against superior pitching, in the sixth they bunched three singles for a run, and though Schultz had already given up five hits to the Phils, they were scattered and came to nothing. The Phils couldn't score till the top of the eighth, when with two out Schultz weakened, walking one man and handing the next a good enough throw to hit for a sharp single, so that there were now men on first and third. Up came Rogers, the Phils' slugger, and hit a fast curve for what looked like no more than a long fly ball, a routine catch, to left center. Now it happened that Bump was nearer to the ball than Flores, who was shifted to the right, but he was feeling horny in the sun and casting about in his mind for who to invite to his bed tonight, when he looked up and noticed this ball coming. He still had time to get under it but then saw Flores going for it like a galloping horse, and the anguished look on the Mexican's face, his black eyes popping, neck like a thick rope, and mouth haunted, fascinated Bump so, he decided to let him have it if he wanted it that bad. At the last minute he tried to take it away from the Mex, risking a head-on collision, but the wind whipped the ball closer to the wall than he had bargained for, so Bump fell back to cover Flores in case he misplayed it.

The ball fell between them, good for a double, and scoring two of the Phils. Pop tore at what was left of his gray hair but couldn't grip it with his oily, bandaged fingers so he pulled at his ears till they were lit like red lamps. Luckily the next Phil smothered the fire by rolling to first, which kept the score at 2–1. When Bump returned to the dugout Pop cursed him from the cradle to the grave and for once Bump had no sassy answers. When it came his time to go out on deck. Pop snarled for him to stay where he was. Flores found a ripe one and landed on first but Pop stuck to his guns and looked down the line past Bump. His eye lit on Roy at the far end of the bench, and he called his name to go out there and hit. Bump turned purple. He grabbed a bat and headed for Roy but half the team jumped on him. Roy just sat there without moving and it looked to everyone like he wouldn't get up. The umpire roared in for a batter to come out, and after a while, as the players fidgeted and Pop fumed, Roy sighed and picked up Wonderboy. He slowly walked up the steps.

'Knock the cover off of it,' Pop yelled.

'Attention, please,' the P.A. man announced. 'Roy Hobbs, number forty-five, batting for Baily.'

A groan rose from the stands and turned into a roar of protest.

Otto Zipp jumped up and down on his seat, shaking his furious little fist at home plate.

'Throw him to the dogs,' he shouted, and filled the air with his piercing curses.

Glancing at the wives' box, Roy saw that Memo had her head turned away. He set his jaw and advanced to the plate. His impulse was to knock the dirt out of his cleats but he refrained because he did not want to harm his bat in any way. Waiting for the pitcher to get set, Roy wiped his palms on his pants and twitched his cap. He lifted Wonderboy and waited rocklike for the throw.

He couldn't tell the color of the pitch that came at him. All he could think of was that he was sick to death of waiting, and tongue-out thirsty to begin. The ball was now a dew drop staring him in the eye so he stepped back and swung from the toes.

Wonderboy flashed in the sun. It caught the sphere where it was biggest. A noise like a twenty-one gun salute cracked the sky. There was a straining, ripping sound and a few drops of rain spattered to the ground. The ball screamed toward the pitcher and seemed suddenly to dive down at his feet. He grabbed it to throw to first and realized to his horror that he held only the cover. The rest of it, unraveling cotton thread as it rode, was headed into the outfield.

Roy was rounding first when the ball plummeted like a dead bird into center field. Attempting to retrieve and throw, the Philly fielder got tangled in thread. The second baseman rushed up, bit the cord and heaved the ball to the catcher but Roy had passed third and made home, standing. The umpire called him safe and immediately a rhubarb boiled. The Phils' manager and his players charged out of the dugout and were joined by the nine men on the field. At the same time, Pop, shouting in defense of the ump, rushed forth with all the Knights but Bump. The umpire, caught between both teams, had a troublesome time of it and was shoved this way and that. He tossed out two men on each side but by then came to the decision that the hit was a ground rules double. Flores had scored and the game was tied up. Roy was ordered back to second, and Pop announced he was finishing the game under protest. Somebody then shouted it was raining cats and dogs. The stands emptied like a yawn and the players piled into the dugouts. By the time Roy got in from second he was wading in water ankle deep. Pop sent him into the clubhouse for a change of uniform but he could have saved himself the trouble because it rained steadily for three days.

The game was recorded as a 2–2 tie, to be replayed later in the season.

In the locker room Pop asked Roy to explain why he thought the cover had come off the ball.

'That's what you said to do, wasn't it?'

'That's right,' said Pop, scratching his bean.

The next day he told Roy he was withdrawing his release and would hereafter use him as a pinch hitter and substitute fielder.

The rain had washed out the Phils' series but the Knights were starting another with the seventh-place Redbirds. In batting practice, Roy, who was exciting some curiosity for his freak hit of yesterday, looked tremendous but so did Bump. For the first time in a long while Roy went out to left field to limber up. Bump was out there too and Earl swatted fungoes to both.

As they were changing into clean uniforms before the start of the game, Bump warned Roy in front of everybody, 'Stay out of my way, busher, or you will get your head bashed.'

Roy squirted spit on the floor.

When Pop later handed the batting order to Stuffy Briggs, the plate umpire, it had Bump's name scribbled on it as usual in the fourth slot, but Pop had already warned him that if he didn't hustle his behind when a ball was hit out to his field, he would rest it a long time on the bench.

Bump made no reply but it was obvious that he took Pop's words to heart, because he was a bang-up fielder that day. He accepted eight chances, twice chasing into center field to take them from Flores. He caught them to his left and right, dove for and came up with a breath-taking shoestringer, and running as if on fire, speared a fantastic catch over his shoulder. Still not satisfied, he pounded like a bull after his ninth try, again in Flores' territory, a smoking ball that sailed up high, headed for the wall. As Bump ran for it he could feel fear leaking through his stomach, and his legs unwillingly slowed down, but then he had this vision of himself as the league's best outfielder, acknowledged so by fans and players alike, even Pop, whom he'd be nothing less than forever respectful to, and in love with and married to Memo. Thinking this way he ran harder, though Zipp's geese honked madly at his back, and with a magnificent twisting jump, he trapped the ball in his iron fingers. Yet the wall continued to advance, and though the redheaded lady of his choice was on her feet shrieking, Bump bumped it with a skull-breaking bang, and the wall embraced his broken body.

*

Though Bump was on the critical list in the hospital, many newspapers contnued to speculate about the ball whose cover Roy had knocked off. It was explained as everything from an optical illusion (neither the ball nor the cover was ever found, the remnant caught by the catcher disappeared, and it was thought some fan had snatched the cover) to a feat of prodigious strength. Baseball records and newspaper files were combed but no one could find any evidence that it had happened before, although some of the older scribes swore it had. Then it leaked out that Pop had ordered Roy to skin the ball and Roy had obliged, but no one took that very seriously. One of the sportswriters suggested that a hard downward chop could shear off the outer covering. He had tried it in his cellar and had split the horsehide. Another pointed out that such a blow would have produced an infield grounder, therefore maybe a tremendous upward slash? The first man proved that would have uncorked a sure pop fly whereas the ball, as everyone knew, had sailed straight out over the pitcher's head. So it had probably resulted from a very very forceful sock. But many a hitter had plastered the ball forcefully before, still another argued, and his idea was that it was defective to begin with, a fact the company that manufactured the ball vigorously denied. Max Mercy had his own theory. He wrote in his column, 'My Eye in the Knot Hole' (the year he'd done the Broadway stint for his paper his eye was in the key hole), that Roy's bat was a suspicious one and hinted it might be filled with something a helluva lot stronger than wood. Red Blow publicly denied this. He said the bat had been examined by league authorities and was found to be less than forty-two inches long, less than two and three-quarters inches thick at its fattest part, and in weight less than two pounds, which made it a legal weapon. Mercy then demanded that the wood be X-rayed but Roy turned thumbs down on that proposition and kept Wonderboy hidden away when the sports columnist was nosing around the clubhouse.

On the day after the accident Pop soberly gave Roy the nod to play in Bump's place. As Roy trotted out to left, Otto Zipp was in his usual seat but looking worn and aged. His face, tilted to the warming rays of the sun, was like a pancake with a cherry nose, and tears were streaming through slits where the eyes would be. He seemed to be waiting for his pre-game kiss on the brow but Roy passed without looking at him.

The long rain had turned the grass green and Roy romped in it like a happy calf in its pasture. The Redbirds, probing his armor, belted the ball to him whenever they could, which was often, because Hill was not too happy on the mound, but Roy took everything they aimed at him. He seemed to know the soft, hard, and bumpy places in the field and just how high a ball would bounce on them. From the flags on the stadium roof he noted the way the wind would blow the ball, and he was quick at fishing it out of the tricky undercurrents on the ground. Not sun, shadow, nor smoke haze bothered him, and when a ball was knocked against the wall he estimated the angle of rebound and speared it as if its course had been plotted on a chart. He was good at gauging slices and knew when to charge the pill to save time on the throw. Once he put his head down and ran ahead of a shot going into the concrete. Though the crowd rose with a thunderous warning, he caught it with his back to the wall and did a little jig to show he was alive. Everyone laughed in relief, and they liked his long-legged loping and that he resembled an acrobat the way he tumbled and came up with the ball in his glove. For his performance that day there was much whistling and applause, except where he would have liked to hear it, an empty seat in the wives' box.

His batting was no less successful. He stood at the plate lean and loose, right-handed with an open stance, knees relaxed and shoulders squared. The bat he held in a curious position, lifted slightly above his head as if prepared to beat a rattlesnake to death, but it didn't harm his smooth stride into the pitch, nor the easy way he met the ball and slashed it out with a flick of the wrists. The pitchers tried something different every time he came up, sliders, sinkers, knucklers, but he swung and connected, spraying them to all fields. He was, Red Blow said to Pop, a natural, though somewhat less than perfect because he sometimes hit at bad ones, which caused Pop to frown.

'I mistrust a bad ball hitter.'

'There are all kinds of hitters,' Red answered. 'Some are bucket foots, and some go for bad throws but none of them bother me as long as they naturally connect with anything that gets in their way.'

Pop spat up over the dugout steps. 'They sometimes make some harmful mistakes.'

'Who don't?' Red asked.

Pop then muttered something about this bad ball hitter he knew who had reached for a lemon and cracked his spine.

But the only thing Roy cracked that day was the record for the number of triples hit in a major league debut and also the one for chances accepted in the outfield. Everybody agreed that in him the Knights had uncovered something special. One reporter wrote, 'He can catch everything in creation,' and Roy just about proved it. It happened that a woman who lived on the sixth floor of an apartment house overlooking the stadium was cleaning out her bird cage, near the end of the game, which the Knights took handily, when her canary flew out of the window and darted down across the field. Roy, who was waiting for the last out, saw something coming at him in the low rays of the sun, and leaping high, bagged it in his glove.

He got rid of the bloody mess in the clubhouse can.

The Four Masters—
And Some Others

GRANTLAND RICE

IN OVER 50 YEARS of wandering about I have run across four master pitchers—pitchers you might label 'super great.' I have seen at least four other great ones.

These four happen to be 'ancients'; three of the next four are what you might call 'moderns.' Believe me, however, I have no special tie with the past that makes me see everything that's old—that occurred when I was a youngster—as necessarily better than what's come since. Around each curve in life I fully expect to meet and to love a 'great champion.' I often find old favorites annoying when they carp and haggle over minute details of events that weren't even clear when they occurred 30 or more years ago. If I didn't look ahead to greater deeds in this speeded up age, I believe I would have withered away long ago.

Incidentally, my first baseball hero was a fellow who never did make the grade in the big leagues. I played baseball with him at Vanderbilt: His name was Joe Sherrill, a gangly sort who must have stood 6 feet 2. He had a shock of black hair and he didn't weight more than 155 pounds. I was a freshman and substitute shortstop. Sherrill, a senior, was our Number 1 pitcher, a right-hander. You must appreciate that back in the 1890s there were precious few baseball heroes to thrill the youngsters who lived away from the big-league cities. There were no wire services to pump out the deeds of Ruth, Cobb, Hoyt, DiMaggio, Williams, Mantle and all the rest for the edification of youngsters from here to Tokyo. We built our own heroes, often from our own contemporaries. And as I say, Joe Sherrill was mine. For a collegian, he had the poise, guts and speed of a champion.

I sat on the bench one Thursday and marveled as Vanderbilt beat

Georgia and watched Sherrill strike out 16 men. I think he gave up two hits. The following Saturday, I watched him defeat Georgia again. I don't remember how many men he fanned but he pitched a one-hitter. This was a good '98 Georgia team that had recently walloped Pennsylvania's strong nine.

Sherrill graduated that June and went straight to the Southern League. In his first assignment he struck out 17 men in seven innings. Then his arm went lame. He never pitched again. He became a doctor. Had his arm remained in one piece, Sherrill would have become a pitching immortal. But that's water long since over the dam.

So who are my Four Masters? In no special order they are: Cy Young, 511 victories; Walter Johnson, 416 victories; Grover Alexander, 373 victories; Christy Mathewson, 373 victories.

The four who are merely great: Rube Waddell, Bob Grove, Carl Hubbell and Herb Pennock. The last three belong to the modern era. Oddly enough, the top four are right-handers and the second four southpaws.

They were all friends of mine, but I knew Mathewson, of the New York Giants, better than any of the others. I first met Matty in 1905, when we were both 25. But I didn't really get to know him well until 1911 when I came to the *New York Evening Mail*.

A graduate of Bucknell University, Matty was just a little bit better at all games than anyone else. He played chess and checkers and poker better, for example, and usually drew in most of the pots. He was smart looking and well dressed.

I played a lot of golf with him—from New York to St Louis. We had a funny argument in Pittsburgh on one trip during the 1911 season. I had Mike Donlin for a partner against Matty and Merkle, Fred Merkle, the old Giant first baseman. I had about a three footer on the first green when Matty spoke to Merkle just as I stroked and missed my putt. Naturally, I squawked.

'What's the matter?' Matty asked, 'We play baseball with thousands yelling and cheering. Yet somebody talks and you can't putt.'

'They are entirely different games,' I said.

'That's a lot of bunk,' Merkle said. I said nothing.

This particular match was at the hilly Schenley Course in Pittsburgh. On the second tee, Matty was at the top of his swing when I spoke to Donlin. Matty lunged and topped his ball into the ravine. He glared at me. Merkle was also at the top of his swing when I spoke again. Merkle's ball followed Matty's into the ravine.

'What's this,' Matty asked, 'a golf match or a talking duel?'

'I thought you said it didn't matter,' I replied. Both quickly agreed to keep quiet if I would. They found golf needs silence just as baseball needs noise.

Mathewson was as fine a companion as I ever knew. That night in Pittsburgh after the match, he asked me to have dinner with him at the Pittsburgh Athletic Club where he was slated to play a chess match. He was to meet 12 opponents. After dinner, walking back and forth from table to table, he won all of his matches, as I recall.

Mathewson had an unusual but sound idea concerning the alibi. 'An alibi is sound and needed in all competition,' he said. 'I mean in the high-up brackets. One of the foundations of success in sport is confidence in yourself. You can't afford to admit that any opponent is better than you are. So, if you lose to him there must be a reason—a bad break. You must have an alibi to show why you lost. If you haven't one, you must fake one. Your self-confidence must be maintained.'

I think there is something in this—but never for the amateur or week-end star. To me, that would be a one-way road towards becoming a complete and insufferable fool. However, devote your life and your living to a sport—be it baseball or golf—and this approach might stand up. Had Sam Snead had more of it after blowing that horrible 8 on the 18th hole in the '39 Open at Philadelphia, he might have won the Open title years ago. Hogan, on the other hand, has a good deal of this attitude although I'm not sure he realizes it when discussing his own game.

Matty's philosophy concerning the alibi went farther, which, to me was the saving grace of his primary thesis. 'Always have that alibi,' he continued. 'But keep it to yourself. That's where it belongs. Don't spread it around. Lose gracefully in the open. To yourself, lose bitterly—but learn! You can learn little from victory. You can learn everything from defeat.'

He was the smartest—all the way around. In the 1905 World Series against the Athletics, during the six days he pitched and won three games, all via shutouts. Mathewson was the greatest pitcher I ever saw. The games were played in October. I believe he could have continued pitching shutouts until Christmas! The A's got 13 singles off him in three games.

'In those games,' Matty said later, 'I had everything you need. Almost as much speed as Johnson, a curve that broke as I wanted it to, and perfect control.'

The next two years, in 1906 and 1907, he had a bad arm. He worked on his fadeaway. In 1908 he won 37 games for the Giants and saved at least 12 others, being responsible for at least 50 Giant victories. He was either pitching or in the bullpen all year.

'When I pitched that extra play-off game against the Cubs,' he told me much later, 'my arm was so sore and stiff I needed an hour's warm-up, I could barely lift it.'

In that game, Cy Seymour's failure to play deep for Joe Tinker, as Matty wanted him to do, cost the Giants the flag—for Tinker's triple was the decisive blow.

I recall another thing about Christy Mathewson. Since he pitched most of the time, he learned to coast. He would get four or five runs ahead and then loaf. 'Let the infielders and outfielders do part of the work,' he'd say. He could loaf and then tighten at a moment's notice. He had no interest in the earned run department. 'The game alone counts,' he remarked. 'I'd rather win nine to seven than lose one to nothing. So when I get ahead, I try to rest my arm.' This would have meant nothing under the modern situation where a lead of three or four runs can be wiped out in an inning. It was different in the day of the dead or unrubbered ball.

In 1908, when Matty won 37 games, with any breaks he could easily have won 43 or 44.

Mathewson, Grover Alexander, Cy Young, and Walter Johnson were entirely different types.

Matty, friendly and companionable with his friends, was aloof with others. For example, he and Babe Ruth were opposites. Here are two examples. Matty was explaining something to me one day in a hotel lobby in Chicago when a stranger came up, interrupted us and asked for his autograph.

'Can't you see that I'm talking to a friend?' Matty asked coldly. The stranger walked away, apparently sore.

'I owe everything I have to them when I'm out on the mound,' he said. 'But I owe the fans nothing and they owe me nothing when I am not pitching.'

Under the same conditions, when I was talking to Ruth, he turned on the stranger and said, 'Sure, I'll give you an autograph; but, you big so-and-so, sit down and wait till I'm through talking to my friend.' The stranger said, 'Sure Babe, I'll wait for you.' And he did—and left smiling.

Alexander, a partly sick man, had unbelievable control. Cy Young had a puzzling delivery—four different ones plus speed and stamina. Johnson had blinding speed. If Walter had ever been wild or had tried to brush a few hitters away from the plate, I don't believe they would ever have hit him, except by luck. One weekend when Washington played New York, Johnson shut out the Highlanders or Yankees three times in four days. He pitched 56 consecutive innings without permitting a run.

They were discussing Walter in various papers, asking what he had. I wrote a piece of verse which only the departed O. B. Keeler remembered. It closed with these two lines –

How do they know what Johnson's got?
Nobody's seen it yet.

Johnson was a big, shy man who rarely had much to say, I never heard him protest to an umpire when he was pitching. Matty, Alexander and Young also rarely complained.

Denton True (Cy) Young, with his vast body, turned his back completely on the hitter with something of a swivel-chair delivery. He never let the ball go until he spun back, almost completely, making his pitch extremely difficult to follow.

'I had four different deliveries,' he told me. He won more than 50 games in five different seasons en route to his 511 winning games.

One night during the 1939 World Series, I introduced Cy, in Cincinnati, to a crowd of baseball writers. 'He won five hundred eleven games,' I added.

'You are wrong,' Cy immediately retorted. 'It was five hundred and twelve games I won. I won one they wouldn't allow me, but I won it.'

Cy had a grand time fanning with the writers. 'How many innings did you say you pitched?' Bob Considine asked. 'Over seven thousand three hundred and something,' Cy replied. 'Good night,' Bob said, 'I'm afraid I'll have to be going.' The actual count was 7,377.

Of the four men, Alexander was the keenest control artist I ever studied. He was a victim of alcohol, a true alcoholic. Yet he won 30 games or more for three years—his earned run average was the lowest of them all—around 1.65 year after year.

Johnny Evers told me he almost cried each time he had to hit against Old Pete. 'I knew in advance it was a hopeless job,' he said.

Alex could throw a ball into a tin cup. I have never seen such control. He would pitch a game in an hour and fifteen minutes—rarely longer than an hour and twenty minutes. He wasted no time staring at the batter or rubbing the ball in his hands, as so many pitchers do today. He pitched like Gene Sarazen plays golf; no fuss and feathers. I remember one year when he pitched 16 shutouts, working mostly in Philadelphia's bandbox park where a soft fly was a home run.

Each of these four had some definite form of greatness to give: Cy Young, his 511 victories—Walter Johnson, his 3,497 strike outs, 113 shutouts, and 416 victories, most of the time with a weak club—Mathewson, three famous 1905 World Series shutouts, 37 wins and 12 saved games in 1908—Alexander, his 373 victories and his stingy earned run mark with a bad club, the Phillies. With the modern Yankees, Alex would have won 40 games many, many times. Alex and I came to the big league the same year—1911, my first baseball season in New York. He won 28 games as a rookie that season.

These pitchers are baseball's greatest. Among them, they won 1,673 games, an average of more than 400 games each; and two of them—Johnson and Alexander—worked for weak clubs.

Waddell, Grove, Pennock, Hubbell and Plank were magnificent, but in my book not quite like Young, Johnson, Alexander and Mathewson. Dizzy Dean? As good as anybody for a short span. He didn't pitch long enough to be rated with these others, who worked so many years. But Dizzy, christened Jay Hanna, was not only a great pitcher. He had more native color than one of his native Ozark sunsets.

In 1931, Diz was a bush rookie up from Texas for spring training with the Cardinals. That day they were playing an exhibition game with the Athletics, who had whipped the Cards in the 1930 Series. Gabby Street, the Cardinal manager, quickly figured Dizzy was more than he could handle. Around the fourth inning, the A's had the bases full, nobody out and Simmons, Foxx and Mickey Cochrane coming up.

'Wish I was out there,' Dean said. 'Those monkeys wouldn't score.'

Catcher Jimmy Wilson, sitting that game out, winked at Street. Street winked back. 'All right, Diz,' he said. 'You're in there! Go to work.'

Without any warm-up Diz proceeded to strike out Simmons, Foxx and Cochrane.

Branch Rickey earmarked Dean back to Houston, Texas. That same evening, Wilson recognized one of his silk shirts on Diz.

'Say, Dean,' Jimmy said, 'isn't that my silk shirt you're wearing? Where'd you get it?'

'Listen Jimmy,' Dean replied. 'You wouldn't want the world's greatest pitcher to wear one shirt for a month would you?'

'What's the answer to that one?' Wilson said to me later.

'There is no answer to anything Dizzy says,' I told Wilson.

'Or anything he does,' Wilson replied.

In 1929, Paul, Diz and father Dean started for Texas riding in two separate, battered old jalopies. Diz, the true pioneer, led the way by a few hundred yards.

'When a freight train came by and separated us, I went on. I musta left Pa and Paul behind,' Diz recalled later. 'They finally turned round and went back home to Arkansas. I went on to Texas. We didn't see each other again for years. I joined the Army and had to be bought from Uncle Sam when Rickey discovered I was the best pitcher in the country.'

It was at spring training in 1933 when Dizzy announced to all within hog-calling distance that he owned a kid brother 'back on the farm' whose high, hard one was even faster than his own. A year later, in '34 he again hollered that 'Me and Paul' would win 45 games. Diz proved better than his word. Between them they won 49 (Diz 30; Paul 19) for the swash-buckling Gas House Gang—and four more from Detroit as the Cards won the World Series four games to three.

Paul (Daffy) always had his big brother's interests at heart. Riding on the train with the Cardinals during that hectic '34 season, Diz and I were sitting on one side with Paul across the aisle swigging a bottle of pop. The train suddenly roared into a long tunnel.

'Diz,' exclaimed Paul. 'You tried any of this stuff?'

'Just fixin' to,' replied Diz. 'Why?'

'Don't!' cautioned Paul. 'I did and I've gone plumb blind.'

Struck on the toe by a line drive off Earl Averill's bat in the 1937 All-Star game, Dean was cut down at 26. Favoring the toe, he pitched without his full stride and injured his shoulder. When bursitis developed, Dean's effectiveness dimmed.

Branch Rickey, shrewdest David Harum ever, peddled Dean to Phil Wrigley for a modest 125,000 dollars. It was as a Chicago Cub in 1938 that Diz made his immortal remark when I questioned him about the arm.

'Well, Grant,' he said, feeling his right shoulder, 'it ain't what it was
... but then, what the hell is?'

At times lately, I'm forced to agree with one of my dearest confeder-
ates, Dizzy Dean, Pitcher-Philosopher Emeritus.

The Merkle 'Boner'— or was it O'Day's?

NEW YORK TIMES

NEW YORK, SEPT. 24, 1908—Censurable stupidity on the part of player Merkle in yesterday's game at the Polo Grounds between the Giants and Chicago placed the New York team's chances of winning the pennant in jeopardy. His usual conduct in the final inning of a great game perhaps deprived New York of a victory that would have been unquestionable had he not committed a breach in baseball play that resulted in Umpire O'Day declaring the game a tie.

With the score tied in the ninth inning at 1 to 1 and New York having a runner, McCormick, on third base and Merkle on first base, Bridwell hit into center field. It was a fair hit ball and would have been sufficient to win the game had Merkle gone on his way down the base path while McCormick was scoring the winning run. But, instead of Merkle going to second base to make sure that McCormick had reached home with the run necessary to a victory, Merkle ran towards the clubhouse, evidently thinking that his share in the game was ended when Bridwell hit the ball into safe territory.

Manager Chance of the Chicago club quickly grasped the situation and directed that the ball be thrown to second base, which would force out Merkle, who had not reached that corner.

Chance, who plays first base, ran to second, and the ball was thrown there, but immediately Pitcher McGinnity interfered in the play and a scramble of players ensued, in which, it is said, McGinnity obtained the ball and threw it into the crowd before Chance could complete a force play on Merkle, who was far away from the base line. Merkle said that he had touched second base, and the Chicago players were equally positive that he had not done so.

Chance then appealed to O'Day, who was head umpire of the game, for a decision on the matter. The crowd, thinking that the Giants had won, swarmed upon the playing field in such a confusion that none of the 'fans' seemed able to grasp the situation, but finally their attitude toward O'Day became so offensive that the police ran into the crowd and protected the umpire, while arguments were being hurled pro and con on the point in question by Chance and McGraw and the umpire.

O'Day finally decided that the run did not count, and, inasmuch as the spectators had gained such large numbers on the field that the game could not be resumed, he declared the game a tie. Although both Umpires O'Day and Emslie, it is claimed, say that they did not see the play at second base, O'Day's action in declaring that McCormick's run did not count was based upon the presumption or fact that a force play was made on Merkle at second base. The rule covering such a point is as follows:

'One run shall be scored every time a base runner, after having legally touched the first three bases, shall legally touch the home base before three men are put out, provided, however, that if he reach home on or during a play in which the third man be forced out or be put out before reaching first base a run shall not count. A force-out can be made only when a base runner legally loses the right to the base he occupies and is thereby obliged to advance as the result of a fair hit ball not caught on the fly.'

The singular ending of the game aroused intense interest throughout the city, and everywhere it was the chief topic of discussion. Early in the evening a report was widely circulated that President Harry C. Pulliam had decided the game was a tie and must be played again. When this rumor reached Mr Pulliam he authorized the following statement:

'I made no decision in the matter at all and I will not do so until the matter is presented to me in proper form. The statement on the 'ticker' that I had decided the game a tie is entirely unauthorized.'

But according to Umpire O'Day the game is a tie and will remain so until either the National League or the National Commission decides the matter. Last night O'Day made an official report of the dispute to President Pulliam. Manager Chance declared that the game was a tie, and the management of the Giants has recorded the game as a 2-to-1 victory.

The result of this game may prove to be the deciding factor in the championship race, and President Pulliam may ask the league to act upon the question or place it in the hands of the National Commission—

the supreme court of baseball.

In any event there will be no double-header this afternoon, and it may be several days before the problem will be decided. The official reporter of the league in New York credits the Giants with a victory, but, of course, this is subject to any action President Pulliam or the league may take in the matter.

President Murphy of the Chicago club last night entered formal claim to yesterday's game in behalf of Chicago. Murphy bases his claim on the ground that Merkle had failed to continue to second when his team-mate scored the winning run from third. Murphy entered his claim in a letter to President Pulliam, wherein Murphy cites in support of his contention the decision rendered in the game at Pittsburgh, Sept. 4, between Pittsburgh and Chicago, in which precisely the same contingency, he asserts, arose. The Chicago club protested the game, but the protest was not allowed, because the single umpire who officiated declared that he had not seen the play. In yesterday's game the omission of Merkle to continue to second, Murphy declares, was noted by Umpire O'Day.

STORY OF THE GAME
by W.W. AULICK

Well, anyway, it was a classy baseball game from the time in the first inning when Roger Bresnahan makes an entrance, accompanied by a dresser, who does him and undoes him in his natty mattress and knee pads, till the end of the ninth, when Bridwell singles safely to center, bringing in what looks like a winning run.

And, from a spectacular point of view, that mix-up at the finish was just the appropriate sensation to a bang-up, all-a-quiver game. They all know they have seen a mighty snappy game of ball; that New York has brought over one more run than the enemy, whether the run counts or not; that McGinnity is holding on to the ball after the ninth-inning run, has done so with the idea that it belongs to the home team, and that good Master O'Day has said, as he exits: 'I didn't see the play on second—the run doesn't count.'

Up to the climactic ninth it was the toss of a coin who would win. For here is our best-beloved Mathewson pitching as only champions pitch, striking out the power and the glory of the Cubs, numbering among his slain, Schulte in the first, Pfeister in the third, Steinfeldt in the fourth. Pfeister in the fifth, Haydon and Schulte in the sixth, Haydon in the eighth and Evers and Schulte in the ninth—these last in one-two order. Proper pitching, and for this and other things we embrace him.

But then, Pfeister is pitching good ball, too. Not so good as the Matty article, for this isn't to be expected, or desired, even. Pfeister doesn't strike anybody out, and Pfeister gives an occasional base on balls, and once he hits a batter, but aside from these irregularities Pfeister must be accounted in the king row of Wednesday matinee pitchers. The gentleman who feels the weight of the delivery, and thereafter takes his base, is the plodsome McCormick. It is in the second inning, and Pfeister whirls up a curve that doesn't break right. In fact, it breaks directly in McCormick's tummy, and Pfeister is forced to figure that the joke's on him. After the heroic Dr Creamer has emptied half a hydrant on the prostrate McCormick the latter walks wanly to first, but he has to wait to walk home till the ninth inning.

Meantime, the game has progressed swiftly, remarkable for excellent plays on either side, and remarkable also for the in-and-out work of Evers at second for Chicago.

It is in the fifth that the Cubs find the solitary run that represents the day's work. Hofman has been thrown out at first by Bridwell, and then the admirable Tinker takes his bat in his hand and faces Matty with determination writ large on his expressive features. Mr Tinker drives the ball away out to right center for what would be a two-bagger if you or I had made it, gentle reader—and this is no disparagement of the Tinker, for he is well seeming in our sight. As the ball approaches Master Donlin this good man attempts to field it with his foot. It's a home run all right, when you get down to scoring, but if this Donlin boy was our boy we'd have sent him to bed without his supper, and ye mind that, Mike.

We found the stick all right in the sixth, and tied the score. Herzog belts boldly to Steinfeldt, and it's a hit all right, but the throw that Steinfeldt makes to first is particularly distressing, and Herzy goes to second. Bresnahan yields up a sacrifice bunt. Donlin hits over second base, Herzog scores, and 18,000 people go out of their minds.

It is at this stage of the game that reputable prophets speak confidently of ten innings, mayhap eleven. We fancy ourselves mightily in the ninth, after Devlin has made a clean single to center. To be sure, Seymour has just gone out at first, but we have a chance.

But here is McCormick, with a drive over to Evers, who throws out Devlin at second, and we're not very far advanced—and two are down and out. Merkle, who failed us the day before in an emergency, is at bat, and we pray of him that he mend his ways. If he will only single we will ignore any errors he may make in the rest of his natural life.

On this condition, Merkle singles. McCormick advances to third, and everybody in the inclosure slaps everybody else and nobody minds. Perfect ladies are screaming like a batch of Coney barkers on the Mardi Gras occasion, and the elderly banker behind us is beating our hat to a pulp with his gold-handled cane. And nobody minds.

Aided by these indications of the popular sentiment, Master Bridwell hits safely to center, McCormick trots home, the reporter boys prepare to make an asterisk under the box score of the game with the line—'Two out when winning run was scored'—the merry villagers flock on the field to worship the hollow where the Mathewson feet have pressed, and all of a sudden there is a doings around second base.

McGinnity, walking off the field with the ball, as is the custom of some member of the winning team, is held up by Tinkler and Evers, who insist that the run does not count, as Merkle has not touched second. And then begins the argument which will keep us in talk for the rest of the season, and then some. Certainly the Cubs have furnished us sport.

The Pitcher and
The Plutocrat

P. G. WODEHOUSE

THE MAIN DIFFICULTY in writing a story is to convey to the reader clearly yet tersely the natures and dispositions of one's leading characters. Brevity, brevity—that is the cry. Perhaps, after all, the playbill style is the best. In this drama of love, baseball, frenzied finance, and tainted millions, then, the principals are as follows, in their order of entry:

Isabel Rackstraw (a peach).
Clarence Van Puyster (a Greek god).
Old Man Van Puyster (a proud old aristocrat).
Old Man Rackstraw (a tainted millionaire).

More about Clarence later. For the moment let him go as a Greek God. There were other sides, too, to Old Man Rackstraw's character; but for the moment let him go as a Tainted Millionaire. Not that it is satisfactory. It is too mild. He was *the* Tainted Millionaire. The Tainted Millions of other Tainted Millionaires were as attar of roses compared with the Tainted Millions of Tainted Millionaire Rackstraw. He preferred his millions tainted. His attitude toward an untainted million was that of the sportsman toward the sitting bird. These things are purely a matter of taste. Some people like Limburger cheese.

It was at a charity bazaar that Isabel and Clarence first met. Isabel was presiding over the Billiken, Teddy Bear, and Fancy Goods stall. There she stood, that slim, radiant girl, buncoing the Younger Set out of its father's hard-earned with a smile that alone was nearly worth the money, when she observed, approaching, the handsomest man she had ever seen. It was—this is not one of those mystery stories—it was Clarence Van Puyster. Over the heads of the bevy of gilded youths who clustered round the stall their eyes met. A thrill ran through Isabel. She dropped her eyes. The next moment Clarence had bucked center;

the Younger Set had shredded away like a mist; and he was leaning toward her, opening negotiations for the purchase of a yellow Teddy Bear at sixteen times its face value.

He returned at intervals during the afternoon. Over the second Teddy Bear they became friendly; over the third, intimate. He proposed as she was wrapping up the fourth Golliwog, and she gave him her heart and the parcel simultaneously. At six o'clock, carrying four Teddy Bears, seven photograph frames, five Golliwogs, and a Billiken, Clarence went home to tell the news to his father.

Clarence, when not at college, lived with his only surviving parent in an old red-brick house at the north end of Washington Square. The original Van Puyster had come over in Governor Stuyvesant's time in one of the then fashionable ninety-four-day boats. Those were the stirring days when they were giving away chunks of Manhattan Island in exchange for trading-stamps; for the bright brain which conceived the idea that the city might possibly at some remote date extend above Liberty Street had not come into existence. The original Van Puyster had acquired a square mile or so in the heart of things for ten dollars cash and a quarter interest in a peddler's outfit. The *Columbus Echo and Vespucci Intelligencer* gave him a column and a half under the heading: 'Reckless Speculator. Prominent Citizens Gamble in Land.' On the proceeds of that deal his descendants had led quiet, peaceful lives ever since. If any of them ever did a day's work, the family records are silent on the point. Blood was their long suit, not Energy. They were plain, homely folk, with a refined distaste for wealth and vulgar bustle. They lived simply, without envy of their richer fellow citizens, on their three hundred thousand dollars a year. They asked no more. It enabled them to entertain on a modest scale; the boys could go to college, the girls buy an occasional new frock. They were satisfied.

Having dressed for dinner, Clarence proceeded to the library, where he found his father slowly pacing the room. Silver-haired old Vansuyther Van Puyster seemed wrapped in thought. And this was unusual, for he was not given to thinking. To be absolutely frank, the old man had just about enough brain to make a jay-bird fly crooked, and no more.

'Ah, my boy,' he said, looking up as Clarence entered. 'Let us go in to dinner. I have been awaiting you for some little time now. I was about to inquire as to your whereabouts. Let us be going.'

Mr Van Puyster always spoke like that. This was due to Blood.

Until the servants had left them to their coffee and cigarettes, the conversation was desultory and commonplace. But when the door had closed, Mr Van Puyster leaned forward.

'My boy,' he said quietly, 'we are ruined.'

Clarence looked at him inquiringly.

'Ruined much?' he asked.

'Paupers,' said his father. 'I doubt if when all is over, I shall have much more than a bare fifty or sixty thousand dollars a year.'

A lesser man would have betrayed agitation, but Clarence was a Van Puyster. He lit a cigarette.

Mr Van Puyster toyed with his coffee spoon. 'I was induced to speculate—rashly, I fear—on the advice of a man I chanced to meet at a public dinner, in the shares of a certain mine. I did not thoroughly understand that matter, but my acquaintance appeared to be well versed in such operations, so I allowed him to—and, well, in fact, to cut a long story short, I am ruined.'

'Daniel Rackstraw!'

Not even Clarence's training and traditions could prevent a slight start as he heard the name.

'Daniel Rackstraw,' repeated his father. 'A man, I fear, not entirely honest. In fact, it seems that he has made a very large fortune by similar transactions. Friends of mine, acquainted with these matters, tell me his behavior toward me amounted practically to theft. However, for myself I care little. We can rough it, we of the old Van Puyster stock. If there is but fifty thousand a year left, well—I must make it serve. It is for your sake that I am troubled, my poor boy. I shall be compelled to stop your allowance. I fear you will be obliged to adopt some profession.' He hesitated for a moment. 'In fact, work,' he added.

Clarence drew at his cigarette.

'Work?' he echoed thoughtfully. 'Well, of course, mind you, fellows do work. I met a man at the club only yesterday who knew a fellow who had met a man whose cousin worked.'

He reflected for a while.

'I shall pitch,' he said suddenly.

'Pitch, my boy?'

'Sign on as a professional ballplayer.'

His father's fine old eyebrows rose a little.

'But, my boy, er—The—ah—family name. Our—shall I say noblesse oblige? Can a Van Puyster pitch and not be defiled?'

'I shall take a new name,' said Clarence. 'I will call myself Brown.'

He lit another cigarette. 'I can get signed on in a minute. McGraw will jump at me.'

This was no idle boast. Clarence had had a good college education, and was now an exceedingly fine pitcher. It was a pleasing sight to see him, poised on one foot in the attitude of a Salome dancer, with one eye on the batter, the other gazing coldly at the man who was trying to steal third, uncurl abruptly like the mainspring of a watch and sneak over a swift one. Under Clarence's guidance a ball could do practically everything except talk. It could fly like a shot from a gun, hesitate, take the first turning to the left, go up two blocks, take the second to the right, bound in mid-air like a jack rabbit, and end by dropping as the gentle dew from heaven upon the plate beneath. Briefly, there was class to Clarence. He was the goods.

Scarcely had he uttered these momentous words when the butler entered with the announcement that he was wanted by a lady at the telephone.

It was Isabel.

Isabel was disturbed.

'Oh, Clarence,' she cried, 'my precious angel wonder-child, I don't know how to begin.'

'Clarence, a terrible thing has happened. I told Papa of our engagement, and he wouldn't hear of it. He was furious. He c-called you a b-b-b—'

'A what?'

'A p-p-p—'

'That's a new one on me,' said Clarence, wondering.

'A b-beggarly p-pauper. I knew you weren't well off, but I thought you had two or three millions. I told him so. But he said no, your father had lost all his money.'

'It is too true, dearest,' said Clarence. 'I am a pauper. But I'm going to work. Something tells me I shall be rather good at work. I am going to work with all the accumulated energy of generations of ancestors who have never done a hand's turn. And some day when I—'

'Goodbye,' said Isabel hastily. 'I hear Papa coming.'

The season during which Clarence Van Puyster pitched for the Giants is destined to live long in the memory of followers of baseball. Probably never in the history of the game has there been such persistent and widespread mortality among the more distant relatives of office boys and junior clerks. Statisticians have estimated that if all the grandmothers alone who perished between the months of April and October that year could have been placed end to end they would have reached considerably further than Minneapolis. And it was Clarence who was responsible for this holocaust. Previous to the opening of the season skeptics had shaken their heads over the Giants' chances for the pennant. It had been assumed that as little new blood would be forthcoming as in other years, and that the fate of Our City would rest, as usual, on the shoulders of the white-haired veterans who were boys with Lafayette.

And then, like a meteor, Clarence Van Puyster had flashed upon the world of fans, bugs, chewing gum, and nuts (pea and human). In the opening game he had done horrid things to nine men from Boston; and from then onward, except for an occasional check, the Giants had never looked back.

Among the spectators who thronged the bleachers to watch Clarence perform there appeared week after week a little, gray, dried-up man, insignificant except for a certain happy choice of language in moments of emotion and an enthusiasm far surpassing that of the ordinary spectator. To the trained eye there is a subtle but well marked difference between the fan, the bug, and—the last phase—the nut of the baseball world. This man was an undoubted nut. It was writ clear across his brow.

Fate had made Daniel Rackstraw—for it was he—a Tainted Millionaire, but at heart he was a baseball spectator. He never missed a game. His library of baseball literature was the finest in the country. His baseball museum had but one equal, that of Mr Jacob Dodson of Detroit. Between them the two had cornered, at enormous expense, the curio market of the game. It was Rackstraw who had secured the glove worn by Neal Ball, the Cleveland shortstop, when he made the only unassisted triple play in the history of the game; but it was Dodson who possessed the bat which Hans Wagner used as a boy. The two men were friends, as far as rival connoisseurs can be friends; and Mr Dodson, when at leisure, would frequently pay a visit to Mr Rackstraw's country home, where he would spend hours gazing wistfully at the Neal Ball glove buoyed up only by the thought of the Wagner bat at home.

Isabel saw little of Clarence during the summer months, except from a distance. She contented herself with clipping photographs of him from the evening papers. Each was a little more unlike him than the last, and this lent variety to the collection. Her father marked her new-born enthusiasm for the national game with approval. It had been secretly a great grief to the old buccaneer that his only child did not know the difference between a bunt and a swat, and, more, did not seem to care to know. He felt himself drawn closer to her. An understanding, as pleasant as it was new and strange, began to spring up between parent and child.

As for Clarence, how easy it would be to cut loose to practically an unlimited extent on the subject of his emotions at this time. One can figure him, after the game is over and the gay throng has dispersed, creeping moodily—but what's the use? Brevity. That is the cry. Brevity. Let us on.

The months sped by. August came and went, and September; and soon it was plain to even the casual follower of the game that, unless something untoward should happen, the Giants must secure the National League pennant. Those were delirious days for Daniel Rackstraw. Long before the beginning of October his voice had dwindled to a husky whisper. Deep lines appeared on his forehead; for it is an awful thing for a baseball nut to be compelled to root, in the very crisis of the season, purely by means of facial expression. In this time of affliction he found Isabel an ever-increasing comfort to him. Side by side they would sit at the Polo Grounds, and the old man's face would lose its drawn look, and light up, as her clear young soprano pealed out above the din, urging this player to slide for second, that to knock the stitching off the ball; or describing the umpire in no uncertain voice as a reincarnation of the late Mr Jesse James.

Meanwhile, in the American League, Detroit had been heading the list with equal pertinacity; and in far-off Michigan Mr Jacob Dodson's enthusiasm had been every whit as great as Mr Rackstraw's in New York. It was universally admitted that when the championship series came to be played, there would certainly be something doing.

But, alas! How truly does Epictetus observe: 'We know not what awaiteth us around the corner, and the hand that counteth its chickens ere they be hatched ofttimes graspeth but a lemon.' The prophets who anticipated a struggle closer than any one record were destined to be proved false.

It was not that their judgement of form was at fault. By every law of averages the Giants and the Tigers should have been the two most evenly matched nines in the history of the game. In fielding there was nothing to choose between them. At hitting the Tigers held a slight superiority; but this was balanced by the inspired pitching of Clarence

Van Puyster. Even the keenest supporters of either side were not confident. They argued at length, figuring out the odds with the aid of stubs of pencils and the backs of envelopes, but they were not confident. Out of all those frenzied millions two men alone had no doubts. Mr Daniel Rackstraw said that he did not desire to be unfair to Detroit. He wished it to be clearly understood that in their own class the Tigers might quite possibly show to considerable advantage. In some rural league down South, for instance, he did not deny that they might sweep all before them. But when it came to competing with the Giants—here words failed Mr Rackstraw, and he had to rush to Wall Street and collect several tainted millions before he could recover his composure.

Mr Jacob Dodson, interviewed by the Detroit *Weekly Rooter,* stated that his decision, arrived at after a close and careful study of the work of both teams, was that the Giants had rather less chance in the forthcoming tourney than a lone gumdrop at an Eskimo tea party. It was his carefully considered opinion that in a contest with the Avenue B Juniors the Giants might, with an effort, scrape home. But when it was a question of meeting a live team like Detroit—here Mr Dodson, shrugging his shoulders despairingly, sank back in his chair, and watchful secretaries brought him round with oxygen.

Throughout the whole country nothing but the approaching series was discussed. Wherever civilization reigned, and in Jersey City, one question alone was on every lip: Who would win? Octogenarians mumbled it. Infants lisped it. Tired businessmen, trampled underfoot in the rush for the West Farms express, asked it of the ambulance attendants who carried them to hospital.

And then, one bright, clear morning, when all Nature seemed to smile, Clarence Van Puyster developed mumps.

New York was in a ferment. I could have wished to go into details, to describe in crisp, burning sentences the panic that swept like a tornado through a million homes. A little encouragement, the slightest softening of the editorial austerity, and the thing would have been done. But no. Brevity. That was the cry. Brevity. Let us on.

The Tigers met the Giants at the Polo Grounds, and for five days the sweat of agony trickled unceasingly down the corrugated foreheads of the patriots who sat on the bleachers. The men from Detroit, freed from the fear of Clarence, smiled grim smiles and proceeded to knock holes through the fence. It was in vain that the home fielders skimmed like swallows around the diamond. They could not keep the score down.

From start to finish the Giants were a beaten side.

Broadway during that black week was a desert. Gloom gripped Lobster Square. In distant Harlem red-eyed wives faced silently scowling husbands at the evening meal, and the children were sent early to bed. Newsboys called the extras in a whisper.

Few took the tragedy more nearly to heart than Daniel Rackstraw. Each afternoon found him more deeply plunged in sorrow. On the last day, leaving the ground with the air of a father mourning over some prodigal son, he encountered Mr Jacob Dodson of Detroit.

Now Mr Dodson was perhaps the slightest bit shy on the finer feelings. He should have respected the grief of a fallen foe. He should have abstained from exulting. But he was in too exhilarated a condition to be magnanimous. Sighting Mr Rackstraw, he addressed himself joyously to the task of rubbing the thing in. Mr Rackstraw listened in silent anguish.

'If we had had Brown—' he said at length.

'That's what they all say,' whooped Mr Dodson. 'Brown! Who's Brown?'

'If we had had Brown, we should have—' He paused. An idea had flashed upon his overwrought mind. 'Dodson,' he said, 'listen here. Wait till Brown is well again, and let us play this thing off again for anything you like a side in my private park.'

Mr Dodson reflected.

'You're on,' he said. 'What side bet? A million? Two million? Three?'

Mr Rackstraw shook his head scornfully.

'A million? Who wants a million? I'll put my Neal Ball glove against your Hans Wagner bat. The best of three games. Does that go?'

'I should say it did,' said Mr Dodson joyfully. 'I've been wanting that glove for years. It's like finding it in one's Christmas stocking.'

'Very well,' said Mr Rackstraw. 'Then let's get it fixed up.'

Honestly, it is but a dog's life, that of the short-story writer. I particularly wished at this point to introduce a description of Mr Rackstraw's country home and estate, featuring the private ball park with its fringe of noble trees. It would have served a double purpose, not only charming the lover of nature, but acting as a fine stimulus to the youth of the country, showing them the sort of home they would be able to buy some day if they worked hard and saved their money. But no. You shall have three guesses as to what was the cry. You give it up? It was 'Brevity! Brevity!' Let us on.

The two teams arrived at the Rackstraw house in time for lunch. Clarence, his features once more reduced to their customary finely chiseled proportions, alighted from the automobile with a swelling heart. He could see nothing of Isabel, but that did not disturb him. Letters had passed between the two. Clarence had warned her not to embrace him in public, as McGraw would not like it; and Isabel accordingly had arranged a tryst among the noble trees which fringed the ball park.

I will pass lightly over the meeting of the two lovers. I will not describe the dewy softness of their eyes, the catching of their breath, their murmured endearments. I could, mind you. It is at just such descriptions that I am particularly happy. But I have grown discouraged. My spirit is broken. It is enough to say that Clarence had reached a level of emotional eloquence rarely met with among pitchers of the National League, when Isabel broke from him with a startled exclamation, and vanished behind a tree; and, looking over his shoulder. Clarence observed Mr Daniel Rackstraw moving toward him.

It was evident from the millionaire's demeanor that he had seen nothing. The look on his face was anxious, but not wrathful. He sighted Clarence and hurried up to him.

'Say, Brown,' he said, 'I've been looking for you. I want a word with you.'

'A thousand, if you wish it.' said Clarence courteously.

'Now, see here,' said Mr Rackstraw. 'I want to explain to you just what this ball game means to me. Don't run away with the idea I've had you fellows down to play an exhibition game just to keep me merry and bright. If the Giants win today, it means that I shall be able to hold up my head again and look my fellow man in the face, instead of crawling around on my stomach and feeling like thirty cents. Do you get that?'

'I am hep,' replied Clarence with simple dignity.

'And not only that,' went on the millionaire. 'There's more to it. I have put up my Neal Ball glove against Mr Dodson's Wagner bat as a side bet. You understand what that means? It means that either you win or my life is soured for keeps. See?'

'I have got you,' said Clarence.

'Good. Then what I wanted to say was this. Today is your day for pitching as you've never pitched before. Everything depends on whether you make good or not. With you pitching like mother used to make it, the Giants are some nine. Otherwise they are Nature's citrons. It's one thing or the other. It's all up to you. Win, and there's twenty thousand dollars waiting for you above what you share with the others.'

Clarence waved his hand deprecatingly.

'Mr Rackstraw,' he said, 'keep your dough, I care nothing for money.'

'You don't?' cried the millionaire. 'Then you ought to exhibit yourself in a dime museum.'

'All I ask of you,' proceeded Clarence, 'is your consent to my engagement with your daughter.'

Mr Rackstraw looked sharply at him.

'Repeat that,' he said. 'I don't think I quite got it.'

'All I ask is your consent to my engagement to your daughter.'

'Young man,' said Mr Rackstraw, not without a touch of admiration, 'you have gall.'

'My friends have sometimes said so,' said Clarence.

'And I admire gall. But there is a limit. That limit you have passed so far that you'd need to look for it with a telescope.'

'You refuse your consent.'

'I never said you weren't a clever guesser.'

'Why?'

Mr Rackstraw laughed. One of those nasty, sharp, metallic laughs that hit you like a bullet.

'How would you support my daughter?'

'I was thinking that you would help to some extent.'

'You were, were you?'

'I was.'

'Oh?'

Mr Rackstraw emitted another of those laughs.

'Well,' he said, 'it's off. You can take that as coming from an authoritative source. No wedding bells for you.'

Clarence drew himself up, fire flashing from his eyes and a bitter smile curving his expressive lips.

'And no Wagner bat for you!' he cried.

Mr Rackstraw started as if some strong hand had plunged an auger into him.

'What!' he shouted.

Clarence shrugged his superbly modeled shoulders in silence.

'Say,' said Mr Rackstraw, 'you wouldn't let a little private difference like that influence you any in a really important thing like this ball game, would you?'

'I would.'

'You would hold up the father of the girl you love?'

'Every time.'

'Her white haired old father?'

'The color of his hair would not affect me.'

'Nothing would move you?'

'Nothing.'

'Then, by George, you're just the son-in-law I want. You shall marry Isabel; and I'll take you into partnership this very day. I've been looking for a good, husky bandit like you for years. You make Dick Turpin look like a preliminary three-round bout. My boy, we'll be the greatest team, you and I, that ever hit Wall Street.'

'Papa!' cried Isabel, bounding happily from behind her tree.

Mr Rackstraw joined their hands, deeply moved, and spoke in low, vibrant tones:

'Play ball!'

Little remains to be said, but I am going to say it, if it snows. I am at my best in these tender scenes of idyllic domesticity.

Four years have passed. Once more we are in the Rackstraw home. A lady is coming down the stairs, leading by the hand her little son. It is Isabel. The years have dealt lightly with her. She is still the same stately, beautiful creature whom I would have described in detail long ago if I had been given half a chance. At the foot of the stairs the child stops and points at a small, wooden object in a glass case.

'Wah?' he says.

'That?' says Isabel. 'That is the bat Mr Wagner used to use when he was a little boy.'

She looks at a door on the left of the hall, and puts a finger to her lip.

'Hush!' she says. 'We must be quiet. Daddy and Grandpa are busy in there cornering wheat.'

And softly mother and child go out into the sunlit garden.

The New Baseball

GARRISON KEILLOR

IF IT WERE merely a sport, baseball would enjoy the permanence and stability of ballet or checkers, but businessmen know that baseball must keep up with the times. Such innovations as artificial turf and the Astrodome were thought up by treasurers and have almost brought the game up to date. (To be precise, they· have brought it up to June 11, 1971, according to the latest figures.) The next decade will see even more radical changes, and one can only wonder whether baseball's farseeing executives are aware of what lies just ahead.

Baseball flourished at a time when most people accepted the doctrine of predestination. Later, during the Depression and in the Second World War, baseball offered certitude to a confused nation. Since then, however, the writings of Sartre and Camus have made untenable our comfortable assumptions about 'safe' and 'out'; the excitement of observing players at a distance has diminished with the development of widescreen movies; and a new time-space consciousness, ushered in by the Apollo moon shots, has rendered 'power hitters' pathetically obsolete. Alas, a home run no longer rates as a 'blast' even if it is 'hit a mile.'

In a simpler era, Ty Cobb came up to the plate in a mood of fierce determination, but today's players, aware of the diminishing importance of hitting the ball, are more content to *experience* at-batness. In the dugout, the athletes no longer discuss batting averages, girls, and the stock market but the swiftly changing dynamics and dialectics of the one-time 'national pastime.' In contemporary baseball, they agree, cause-and-effect sequentiality is giving way to simple concurrence of phenomena as the crisis in baseball's system of linear reaction brings on a new 'system' of concentric and reflexive response, and the old stately inwardness of the game is losing out to, or giving in to, outwardness, or rather *away* ness; the static balance of baseball—pitcher vs batter, base runner vs infielder—will shortly slither into flow, and the crowd, not content to cheer the artifice of great hitters and pitchers, will rise in tribute to the natural organic unity of a scoreless game.

In a few years, the ultra-lively ball will be introduced, ending the game as we know it. Baseball fans will quickly tire of seeing thirty home runs in one game and will demand a complete restructuring. The first barrier to fall will be the outfield fence. The outfield will be extended up to ten or twelve miles, depending on local zoning. Baseball, which has always concentrated on the pitcher, will look outward to the horizon, and a period of exploration will occur as players wander over the hill to search for the ball. The 'home-base' concept will be scrapped next, of course, along with the ball-and-strike construct, and the infield will become a mere appendix—staging area or ondeck circle, as it were. Infielders will wait there for their turn, which, as often as not, will never come. Outfielders, on the other hand, will be free as antelope, roaming the farther regions for fly balls or, as the case may be, not for fly balls, the ball itself having changed. Its flight will be erratic and mysterious; a player will no longer be said to be 'on the ball' or even 'under the ball' but rather 'near the ball'—in sight of it, perhaps circling it or viewing it curiously. The time scheme of baseball—three outs to a side, two sides to an inning, nine innings to a game—will be simplified by eliminating outs, sides, and innings, thus leaving the idea of the game itself whole and round, and people will play until the sun goes down or the cows come home.

In time, of course, the entire stadium setup will become useless as spectators are drawn into the playing area, and free participation will evolve as tasks become less specialized. This will lead to the disappearance of ballplayers as a performing elite. Players and spectators alike will wonder 'What is happening?' and 'Will it happen?' and 'What do I do in either eventuality?' The umpires, who will have disappeared along with home plate, will return to baseball as friendly advisers, suggesting alternative courses or action, turns of phrase, avenues of thought. People will enjoy great freedom of opportunity, and some real-estate speculation will take place in deep center, most likely multiple-family housing and light commercial development.

The Baseball Hall of Fame

BILL BRYSON

I SPENT THE night in Cobleskill, New York, on the northern fringes of
the Catskills, and in the morning drove to Cooperstown, a small resort
on Lake Otsego. Cooperstown was the home of James Fenimore Cooper,
from whose family the town takes its name. It was a handsome town,
as handsome as any I had seen in New England, and more replete with
autumn color, with a main street of square-topped brick buildings,
old banks, a movie theater, family stores. The Cooperstown Diner, where
I went for breakfast, was busy, friendly and cheap—all that a diner should
be. Afterwards I went for a stroll around the residential streets, shuffling
hands-in-pockets through the dry leaves, and down to the lakeside.
Every house in town was old and pretty; many of the larger ones had
been converted into inns and expensive B & Bs. The morning sunlight
filtered through the trees and threw shadows across the lawns and
sidewalks. This was as nice a little town as I had seen on the trip; it
was almost Amalgam.

The only shortcoming with Cooperstown is that it is full of tourists,
drawn to the town by its most famous institution, the Baseball Hall
of Fame, which stands by a shady park at the far end of Main Street.
I went there now, paid $8.50 admission and walked into its cathedral-like
calm. For those of us who are baseball fans and agnostics, the Hall
of Fame is as close to a religious experience as we may ever get. I walked
serenely through its quiet and softly-lit halls, looking at the sacred vest-
ments and venerated relics from America's national pastime. Here,
beautifully preserved in a glass case, was 'the shirt worn by Warren
Spahn when registering win No. 305, which tied him with Eddie Plank
for most by a left-hander.' Across the aisle was 'the glove used by Sal

Maglie on September 25, 1958, no-hitter vs Phillies.' At each case people gazed reverently or spoke in whispers.

One room contained a gallery of paintings commemorating great moments in baseball history, including one depicting the first professional night game under artificial lighting played in Des Moines, Iowa, on May 2, 1930. This was exciting news to me. I had no idea that Des Moines had played a pivotal role in the history of both baseball and luminescence. I looked closely to see if the artist had depicted my father in the press-box, but then I realised that my father was only fifteen years old in 1930 and still in Winfield. This seemed kind of a pity.

In an upstairs room I suppressed a whoop of joy at the discovery of whole cases full of baseball cards that my brother and I had so scrupulously collected and catalogued, and which my parents, in an early flirtation with senility, had taken to the dump during an attic springcleaning in 1981. We had the complete set for 1959 in mint condition; it is now worth something like $1,500. We had Mickey Mantle and Yogi Berra as rookies. Ted Williams from the last year he hit .400, the complete New York Yankees teams for every year between 1956 and 1962. The whole collection must have been worth something like $8,000—enough, at any rate, to have sent Mom and Dad for a short course of treatment at a dementia clinic. But never mind! We all make mistakes. It's only because everyone throws these things out that they grow so valuable for the lucky few whose parents don't spend their retirements getting rid of all the stuff they spent their working lives accumulating. Anyway it was a pleasure to see all the old cards again. It was like visiting a friend in hospital.

The Hall of Fame is surprisingly large, much larger than it looks from the road, and extremely well presented. I wandered through it in a state of complete contentment, reading every label, lingering at every display, reliving my youth, cocooned in a happy nostalgia, and when I stepped back out on to Main Street and glanced at my watch I was astonished to discover that three hours had elapsed.

Next door to the Hall of Fame was a shop selling the most wonderful baseball souvenirs. In my day all we could get were pennants and baseball cards and crummy little pens in the shape of baseball bats that stopped working about the second time you tried to sign your name with them. But now little boys could get everything with their team's logo on it—lamps, towels, clocks, throw rugs, mugs, bedspreads and even Christmas tree ornaments, plus of course pennants, baseball cards

and pens that stop working about the second time you use them. I
don't think I have ever felt such a pang of longing to be a child again.
Apart from anything else, it would mean I'd get my baseball cards back
and I could put them somewhere safe where my parents couldn't get
at them; then when I got to my age I could buy a Porsche.

I was so taken with all the souvenirs that I began to fill my arms
with stuff, but then I noticed that the store was full of Do Not Touch
signs and on the counter by the cash register had been taped a notice
that said 'Do Not Lean on Glass—If You Break, Cost to You Is $50'
What a jerky thing to say on a sign. How could you expect kids to
come into a place full of wonderful things like this and not touch them?
This so elevated my hackles that I deposited my intended purchases
on the counter and told the girl I didn't want them after all. This was
perhaps just as well because I'm not altogether sure that my wife would
have wanted St Louis Cardinals pillowcases.

My ticket to the Hall of Fame included admission to a place on the
edge of town called the Farmers Museum, where a couple of dozen
old buildings—a schoolhouse, a tavern, a church and the like—have
been preserved on a big site. It was about as exciting as it sounds, but
having bought the ticket I felt obliged to go and have a look at it. If
nothing else, the walk through the afternoon sunshine was pleasant.
But I was relieved to get back in the car and hit the road again. It was
after four by the time I left town. I drove on across New York State
for several hours, through the Susquehanna Valley, which was very
fetching, especially at this time of day and year in the soft light of an
autumn afternoon: watermelon-shaped hills, golden trees, slumbering
towns. To make up for my long day in Cooperstown, I drove later than
usual, and it was after nine by the time I stopped at a motel on the
outskirts of Elmira.

Dizzy Dean's Day

RED SMITH

THROUGH THE MURK of cigarette smoke and liniment fumes in the Cardinals clubhouse a radio announcer babbled into a microphone.

'And now,' he read with fine spontaneity from a typewritten sheet prepared hours in advance, 'and now let's have a word from the Man of the Hour, Manager Frank Frisch.'

The Man of the Hour shuffled forward. He had started changing clothes. His shirttail hung limply over bare thighs. The Man of the Hour's pants had slipped down and they dragged about his ankles. You could have planted petunias in the loam on his face. The Man of the Hour looked as though he had spent his hour in somebody's coal mine.

Beside him, already scrubbed and combed and natty in civilian clothes, awaiting his turn to confide to a nationwide audience that 'the Cardinals are the greatest team I ever played with and I sure am glad we won the champeenship today and I sure hope we can win the World Series from Detroit,' stood Dizzy Dean, destiny's child.

There was a conscious air of grandeur about the man. He seemed perfectly aware of and not at all surprised at the fact that just outside the clubhouse five thousand persons were pressing against police lines, waiting to catch a glimpse of him, perhaps even to touch the hem of his garment.

He couldn't have known that in that crowd one woman was weeping into the silver fox fur collar of her black cloth coat, sobbing, 'I'm so happy! I can't stand it!' She was Mrs Dizzy Dean.

All afternoon Dizzy Dean had seemed surrounded by an aura of greatness. A crowd of 37,402 persons jammed Sportsman's Park to see the game that would decide the National League pennant race. To this reporter it did not appear that they had come to see the Cardinals win the championship. Rather, they were there to see Dizzy come to glory.

It was Dean's ball game. He, more than anyone else, had kept the Cardinals in the pennant race throughout the summer. He had won two games in the last five days to help bring the Red Birds to the top of the league. Here, with the championship apparently hinging upon the outcome of this game, was his chance to add the brightest jewel to his crown, and at the same time to achieve the personal triumph of becoming the first National League pitcher since 1917 to win 30 games in a season.

And it was Dizzy's crowd. Although the game was a box office 'natural', it is doubtful that, had it not been announced that Dean would pitch, fans would have been thronged before the Dodier street gate when the doors were opened at 9.30 a.m. They were, and from then until game time they came in increasing numbers. Eventually, some had to be turned away from lack of space.

Packed in the aisles, standing on the ramps and clinging to the grandstand girders, the fans followed Dizzy with their eyes, cheered his every move.

They whooped when he rubbed resin on his hands. They yowled when he fired a strike past a batter. They stood and yelled when he lounged to the plate, trailing his bat in the dust. And when, in the seventh inning, with the game already won by eight runs, he hit a meaningless single, the roar that thundered from the stands was as though he had accomplished the twelve labors of Hercules.

The fact was, the fans were hungry for drama, and that was the one ingredient lacking. With such a stage setting as that crowd provided, with such a buildup as the National League race, with such a hero as Dizzy, Mr Cecil B. DeMille would have ordered things better.

He would have had the New York Giants beat Brooklyn and thus make a victory essential to the Cards' pennant prospects. He would have had Cincinnati leading St Louis until the eighth inning, when a rally would have put the Red Birds one run ahead. Then Mr DeMille would have sent ex-St Louis Hero Jim Bottomley, now one of the enemy, to bat against Hero Dean, with Cincinnati runners on every base. And he would have had Dizzy pour across three blinding strikes to win the ball game.

In the real game there was no suspense. Cincinnati tried, but the Cards couldn't be stopped. They just up and won the game, 9–0, and the pennant, and to blazes with drama.

Still, drama is where you find it. The crowd seemed to find it in the gawky frame of Mr Dean and in the figures on the scoreboard which showed Brooklyn slowly overhauling the Giants in their game in the east.

Dean was warming up in front of the Cardinal dugout when the first-inning score of the New York–Brooklyn game was posted, showing four runs for the Giants and none for the Dodgers. As an apprehensive 'Oooooh!' from the fans greeted the score, Dizzy glanced toward the scoreboard. Watching through field glasses, this reporter saw his eyes narrow slightly. That was all. A moment later he strolled to the plate, entirely at ease, to accept a diamond ring donated by his admirers.

Then the game started, and for a few minutes the customers' attention was diverted from their hero by the exploits of some of his mates.

In the first inning Ernie Orsatti, chasing a low drive to right center by Mark Koenig, raced far to his left, dived forward, somersaulted, and came up with the ball. To everyone except the fans in the right field seats it seemed a miraculous catch. The spectators closest to the play were sure they saw Orsatti drop the ball and recover it while his back was toward the plate. But everyone screamed approbation.

Magnificent plays, one after another, whipped the stands into a turmoil of pleasure. In Cincinnati's second inning, after Bottomley had singled, Leo Durocher scooted far to his right to nail a grounder by Pool and, in one astonishingly swift motion, he pivoted and whipped the ball to Frisch for a forceout of Bottomley.

Again in the fourth inning, there was a play that brought the fans whooping to their feet. This time Frisch scooped up a bounder from Pool's bat and beat Koenig to second base, Durocher hurdling Frisch's prostrate body in order to avoid ruining the play. A few minutes earlier Frisch had brought gasps and cheers from the stands by stretching an ordinary single into a two-base hit, reaching second only by the grace of a breakneck headfirst slide.

Play by play, inning by inning, the crowd was growing noisier, more jubilant. Cheer followed exultant cheer on almost every play.

Meanwhile the Cards were piling up a lead. Meanwhile, too, Brooklyn was chiseling runs off New York's lead, and the scoreboard became a magnet for all eyes. When Brooklyn scored two runs in the eighth inning to tie the Giants, Announcer Kelly didn't wait for the scoreboard to flash the news. He shouted it through his megaphone, and as fans in each succeeding section of seats heard his words, waves of applause echoed through the stands.

Shadows were stretching across the field when Cincinnati came to bat in the ninth inning. The National League season was within minutes of its end. The scoreboard long since had registered the final tallies for all other games. Only the tied battle in New York and the contest on this field remained unfinished.

Dean lounged to the pitching mound. The man was completing his third game in six days. He was within three putouts of his second shutout in those six days. He didn't seem tired. He hardly seemed interested. He was magnificently in his element, completely at ease in the knowledge that every eye was on him.

The first two Cincinnati batters made hits. Dizzy was pitching to Adam Comorosky when a wild yell from the stands caused him to glance at the scoreboard. The Dodgers had scored three runs in the tenth. New York's score for the inning had not been posted.

Seen through field glasses, Dean's face was expressionless. He walked Comorosky. The bases were filled with no one out. Was Dizzy tiring, or was he deliberately setting the stage for the perfect melodramatic finish.

The scoreboard boy hung up a zero for the Giants. The pennant belonged to the Cardinals. Most pitchers would have said, 'the hell with it,' and taken the course of least resistance, leaving it to the fielders to make the putouts.

But this was Dean's ball game. Seen through a haze of fluttering paper, cushions and torn scorecards, he seemed to grow taller. He fanned Clyde Manion. A low roar rumbled through the stands. The fans saw what was coming. Dizzy was going to handle the last three batters himself.

Methodically, unhurriedly, he rifled three blinding strikes past Pinch-Hitter Petoskey. Was that a faint grin on Dizzy's face? The roar from the stands had become rolling thunder. The outfielders foresaw what was coming. They started in from their positions as Dizzy began pitching to Sparky Adams.

They were almost on the field when Adams, in hopeless desperation, swung at a pitch too fast for him to judge. His bat just tipped the ball, sending it straight upward in a wobbly, puny foul fly to DeLancey.

Dean didn't laugh. He didn't shout or caper. the man who had been at times a gross clown was in this greatest moment a figure of quiet dignity. Surrounded by his players he walked slowly to the dugout, a mad, exultant thunder drumming in his ears.

You Could Look It Up

JAMES THURBER

IT ALL BEGAN when we dropped down to C'lumbus, Ohio, from Pittsburgh to play a exhibition game on our way out to St Louis. It was gettin' on into September, and though we'd been leadin' the league by six, seven games most of the season, we was now in first place by a margin you could 'a' got it into the eye of a thimble, bein' only a half a game ahead of St Louis. Our slump had given the boys the leapin' jumps, and they was like a bunch a old ladies at a lawn fete with a thunderstorm comin' up, runnin' around snarlin' at each other, eatin' bad and sleepin' worse, and battin' for a team average of maybe, .186. Half the time nobody'd speak to nobody else, without it was to bawl 'em out.

Squawks Magrew was managin' the boys at the time, and he was darn near crazy. They called him 'Squawks' 'cause when things was goin' bad he lost his voice, or perty near lost it, and squealed at you like a little girl you stepped on her doll or somethin'. He yelled at everybody and wouldn't listen to nobody, without maybe it was me. I'd been trainin' the boys for ten year, and he'd take more lip from me than from anybody else. He knowed I was smarter'n him, anyways, like you're goin' to hear.

This was thirty, thirty-one year ago; you could look it up, 'cause it was the same year C'lumbus decided to call itself the Arch City, on account of a lot of iron arches with electric-light bulbs into 'em which stretched across High Street. Thomas Albert Edison sent 'em a telegram, and they was speeches and maybe even President Taft opened the celebration by pushin' a button. It was a great week for the Buckeye capital, which was why they got us out there for this exhibition game.

Well, we just lose a double-header to Pittsburgh, 11 to 5 and 7 to 3, so we snarled all the way to C'lumbus where we put up at the Chittaden Hotel, still snarlin'. Everybody was tetchy, and when Billy Klinger took a sock at Whitey Cott at breakfast, Whitey throwed marmalade all over his face.

'Blind each other, whatta I care?' says Magrew. 'You can't see nothin' anyways.'

C'lumbus won the exhibition game, 3 to 2, whilst Magrew set in the dugout, mutterin' and cursin' like a fourteen-year-old Scotty. He bad-mouthed everybody on the ball club and he bad-mouthed everybody off a the ball club, includin' the Wright brothers, who, he claimed, had yet to build a airship big enough for any of our boys to hit it with a ball bat.

'I wisht I was dead,' he says to me. 'I wisht I was in heaven with the angels.'

I told him to pull hisself together, 'cause he was drivin' the boys crazy, the way he was goin' on, sulkin' and bad-mouthin' and whinin'. I was older'n he was and smarter'n he was, and he knowed it. I was ten times smarter'n he was about this Pearl du Monville, first time I ever laid eyes on the little guy, which was one of the saddest days of my life.

Now, most people name of Pearl is girls, but this Pearl du Monville was a man if you could call a fella a man who was only thirty-four, thirty-five inches high. Pearl du Monville was a midget. He was part French and part Hungarian, and maybe even part Bulgarian or somethin'. I can see him now, a sneer on his little pushed-in pan, swingin' a bamboo cane and smokin' a big cigar. He had a gray suit with a big black check into it, and he had a gray felt hat with one of them rainbow-colored hatbands onto it, like the young fellas wore in them days. He talked like he was talkin' into a tin can, but he didn't have no foreign accent. He mighta been fifteen or he mighta been a hundred, you couldn't tell. Pearl du Monville.

After the game with C'lumbus, Magrew headed straight for the Chittaden bar—the train for St Louis wasn't goin' for three, four hours—and there he set, drinkin' rye and talkin' to this bartender.

'How I pity me, brother,' Magrew was tellin' this bartender. 'How I pity me.' That was alwuz his favorite tune. So he was settin' there, tellin' this bartender how heartbreakin' it was to be manager of a bunch of blindfolded circus clowns, when up pops this Pearl du Monville outa nowheres.

It give Magrew the leapin' jumps. He thought at first maybe the D.T.'s had come back on him; he claimed he'd had 'em once, and little guys had popped up all around him, wearin' red, white and blue hats.

'Go on, now!' Magrew yells. 'Get away from me!'

But the midget clumb up on a chair acrost the table from Magrew and says, 'I seen that game today, Junior, and you ain't got no ball club. What you got there, Junior,' he says, 'is a side show.'

'Whatta ya mean, "Junior"?' says Magrew touchin' the little guy to satisfy hisself he was real.

'Don't pay him no attention, mister,' says the bartender. 'Pearl calls everybody 'Junior,' 'cause it alwuz turns out he's a year older'n anybody else.'

'Yeh?' says Magrew. 'How old is he?'

'How old are you, Junior?' says the midget.

'Who, me? I'm fifty-three,' says Magrew.

'Well, I'm fifty-four,' says the midget.

Magrew grins and asts him what he'll have, and that was the beginnin' of their beautiful friendship, if you don't care what you say.

Pearl du Monville stood up on his chair and waved his cane around and pretended like he was ballyhooin' for a circus. 'Right this way, folks!' he yells. 'Come on in and see the greatest collection of freaks in the world! See the armless pitchers, see the eyeless batters, see the infielders with five thumbs!' and on and on like that, feedin' Magrew gall and handin' him a laugh at the same time, you might say.

You could hear him and Pearl du Monville hootin' and hollerin' and singin' way up to the fourth floor of the Chittaden, where the boys was packin' up. When it come time to go to the station, you can imagine how disgusted we was when we crowded into the doorway of that bar and seen them two singin' and goin' on.

'Well, well, well,' says Magrew, lookin' up and spottin' us. 'Look who's here . . . Clowns, this is Pearl du Monville, a monseer of the old, old school . . . Don't shake hands with 'em, Pearl, 'cause their fingers is made of chalk and would bust right off in your paws,' he says, and he starts guffawin' and Pearl starts titterin' and we stand there givin' 'em the iron eye, it bein' the lowest ebb a ball club manager'd got hisself down to since the national pastime was started.

Then the midget begun givin' us the ballyhoo. 'Come on in!' he says, wavin' his cane. 'See the legless base runners, see the outfielders with the butterfingers, see the southpaw with the arm of a chee-ild!'

Then him and Magrew begun to hoop and holler and nudge each other till you'd 'a' thought this little guy was the funniest guy than even Charlie Chaplin. The fellas filed outa the bar without a word and went on up to the Union Depot, leavin' me to handle Magrew and his new-found crony.

Well, I got 'em outa there finely. I had to take the little guy along, 'cause Magrew had a holt onto him like a vise and I couldn't pry him loose.

He's comin' along as masket,' says Magrew, holdin' the midget in the crouch of his arm like a football. And come along he did, hollerin' and protestin' and beatin' at Magrew with his little fists.

'Cut it out, will ya, Junior?' the little guy kept whinin'. 'Come on, leave a man loose, will ya, Junior?'

But Junior kept a holt onto him and begun yellin', 'See the guys with the glass arm, see the guys with the cast-iron brains, see the infielders with the feet on their wrists!'

So it goes, right through the whole Union Depot, with people starin' and catcallin', and he don't put the midget down till he gets him through the gates.

'How'm I goin' to go along without no toothbrush?' the midget asts. 'What'm I goin' to do without no other suit?' he says.

'Doc here,' says Magrew, meanin' me—'doc here will look after you like you was his own son, won't you, doc?'

I give him the iron eye, and he finely got on the train and prob'ly went to sleep with his clothes on.

This left me alone with the midget. 'Lookit,' I says to him. 'Why don't you go on home now? Come mornin', Magrew'll forget all about you. He'll prob'ly think you was somethin' he seen in a nightmare maybe. And he ain't goin' to laugh so easy in the mornin' neither,' I says. 'So why don't you go on home?'

'Nix,' he says to me. 'Skiddoo,' he says, 'twenty-three for you,' and he tosses his cane up into the vestibule of the coach and clam'ers on up after it like a cat. So that's the way Pearl du Monville come to go to St.Louis with the ball club.

I seen 'em first at breakfast the next day, settin' opposite each other; the midget playin' Turkey in the Straw on a harmonium and Magrew starin' at his eggs and bacon like they was a uncooked bird with its feathers still on.

'Remember where you found this?' I says, jerkin' my thumb at the midget. 'Or maybe you think they come with breakfast on these trains,' I says, bein' a good hand at turnin' a sharp remark in them days.

The midget puts down the harmonium and turns on me. 'Sneeze,' he says, 'your brains is dusty.' Then he snaps a couple of drops of water at me from a tumbler. 'Drown,' he says, tryin' to make his voice deep.

Now, both them cracks is Civil War cracks, but you'd 'a' thought they was brand new and the funniest than any crack Magrew'd ever heard in his whole life. He started hoopin' and hollerin', and the midget started hoopin' and hollerin', so I walked on away and set down with Bugs Courtney and Hank Metters, payin' no attention to this weak-minded Damon and Phidias acrost the aisle.

Well, sir, the first game with St Louis was rained out, and there we was facin' a double-header next day. Like maybe I told you, we lose the last three double-headers we play, makin' maybe twenty-five errors in the six games, which is all right for the intimates of a school for the blind, but is disgraceful for the world's champions. It was too wet to go to the zoo, and Magrew wouldn't let us go to the movies, 'cause they flickered so bad in them days. So we just set around, stewin' and frettin'.

One of the newspaper boys come over to take a pitture of Billy Klinger and Whitey Cott shakin' hands—this reporter'd heard about the fight—and whilst they was standin' there, toe to toe, shakin' hands, Billy give a back lunge and a jerk, and throwed Whitey over his shoulder into a corner of the room, like a sack of salt. Whitey come back at him with a chair, and Bethlehem broke loose in that there room. The camera was tromped to pieces like a berry basket. When we finely got 'em pulled apart, I heard a laugh, and there was Magrew and the midget standin' in the door and givin' us the iron eye.

'Wrasslers,' says Magrew, cold-like, 'that's what I got for a ball club, Mr du Monville, wrasslers—and not very good wrasslers at that, you ast me.'

'A man can't be good at everythin',' says Pearl, 'but he oughta be good at somethin'.'

This set Magrew guffawin' again, and away they go, the midget taggin' along by his side like a hound dog and handin' him a fast line of so-called comic cracks.

When we went out to face that battlin' St Louis club in a double-header the next afternoon, the boys was jumpy as tin toys with keys in their back. We lose the first game, 7 to 2, and are trailin', 4 to o when the second game ain't but ten minutes old. Magrew set there like a stone statue, speakin' to nobody. Then, in their half a the fourth, somebody singled to center and knocked in two more runs for St Louis.

That made Magrew squawk. 'I wisht one thing,' he says. 'I wisht I was manager of a old ladies' sewin' circus 'stead of a ball club.'

'You are, Junior, you are,' says a familyer and disagreeable voice that I am not happy to hear.

It was that Pearl du Monville again, poppin' up outa nowheres, swingin' his bamboo cane and smokin' a cigar, that's three sizes too big for his face. By this time we'd finely got the other side out, and Hank Metters slithered a bat acrost the ground, and the midget had to jump to keep both his ankles from bein' broke.

I thought Magrew'd bust a blood vessel. 'You hurt Pearl and I'll break your neck!' he yelled.

Hank muttered somethin' and went on up to the plate and struck out.

We managed to get a couple runs acrost in our half a the sixth, but they come back with three more in their half a the seventh, and this was too much for Magrew.

'Come on, Pearl,' he says. 'We're gettin' outa here.'

'Where you think you're goin'?' I ast him.

'To the lawyer's again,' he says cryptly.

'I didn't know you'd been to the lawyers once, yet,' I says.

'Which that goes to show how much you don't know,' he says.

With that, they was gone, and I didn't see 'em the rest of the day, nor know what they was up to, which was a God's blessin'. We lose the nightcap, 9 to 3, and that puts us into second place plenty, and as low in our mind as a ball club can get.

The next day was a horrible day, like anybody that lived through it can tell you. Practice was just over and the St Louis club was takin' the field, when I hears this strange sound from the stands. It sounds like the nervous whickerin' a horse gives when he smells somethin' funny on the wind. It was the fans ketchin' sight of Pearl du Monville, like you have prob'ly guessed. The midget had popped up onto the field all dressed up in a minacher club uniform, sox, cap, little letters sewed onto his chest, and all. He was swingin' a kid's bat and the only thing kept him from lookin' like a real ballplayer seen through the wrong end of a microscope was this cigar he was smokin'.

Bugs Courtney reached over and jerked it outa his mouth and throwed it away. 'You're wearin' that suit on the playin' field,' he says to him, severe as a judge. 'You go insultin' it and I'll take you out to the zoo and feed you to the bears.'

Pearl just blowed some smoke at him which he still has in his mouth.

Whilst Whitey was foulin' off four or five prior to strikin' out, I went on over to Magrew. 'If I was as comic as you,' I says, 'I'd laugh myself to death,' I says. 'Is that any way to treat the uniform, makin' a mockery out of it?'

'It might surprise you to know I ain't makin' no mockery outa the uniform,' says Magrew, 'Pearl du Monville here has been made a bone-of-fida member of this so-called ball club. I fixed it up with the front office by long-distance phone.'

'Yeh?' I says. 'I can just hear Mr Dillworth or Bart Jenkins agreein' to hire a midget for the ball club. I can just hear 'em.' Mr Dillworth was the owner of the club and Bart Jenkins was the secretary, and they never stood for no monkey business. 'May I be so bold as to inquire,' I says, 'just what you told 'em?'

'I told 'em,' he says, 'I wanted to sign up a guy they ain't no pitcher in the league can strike him out.'

'Uh-huh,' I says, 'and did you tell 'em what size of a man he is?'

'Never mind about that,' he says. 'I got papers on me, made out legal and proper, constitutin' one Pearl du Monville a bone-of-fida member of this former ball club. Maybe that'll shame them big babies into gettin' in there and swingin', knowin' I can replace any one of 'em with a midget, if I have a mind to. A St Louis lawyer I seen twice tells me it's all legal and proper.'

'A St Louis lawyer would,' I says, 'seein' nothin' could make him happier than havin' you makin' a mockery outa this one-time baseball outfit,' I says.

Well, sir, it'll all be there in the papers of thirty, thirty-one year ago, and you could look it up. The game went along without no scorin' for seven innings, and since they ain't nothin' much to watch but guys poppin' up or strikin' out, the fans pay most of their attention to the goin's-on of Pearl du Monville. He's out there in front a the dugout, turnin' handsprings, balancin' his bat on his chin, walkin' a imaginary line, and so on. The fans clapped and laughed at him, and he ate it up.

So it went up to the last a the eighth, nothin' to nothin', not more'n seven, eight hits all told, and no errors on neither side. Our pitcher gets the first two men out easy in the eighth. Then up come a fella name of Porter or Billings, or some such name, and he lammed one up against the tobacco sign for three bases. The next guy up slapped the first ball out into left for a base hit, and in come the fella from third for the only run of the ball game so far. The crowd yelled, the look a death come onto Magrew's face again, and even the midget quit his tomfoolin'. Their next man fouled out back a third, and we come up for our last bats like a bunch a schoolgirls steppin' into a pool of cold water. I was lower in my mind than I'd been since the day in nineteen-four when Chesbro throwed the wild pitch in the ninth inning with a man on third and lost the pennant for the Highlanders. I knowed something just as bad was goin' to happen, which shows I'm a clairvoyun, or was then.

When Gordy Mills hit out to second, I just closed my eyes. I opened 'em up again to see Dutch Muller standin' on second, dustin' off his pants, him havin' got his first hit in maybe twenty time to the plate. Next up was Harry Loesing, battin' for our pitcher, and he got a base on balls, walkin' on a fourth one you could 'a' combed your hair with.

Then up come Whitey Cott, our lead-off man. He crotches down in what was prob'ly the most fearsome stanch in organized ball, but all he can do is pop out to short. That brung up Billy Klinger, with two down and a man on first and second. Billy took a cut at one you could 'a' knocked a plug hat offa this here Carnera with it, but then he gets sense enough to wait 'em out, and finely he walks, too, fillin' the bases.

Yes, sir, there you are; the tyin' run on third and winnin' run on second, first a the ninth, two men down, and Hank Metters comin' to the bat. Hank was built like a Pope-Hartford and he couldn't run no faster'n President Taft, but he had five home runs to his credit for the season, and that wasn't bad in them days. Hank was still hittin' better'n anybody else on the ball club, and it was mighty heartenin', seein' him stridin' up towards the plate. But he never got there.

'Wait a minute!' yells Magrew, jumpin' to his feet. 'I'm sendin' in a pinch hitter!' he yells.

You could 'a' heard a bomb drop. When a ballclub manager says he's sendin' in a pinch hitter for the best batter on the club, you know and I know and everybody knows he's lost his holt.

'They're goin' to be sendin' the funny wagon for you, if you don't watch out,' I says, grabbin' a holt of his arm.

But he pulled away and run out towards the plate, yellin'. 'Du Monville battin' for Metters!'

All the fellas begun squawlin' at once, except Hank, and he just stood there starin' at Magrew like he'd gone crazy and was claimin' to be Ty Cobb's grandma or somethin'. Their pitcher stood out there with his hands on his hips and a disagreeable look on his face, and the plate umpire told Magrew to go on and get a batter up. Magrew told him again du Monville was battin' for Metters, and the St Louis manager finely got the idea. It brung him outa his dugout, howlin' and bawlin' like he'd lost a female dog and her seven pups.

Magrew pushed the midget towards the plate and he says to him, he says, 'Just stand up there and hold that bat on your shoulder. They ain't a man in the world can throw three strikes in there 'fore he throws four balls,' he says.

'I get it, Junior,' says the midget. 'He'll walk me and force in the tyin' run!' And he starts on up to the plate as cocky as if he was Willie Keeler.

I don't need to tell you Bethlehem broke loose on that there ball field. The fans got onto their hind legs, yellin' and whistlin', and everybody on the field began wavin' their arms and hollerin' and shovin'. The plate umpire stalked over to Magrew like a traffic cop, waggin' his jaw and pointin' his finger, and the St Louis manager kept yellin' like his house was on fire. When Pearl got up to the plate and stood there, the pitcher slammed his glove down onto the ground and started stompin' on it, and they ain't nobody can blame him. He's just walked two normal-sized human bein's, and now here's a guy up to the plate they ain't more'n twenty inches between his knees and his shoulders.

The plate umpire called in the field umpire, and they talked a while, like a couple doctors seein' the bucolic plague or somethin' for the first time. Then the plate umpire come over to Magrew with his arms folded acrost his chest, and he told him to go on and get a batter up, or he'd forfeit the game to St Louis. He pulled out his watch, but somebody batted it outa his hand in the scufflin', and I thought there'd be a free-for-all, with everybody yellin' and shovin' except Pearl du Monville, who stood up at the plate with his little bat on his shoulder, not movin' a muscle.

Then Magrew played his ace. I seen him pull some papers outa his pocket and show 'em to the plate umpire. The umpire begun lookin' at 'em like they was bills for somethin' he not only never bought it, he never even heard of it. The other umpire studied 'em like they was a death warren, and all this time the St Louis manager and the fans and the players is yellin' and hollerin'.

Well, sir, they fought about him bein' a midget, and they fought about him usin' a kid's bat, and they fought about where'd he been all season. They was eight or nine rule books brung out and everybody was thumbin' through 'em, tryin' to find out what it says about midgets, but it don't say nothin' about midgets, 'cause this was somethin' never'd come up in the history of the game before, and nobody'd ever dreamed about it, even when they has nightmares. Maybe you can't send no midgets in to bat nowadays, 'cause the old game's changed a lot, mostly for the worst, but you could then, it turned out.

The plate umpire finely decided the contrack papers was all legal and proper, like Magrew said, so he waved the St Louis players back to their places and he pointed his finger at their manager and told him to quit hollerin' and get on back in the dugout. The manager says the game is percedin' under protest, and the umpire bawls, 'Play ball!', over 'n' above the yellin' and booin', him havin' a voice like a hogcaller.

The St Louis pitcher picked up his glove and beat at it with his fist six or eight times, and then got set on the mound and studied the situation. The fans realized he was really goin' to pitch to the midget, and they went crazy, hoopin' and hollerin' louder'n ever, and throwin' pop bottles and hats and cushions down onto the field. It took five, ten minutes to get the fans quieted down again, whilst our fellas that we on base set down on the bags and waited. And Pearl du Monville kept standin' up there with the bat on his shoulder, like he'd been told to.

So the pitcher starts studyin' the setup again, and you got to admit it was the strangest setup in a ball game since the players cut off their beards and begun wearin' gloves. I wisht I could call the pitcher's name – it wasn't old Barney Pelty nor Nig Jack Powell nor Harry Howell. He was a big right-hander, but I can't call his name. You could look it up. Even in a crotchin' position, the ketcher towers over the midget like the Washington Monument.

The plate umpire tries standin' on his tiptoes, then he tries crotchin' down, and he finely gets hisself into a stanch nobody'd ever seen on a ball field before, kinda squattin' down on his hanches.

Well, the pitcher is sore as a old buggy horse in fly time. He slams in the first pitch, hard and wild, and maybe two foot higher'n the midget's head.

'Ball one!' hollers the umpire over 'n' above the racket, 'cause everybody is yellin' worsten ever.

The ketcher goes on out towards the mound and talks to the pitcher and hands him the ball. This time the big right-hander tries to undershoot, and it comes in a little closer, maybe no higher'n a foot, foot and a half above Pearl's head. It would 'a' been a strike with a human bein' in there, but the umpire's got to call it, and he does.

'Ball two!' he bellers.

The ketcher walks on out to the mound again, and the whole infield comes over and gives advice to the pitcher about what they'd do in a case like this, with two balls and no strikes on a batter that oughta be in a bottle of alcohol 'stead of up there at the plate in a big-league game between the teams that is fightin' for first place.

For the third pitch, the pitcher stands there flat-footed and tosses up the ball like he's playin' ketch with a little girl.

Pearl stands there motionless as a hitchin' post, and the ball comes in big and slow and high—high for Pearl, that is, it bein' about on a level with his eyes, or a little higher'n a grown man's knees.

They ain't nothin' else for the umpire to do, so he calls, 'Ball three!'

Everybody is onto their feet, hoopin' and hollerin' as the pitcher sets to throw ball four. The St Louis manager is makin' signs and faces like he was a contorturer, and the infield is givin' the pitcher some more advice about what to do this time. Our boys who was on base stick right onto the bag, runnin' no risk of bein' nipped for the last out.

Well, the pitcher decides to give him a toss again, seein' he come closer with that than with a fast ball. They ain't nobody ever seen a slower ball throwed. It came in big as a balloon and slower'n any ball every throwed before the major leagues. It come right in over the plate in front of Pearl's chest, lookin' prob'ly big as a full moon to Pearl. They ain't never been a minute like the minute that followed since the United States was founded by the Pilgrim grandfathers.

Pearl du Monville took a cut of that ball, and he hit it! Magrew give a groan like a poleaxed steer as the ball rolls out in front a the plate into fair territory.

'Fair ball!' yells the umpire, and the midget starts runnin' for the first, still carryin' that little bat, and makin' maybe ninety foot an hour. Bethlehem breaks loose on the ball field and in them stands. They ain't never been nothin' like it since creation was begun.

The ball's rollin' slow, on down towards third, goin' maybe eight, ten foot. The infield comes in fast and out boys break from their bases like hares in a brushfire. Everybody is standin' up, yellin' and hollerin', and Magrew is tearin' his hair outa his head, and the midget is scamperin' for the first with all the speed of one of them little dashhounds carryin' a satchel in his mouth.

The ketcher gets to the ball first, but he boots it on out past the pitcher's box, the pitcher fallin' on his face tryin' to stop it, the shortstop sprawlin' after it full length and zaggin' it on over towards the second baseman, whilst Muller is scorin' with the tyin' run and Loesing is roundin' third with the winnin' run. Ty Cobb could 'a' made a three-bagger outa that bunt, with everybody fallin' over theirself tryin' to pick the ball up. But Pearl is still maybe fifteen, twenty feet from the bag, toddlin' like a baby and yeepin' like a trapped rabbit, when the second baseman finely gets a holt o' that ball and slams it over to first. The first baseman ketches it and stomps on the bag, the base umpire waves Pearl out, and there goes your old ball game, the craziest ball game every played in the history of the organized world.

Their players start runnin' in and then I see Magrew. He starts after Pearl, runnin' faster'n any man every run before. Pearl sees him comin' and runs behind the base umpire's legs and gets a holt onto 'em. Magrew comes up, pantin' and roarin', and him and the midget play ring-around-a-rosy with the umpire, who keeps shovin' at Magrew with one hand and tryin' to slap the midget loose from his legs with the other.

Finely Magrew ketches the midget, who is still yeepin' like a stuck sheep. He gets holt of that little guy by both his ankles and starts whirlin' him round and round his head like Magrew was a hammer thrower and Pearl was the hammer. Nobody can stop him without gettin' their head knocked off so everybody just stands there and yells. Then Magrew lets the midget fly. He flies on out towards second, high and fast, like a human home run, headed for the soap sign in center field.

Their shortstop tries to get to him, but he can't make it, and I knowed the little fella was goin' to bust to pieces like a dollar watch on a asphalt street when he hit the ground. But it so happens their center fielder is just crossin' second, and he starts runnin' back, tryin' to get under the midget, who had took to spiralin' like a football 'stead of turnin' head over foot, which give him more speed and more distance.

I know you never seen a midget ketched, and you prob'ly never ever seen one throwed. To ketch a midget that's been throwed by a heavy-muscled man and is flyin' through the air, you got to run under him and with him and pull your hands and arms back and down when you ketch him, to break the compact of his body, or you'll bust him in two like a matchstick. I see Bill Lange and Willie Keeler and Tris Speaker make some wonderful ketches in my day, but I never seen nothin' like that center fielder. He gets back and back and still further back and he pulls that midget down outa the air like he was liftin' a sleepin' baby from a cradle. They wasn't a bruise onto him, only his face was the color of cat's meat and he ain't got no air in his chest. In his excitement, the base umpire, who was runnin' back with the center fielder when he ketched Pearl, yells, 'Out!' and that give hysterics to the Bethlehem which was ragin' like Niagry on that ball field.

Everybody was hoopin' and hollerin' and yellin' and runnin', with the fans swarmin' onto the field, and the cops tryin' to keep order, and some guys laughin' and some of the women fans cryin', and six or eight of us holdin' onto Magrew to keep him from gettin' at that midget and finishin' him off. Some of the fans picks up the St Louis pitcher and the center fielder, and starts carryin' 'em around on their shoulders, and they was the craziest goin's-on knowed in the history of organized ball on this side of the 'Lantic Ocean.

I seen Pearl du Monville strugglin' in the arms of a lady fan with a ample bosom, who was laughin' and cryin' at the same time, and him beatin' at her with his little fists and bawlin' and yellin'. He clawed his way loose finely and disappeared in the forest of legs which made that ball field look like it was Coney Island on a hot summer's day.

That was the last I ever seen of Pearl du Monville. I never seen hide nor hair of him from that day to this, and neither did nobody else. He just vanished into the thin air, as the fella says. He was ketched for the final out of the ball game and that was the end of him, just like it was the end of the ball game, you might say, and also the end of our losin' streak, like I'm goin' to tell you.

That night we piled onto a train for Chicago, but we wasn't snarlin' and snappin' any more. No, sir, the ice was finely broke and a new spirit come into that ball club. The old zip came back with the disappearance of Pearl du Monville, and 'fore long Magrew was laughin' with us. He got a human look onto his pan again, and he quit whinin' and complainin' and wishin' he was in heaven with the angels.

Well, sir, we wiped up that Chicago series, winnin' all four games, and makin' seventeen hits in one of 'em. Funny thing was, St Louis was so shook up by that last game with us, they never did hit their stride again. Their center fielder took to misjudgin' everything that come his way, and the rest a the fellas followed suit, the way a club'll do when one guy blows up.

'Fore we left Chicago, I and some of the fellas went out and bought a pair of them little baby shoes, which we had 'em golded over and give 'em to Magrew for a souvenir, and he took it all in good spirit. Whitey Cott and Billy Klinger made up and was fast friends again, and we hit our home lot like a ton of dynamite and they was nothin' could stop us from then on.

I don't recollect things as clear as I did thirty, forty years ago. I can't read no fine print no more, and the only person I got to check with on the golden days of the national pastime, as the fella says, is my friend, old Milt Kline, over in Springfield, and his mind ain't as strong as it once was.

He gets Rube Waddell mixed up with Rube Marquard, for one thing, and anybody does that oughta be put away where he won't bother nobody. So I can't tell you the exact margin we win the pennant by. Maybe it was two and a half games, or maybe it was three and a half. But it'll all be there in the newspapers and record books of thirty, thirty-one year ago and, like I was sayin', you could look it up.

Snodgrass' World Series Muff

NEW YORK TIMES

BOSTON, OCT. 16, 1912 (SPECIAL)—Write in the pages of world series base-ball history the name of Snodgrass. Write it large and black. Not as a hero; truly not. Put him rather with Merkle, who was in such a hurry that he gave away a National League championship. Snodgrass was in such a hurry that he gave away a world championship. It was because of Snodgrass' generous muff of an easy fly in the tenth inning that the decisive game in the world series went to the Boston Red Sox this afternoon by a score of 3 to 2 instead of to the New York Giants by a score of 2 to 1.

It is the tenth inning of the eighth game of the series. The score in games is 3 to 3 (the second game was a tie), and the score of this contest is 1 to 1. Mathewson, the veteran, has given the lie to his own announce-ment that he could never again pitch in such a contest, by holding the Red Sox enemy at bay for nine innings in decisive fashion. One run has been made off him, through the fortunate hit of a youngster who had never faced him before. The regular members of the Boston team have been helpless in the face of his speed and his elusive fadeaway. They have been outfought, outgeneraled, outspeeded, and their only hope is that Wood, who had gone in fresh only two innings before, will hold out until the veteran shall give way to the strain.

And who is this that comes to bat for the Giants? 'Tis 'Red' Murray—once the hitless. And what does he do? He pierces the mark of one of the smokiest of Wood's shoots and puts the ball far over the head of Speaker into the left-field stands. It is a home-run hit, but ground rules limit it to two bases. Yet what is the difference? Merkle also sees through the smoke, and the ball which Wood has sent so speedily toward him is returned so fast that Wood can hardly see it as it goes toward center field. So Murray is in with the run that un-ties the score, and it only remains for Mathewson to hold himself for one more inning and New York has a world championship and the Giant players the lion's share of the big purse hung up for the players, a difference of $29,514.

Is Mathewson apprehensive as he walks to the box? He is not. All the confidence that was his when the blood of youth ran strong in his supple muscles is his now. Even though the mountainous Clyde Engle faces him—this Engle who brought in the two runs of the Red Sox on Monday—he shows not a quiver, and he is right. All that Engle can do with the elusive drop served up is to hoist it high between center and right fields. Snodgrass and Murray are both within reach of it, with time to spare. Snodgrass yells, 'I've got it,' and sets himself to take it with ease, as he has taken hundreds of that sort. Murray stops, waiting for the play that will enable him to line the ball joyfully to the infield just to show that his formidable right wing is still in working order.

And now the ball settles. It is full and fair in the pouch of the padded glove of Snodgrass. But he is too eager to toss it to Murray and it dribbles to the ground. Before Snodgrass can hurl the ball to second, Engle is perching there.

Mathewson stands in the box, stunned for a moment, then swings his gloved hand in a gesture that is eloquent of his wrath. He has lost none of his courage and determination, but it can be seen as he faces Hooper that there is just a bit of uncertainty in his bearing. Proof comes that he has lost some of his cunning, for Hooper hits the ball so hard that Snodgrass has to sprint and reach to pull down his liner. For Yerkes, Matty cannot put them over at all, and two Red Sox are on the bases.

And now that something which upsets a ball team—which McGraw has called an explosion—becomes evident. Speaker pops up a high foul near first base, and Merkle, Meyers and Mathewson converge on it, with none collected enough to say which shall take it, and it drops among them. The three who have made the muss walk to the box arguing. Mathewson saying things which he emphasizes with angry gestures.

Now the Boston throng calls for the blood of the veteran—and gets it.

His control is gone, and Speaker, saved by a blunder, hammers the ball hard for a single to right field and Engle is over the plate. Lewis stands still while four bad ones pass him, and then Gardner steps up and puts all his weight against the ball, and it goes far out to Devore, too far for him to stop Yerkes with the winning run, even though his throw comes true as a bullet.

Too bad! Too bad! The world championship belongs in New York and Boston is perfectly aware of it. Here as well as there admiration is ungrudging for a team that could come from behind, win two decisive victories on its gameness, and deserve to win a third; and sympathy is widespread for a gallant pitcher and his gallant mates, who were cheated of their triumph by a bit of bravado. After the game the Red Sox rooters gave hearty cheers 'for the best player on the Giants' team – Snodgrass.'

Most of all the sympathy is due Mathewson. Three times he has given prodigally of his waning vigor to bring the world championship to New York, and three times he has deserved victory but has had it denied because his team has failed to play its real game behind him. What it meant to him to pitch the game today he only knows.

As he sat in the corridor of his hotel this morning it could be seen that he had little left to give. The skin was drawn tightly over the bone on his jaw and chin, and in his hollowed cheeks the furrows that have been graven by hard campaigns of recent years were startling in their depth. As he warmed up, his gauntness was evident, and the Boston fans gloated over the thought that he could not long stand the rush of their sluggers.

Yet up to that disastrous tenth he was 'Big Six' at his best. His fast ball shot with a thud into the glove of Meyers, his drop shot down in front of the batters and his fadeaway had the best of them breaking their backs. Now and again he seemed in trouble, but no sign of a crack appeared, and only eight safe hits were made off him in the ten periods.

He went along to the seventh holding the game as he wished, and it was only in this round that two hits were bunched on him. That luck had some part here cannot be denied. Stahl got on with a pop up, and Wagner walked, but it seemed as though nothing would come of it when 'Big Six', with two out, had fooled Henriksen, batting for Bedient, twice on strikes and had started a fadeaway over the plate. Henriksen had never faced him before but his bat happened to connect with the ball as he made a wide swing, and the sphere shot over third base for a double bringing in Stahl.

In the eighth and ninth the Sox hit him hard, but could not place the ball out of reach of the Giant fielders. In the fatal tenth the whole

Boston side should have been put out on flies and none should have reached first base.

Yet credit must not be denied to young Bedient. When he went to the box Gardner, Stahl and Cady were as solicitous for his welfare as though he were an only child with the croup. Whatever nervousness he might have had at first, it was not long before both his feet were firmly planted on the ground. He was dangerously wild at times, but in the pinches he was as cool as the east wind that wafted its chilling way across the field. His departure from the mound after the seventh inning was a matter of batting strategy, not of necessity.

The one run scored against him in the third inning had in it elements of luck and misfortune. He let Devore walk to first, but a double play would have been possible had not Gardner fumbled Doyle's swift grounder. Murray's drive to left-center which scored Devore was just missed by Speaker. In the fourth Bedient showed his class. With Herzog on third and only one out he forced Fletcher and Mathewson to send up high flies.

Wood, who went to the box in the eighth, gave promise at first, showing the form of the first two games he won. In the ninth, however, the Giants showed that they could find his smoke ball, and in the tenth they made it plainly evident that he could not last long. He gave plain indication of distress and was legally out of the game. Engle having batted for him in the last half of the tenth. Collins was warming up to take his place when the Giants exploded.

At the bat, in the field and in base running the Giants excelled. They got nine hits off Bedient and Wood, to eight off Mathewson. In the error column they showed up 2 to 5, and in the base running they were fast, while the Sox at times were slow and blundering.

A peculiar piece of hard luck for the Giants resulted from a protest that had been made by Manager McGraw. In Saturday's game Lewis scored one of the Red Sox runs because of a triple he drove into a blind alley off the left-field bleachers. McGraw insisted that thereafter such a hit should be good for only two bases, and the rule was made. Herzog, in the fourth with nobody out, drove a vicious ball into this same alley, and was waved back to second after easily getting to the third sack. He did not get home, as he probably would have except for McGraw's protest. With his run scored the series would have been won by the Giants in the ninth, and there would have been no fatal tenth inning.

The setting for the most stirring finish of a world championship in the history of baseball was not calculated to be inspiring. There was an atmosphere of dreariness about the affair. The ramshackle structures of the Boston field did not look good to one who had been used to the glories of Brush Stadium.

The Royal Rooters were not there. Offended by the neglect to recognize their unwavering loyalty by providing seats for them the day before, they boycotted the game and thousands of others did the same thing. Then, too, there was a general feeling among the Boston rooters that the series had been lost by the routs of Monday and Tuesday.

Of the 17,000 odd who were present, however, many were loyal to the team and were quite willing to show it when the occasion arose. When the game was over hundreds of fans made a rush on the Red Sox bench, where they cooped the players in almost suffocating confinement and insisted on cheering them again and again, not even forgetting Snodgrass of the Giants.

After the game was finished Manager McGraw ran over to the Red Sox bench to shake hands with Manager Stahl and congratulate him on his victory and sportsmanship.

Boston has shown no great jubilation tonight over the victory. Fans admit that the Sox were played to a standstill and that no large honor accrues to them. Beyond the cheering at the grounds there has been no demonstration in the city.

Vick Shore and
The Good of The Game

ERSKINE CALDWELL

EVERYBODY IN DELTA knew Vick Shore, and if anybody in town had a dislike for him or held a grudge against him, it had been a well-kept secret for the past twelve or fifteen years. He was an easy-going good natured, chubby-faced bachelor in his late forties who owned a one-chair barber's shop next door to the post office. In fact, Delta being as small as it was, Vick's barber's shop was the only one in town. Vick Shore liked barbering, saying that it gave him the privilege to do things for other people that they would have had a devilish hard time doing for themselves, but he rarely trimmed his own hair, and his tawny forelock drooped lower and lower over his face each year.

When Vick did not feel like barbering, he had the habit of locking the front door of his shop and pulling the green window-shade half-way down. After that he would sit in the barber's chair and tilt it backward the way he did when he was shaving a customer. Then he would spend the remainder of the day stretched out comfortably on his back with his feet propped up high while he read the official league baseball rule book, memorising the rules page by page and then repeating them to himself with his eyes closed. It made no difference to Vick Shore how many customers banged on the front door and shouted at him, saying they were going to a wedding or a funeral and just had to have a haircut or shave, and he paid no attention whatever to the clamor they made.

During the hot summer months from May to September, Vick frequently locked up the barber's shop—as often as not it was a busy Saturday afternoon, too—and umpired a baseball game between semi-pro teams in Delta or in one of the other small towns in the country.

The principal reason why he was always being asked to umpire a game—aside from the fact that he never expected to be paid for his services, saying that he liked to umpire for the good of the game—was because he never failed to try to please both teams. If one side did not like one of his decisions, such as a tight play at second base or a close call on a ball or strike at home plate, Vick would stop the game then and there and let the players on both sides swear at him as much as they pleased and call him the worst names they could think of until they were tired of arguing and bickering and wanted to get back to playing ball. In all those years of umpiring, Vick had never even talked back to a wrangling player, much less ordered him off the field. He always said that the good of the game was too important to let his own personal feelings influence his conduct as an umpire.

There had been a lot of times when a game was held up for half an hour or longer while Vick sat down on the pitcher's mound, shoved his umpire's cap to the back of his head, and then, taking his baseball rule book from his hip pocket, sat there reading the rules to himself until all the players got tired of arguing and said they were willing to let the decision stand. Regardless of that, Vick always made up for the disputed decision by favoring the other side the next time he had a chance to make a close choice between calling a base runner safe or out. In that way, during the course of nine innings, he evened matters for both sides and made everybody feel happy by the time the last out of the game was called.

After the game was over, and when he had gone back to the barber's shop, a crowd of fans always got together in the shop and talked and argued about the way Vick had called some of the plays. No matter what the argument was about, Vick always told them that umpiring a baseball game was just like cutting a customer's hair.

'You've got to please one customer at a time to be a good reliable barber,' he would explain to them, 'and when you umpire a baseball game, the thing to do is to please one team at a time.'

'But what about all that fussing and cussing at you, Vick?' somebody would ask. 'You know yourself that baseball players can think of the worst thing in the world to call an umpire, and they do it, too. Doesn't that bother you at all? Looks to me like you'd get mad and lose your temper over some of the things they call you and chase them out of the game.'

'I'm a sportsman, and I'm used to that kind of talk by now,' Vick would tell them. 'It doesn't bother me one little bit. I've heard everything there is that a player can think of to call an umpire on a baseball diamond. Besides, all the cussing and name calling is as much a part of baseball as a catcher's chest protector and shin guards, and if I tried to stop it, it wouldn't be for the good of the game.'

The big event of the summer that year was when two barnstorming teams of girl softball players came to Delta to play an exhibition game about a week after the Fourth of July. A few days before the game, the manager of the barnstorming tour came to Delta and put up signs all over town advertising the game between the Louisiana Queens and the Florida Orange Blossoms.

The baseball park had seats for about five hundred people, including both the grandstand and the bleachers, but nearly twice that many tickets had been sold by game time, and about half the spectators had to sit on the ground along the side lines or else perch on the fence around the baseball park. The manager of the tour said he wanted to hire a local umpire for the game, just to prove to the fans that the game was going to be played fairly and squarely, and, as soon as he heard about Vick Shore, it was only natural that he asked Vick to umpire.

Since Vick knew practically everything there was to know about the rules of baseball and softball, because he had studied the official rules of both games all those years, it was not difficult at all for him to umpire the softball game between the two girls' teams. The game was called promptly at two o'clock that July afternoon, and the Louisiana Queens and the Florida Orange Blossoms got ready to play ball.

Very few people in Delta had ever seen a professional softball game between two girls' teams, but the game was played so much like baseball that by the end of the first innings nearly everybody in the park had picked one of the teams to root for, and after that there was a lot of cheering every time a good play was made by one of the girls. Besides that, after watching men play baseball in baggy uniforms all those years, everybody was interested in the way the bare-legged girls ran around the playing field in their brightly colored tight silk shorts.

The game went along smoothly for the first four innings, and there had not been a single protest or argument over Vick Shore's decisions, even though he had made some close ones that would certainly have caused an argument if two teams of men had been playing baseball. However, in the first half of the fifth innings, a slender dark haired girl on the Orange Blossoms team hit a slow-rolling infield grounder and she was thrown out at first base. At least, Vick Shore called her out. Everybody admitted that it was a close play, and most of the fans thought Vick had called it fairly as he saw it.

The Queens pitcher was waiting for the next Orange Blossoms hitter to walk up to the batter's box when suddenly there was a loud uproar on the Orange Blossoms bench. Immediately after that, the captain of the Orange Blossoms team ran out on the field waving her arms excitedly and loudly protesting at Vick Shore's decision on the play at first base.

Vick looked surprised to see the girl behaving the way she was and he acted as though he did not know what to do in a case like that. He was still standing there with a dumbfounded expression on his chubby red face when he realised that he was completely surrounded by all the girls on the Orange Blossoms team. There was so much excitement on the field by that time that nobody in the park could hear what was being said, but most people sat back and waited for the confusion to end, thinking it was merely a momentary delay of the game. Probably everybody there thought that Vick Shore, being the experienced umpire that he was, would quickly pacify the excited girls and in a few minutes the Orange Blossoms would go back to their bench and let the game continue.

However, that was exactly what did not happen. In the midst of all the commotion, Vick suddenly jerked off his umpire's cap, flung it on the ground with all his might, and walked stiffly off the field without even once looking backwards over his shoulder.

There was scarcely a sound in the whole park when Vick leaped over the left-field fence and disappeared in the direction of his barber's shop. Probably because it was such an unusual thing to see an umpire quit like that in the middle of a game and walk off the field, it was a long time before people realized what had happened. Finally, though, after a delay of about twenty minutes, the game was resumed. The manager of the barnstorming tour persuaded the athletic coach of the Delta high school, who was one of the spectators in the grandstand, to finish umpiring the game and there was not a single protest by either team after that. The Louisiana Queens won the game by the score of five to three.

As soon as the game was over, a crowd of men hurried down-town to Vick Shore's barber's shop. Vick had tilted the barber's chair backward and he had stretched himself out comfortably while he read the baseball rule book. Twelve or fourteen men had crowded into the small barber's shop by that time and nearly that many more were standing in the doorway or looking through the window.

'What in the world happened, Vick?' one of the men asked him. 'What made you quit umpiring right in the middle of the game like that? I never saw an umpire quit before in my life.'

'I'm a sportsman,' Vick said calmly, glancing away from the rule book. 'That's the one thing I always try to be when I'm umpiring. I conduct myself like a sportsman, because I think it's for the good of the game. But those ladies—those lady softball players—those——'

'What did they say to you, Vick?' somebody else asked him. 'Did they cuss at you?'

'Of course not,' he answered, solemnly shaking his head. 'They're ladies. Ladies wouldn't cuss out an umpire.'

'Then what was it they said to you that made you quit like that, Vick?' another man asked.

Releasing the lever on the barber's chair and propelling himself upward, he was suddenly sitting stiffly erect. He put the baseball rule book into his hip pocket.

'I'll tell you what they said,' he answered, nodding at all the men around him. 'One of those girls—she was that good-looking red-haired girl with the green ribbon tied around her head—anyway, she came up to me real close and held out her hand. I asked her what she was doing that for, and she said if I'd take out my glass eyes, she'd dust them off for me. Then another girl—she was the blonde-haired one who curved out so much in front—well, that one came up real close and asked me if I'd had trouble sleeping the past few nights. I asked her why she wanted to know that, and she said because I acted like I was trying to make up for all the sleep I'd lost sometime or other. There was a lot more talk along those lines, and there would've been a heap more of it if I hadn't walked off the field when I did.'

'Shucks, Vick,' somebody in the crowd said, laughing a little, 'that's nothing. I've heard baseball players get hot under the collar and say things to an umpire that were a thousand times worse than that. You've had real old-fashioned cussing out, and you know it.'

'That's true,' Vick agreed, nodding slowly. 'I know it doesn't amount to much when a baseball player says things like that, and worse, but it's different when a girl says it.'

'How is it different, Vick?' another man asked.

'It's different because those girls smiled when they said it, that's why.

Every last one of those girls came up real close and smiled just as nice and pretty as she could when she said something to me. I just couldn't stand that, because that could only mean that she meant what she was saying and was in dead earnest about it. I can stand it when men baseball players cuss me out, and I think nothing of it, because I know they're convinced they're doing it for the good of the game. But those girl softball players—they didn't care a hoot about the good of the game! All they cared about was winning it!'

A Letter to A. G. Spalding

FRED W. THAYER

116 FEDERAL STREET
BOSTON, MAY 18, 1911

MY DEAR MR SPALDING:

I am in receipt of your favor of the 9th instant. You shall have the facts in regard to the catcher's mask, and I think you can feel assured that the data are all correct.

In order to give you the whole story I shall have to ask you to go back to the year '76 that you may know what the conditions were in Harvard Base Ball matters.

Thatcher was the catcher in the season of '76. He left college at the end of the year.

You will recall the fact that college nines especially had rarely more than one, possibly two, substitutes, and these were 'general utility' men.

Tyng was the best all-around natural ballplayer of my time. He had played third base, center field, and helped out in other positions, including catcher, in the season of '76. In one or two games in which he caught behind the bat he had been hit by foul tips and had become more or less timid.

He was, by all odds, the most available man as catcher for the season of '77, and it was up to me to find some way to bring back his confidence.

The fencing mask naturally gave me the hint as to the protection for the face, and then it was up to me to devise some means of having the impact of the blow kept from driving the mask onto the face, The forehead and chin rest accomplished this and also made it possible for me to secure a patent, which I did in the winter of 1878.

Tyng practiced catching with the mask, behind the bat, in the gymnasium during the winter of '77, and became so thoroughly proficient that foul tips had no further terrors for him.

The first match game in which the mask was used was on Fast Day, in Lynn, against the Live Oaks, in April 1877. Thereafter the Harvard catcher used it in all games.

I hope this will give you the data which you wish. At all events it gives you the real facts in regard to the Base Ball mask.

Yours faithfully

(signed) FRED W. THAYER

Casey at the Bat

ERNEST LAWRENCE THAYER

The outlook wasn't brilliant for the Mudville nine that day;
The score stood four to two with but one inning more to play.
So when Cooney died at second, and Burrows did the same,
A pallor wreathed the features of the patrons of the game.
A straggling few got up to go in deep despair. The rest
Clung to the hope which springs eternal in the human breast;
They thought, 'If only Casey could but get a whack at that—
We'd put up even money now with Casey at the bat.'
But Flynn preceded Casey, as did also Jimmy Blake,
And the former was a lulu and the latter was a fake;
So upon that stricken multitude a deathlike silence sat,
For there seemed but little chance of Casey's getting to the bat.
But Flynn let drive a single, to the wonderment of all,
And Blake, the much despis-ed, tore the cover off the ball;
And when the dust had lifted, and the men saw what had occurred.
There was Jimmy safe at second and Flynn a-hugging third.
Then from five thousand throats and more there rose a lusty yell;
It rumbled in the mountaintops, it rattled in the dell;
It knocked upon the hillside and recoiled upon the flat,
For Casey, mighty Casey, was advancing to the bat.
There was ease in Casey's manner as he stepped into his place;
There was pride in Casey's bearing and a smile on Casey's face.
And when, responding to the cheers, he lightly doffed his hat,
No stranger in the crowd could doubt 'twas Casey at the bat.
Ten thousand eyes were on him as he rubbed his hands with dirt;
Five thousand tongues applauded when he wiped them on his shirt.
Then while the writhing pitcher ground the ball into his hip,

Defiance gleamed in Casey's eye, a sneer curled Casey's lip.
And now the leather-covered sphere came hurtling through the air,
And Casey stood a-watching it in haughty grandeur there.
Close by the sturdy batsman the ball unheeded sped—
'That ain't my style,' said Casey—'Strike one,' the Umpire said.
From the benches black with people, there went up a muffled roar,
Like the beating of the storm waves on a stern and distant shore.
'Kill him! kill the umpire!' shouted someone on the stand;
And it's likely they'd have killed him had not Casey raised his hand.
With a smile of Christian charity great Casey's visage shone;
He stilled the rising tumult; he bade the game go on;
He signalled to the pitcher, and once more the spheroid flew;
But Casey still ignored it, and the Umpire said, 'Strike two.'
'Fraud!' cried the maddened thousands, and the echo answered,
    'Fraud!'
But one scornful look from Casey and the multitude was awed.
They saw his face grow stern and cold, they saw his muscles strain,
And they knew that Casey wouldn't let that ball go by again.
The sneer is gone from Casey's lip, his teeth are clenched in hate;
He pounds with cruel violence his bat upon the plate.
And now the pitcher holds the ball, and now he lets it go,
And now the air is shattered by the force of Casey's blow.
Oh, somewhere in this favored land the sun is shining bright;
The band is playing somewhere, and somewhere hearts are light,
And somewhere men are laughing, and somewhere children shout;
But there is no joy in Mudville—mighty Casey has struck out.

braves 10, giants 9

SHIRLEY JACKSON

BEFORE THE CHILDREN were able to start counting days till school was out, and before Laurie had learned to play more than a simple scale on the trumpet, and even before my husband's portable radio had gone in for its annual checkup so it could broadcast the Brooklyn games all summer, we found ourselves deeply involved in the Little League. The Little League was new in our town that year. One day all the kids were playing baseball in vacant lots and without any noticeable good sportsmanship, and the next day, almost, we were standing around the grocery and the post office wondering what kind of a manager young Johnny Cole was going to make, and whether the Weaver boy—the one with the strong arm—was going to be twelve this August, or only eleven as his mother said, and Bill Cummings had donated his bulldozer to level of the top of Sugar Hill, where the kids used to go sledding, and we were all sporting stickers on our cars reading 'We have contributed' and the fund-raising campaign was over the top in forty-eight hours. There are a thousand people in our town, and it turned out, astonishingly, that about sixty of them were boys of Little League age. Laurie thought he'd try out for pitcher and his friend Billy went out for catcher. Dinnertime all over town got shifted to eight-thirty in the evening, when nightly baseball practice was over. By the time our family had become accustomed to the fact that no single problem in our house could be allowed to interfere in any way with the tempering of Laurie's right arm, the uniforms had been ordered, and four teams had been chosen and named, and Laurie and Billy were together on the Little League Braves. My friend Dot, Billy's mother, was learning to keep a box score. I announced in family assembly that there would be no more oiling of baseball gloves in the kitchen sink.

We lived only a block or so from the baseball field, and it became the amiable custom of the ballplayers to drop in for a snack on their way to the practice sessions. There was to be a double-header on Memorial Day, to open the season. The Braves would play the Giants; the Red Sox would play the Dodgers. After one silent, apoplectic moment my husband agreed, gasping, to come to the ball games and root against the Dodgers. A rumor got around town that the Red Sox were the team to watch, with Butch Weaver's strong arm, and several mothers believed absolutely that the various managers were putting their own sons into all the best positions, although everyone told everyone else that it didn't matter, really, *what* position the boys held so long as they got a chance to play ball, and show they were good sports about it. As a matter of fact, the night before the double-header which was to open the Little League, I distinctly recall that I told Laurie it was only a game. 'It's only a game, fella,' I said. 'Don't *try* to go to sleep; read or something if you're nervous. Would you like an aspirin?'

'I forgot to tell you,' Laurie said, yawning. 'He's pitching Georgie tomorrow. Not me.'

'*What?*' I thought, and then said heartily, 'I mean, he's the manager, after all. I know you'll play your best in *any* position.

'I could go to sleep now if you'd just turn out the light,' Laurie said patiently. 'I'm really quite tired.'

I called Dot later, about twelve o'clock, because I was pretty sure she'd still be awake, and of course she was, although Billy had gone right off about nine o'clock. She said she wasn't the least bit nervous, because of course it didn't really matter except for the kids' sake, and she hoped the best team would win. I said that that was just what I had been telling my husband, and she said *her* husband had suggested that perhaps she had better not go to the game at all because if the Braves lost she ought to be home with a hot bath ready for Billy and perhaps a steak dinner or something. I said that even if Laurie wasn't pitching I was sure the Braves would win, and of course I wasn't one of those people who always wanted their own children right out in the center of things all the time but if the Braves lost it would be my opinion that their lineup ought to be revised and Georgie put back into right field where he belonged. She said *she* thought Laurie was a better pitcher, and I suggested that she and her husband and Billy come over for lunch and we could all go to the game together.

I spent all morning taking movies of the Memorial Day parade, particularly the Starlight 4-H Club, because Jannie was marching with them, and I used up almost a whole film magazine on Sally and Barry, standing at the curb, wide-eyed and rapt, waving flags. Laurie missed the parade because he slept until nearly twelve, and then came downstairs and made himself an enormous platter of bacon and eggs and toast, which he took out to the hammock and ate lying down.

'How do you feel?' I asked him, coming out to feel his forehead. 'Did you sleep all right? How's your arm?'

'Sure,' he said.

We cooked lunch outdoors, and Laurie finished his breakfast in time to eat three hamburgers. Dot had only a cup of coffee, and I took a little salad. Every now and then she would ask Billy if he wanted to lie down for a little while before the game, and I would ask Laurie how he felt. The game was not until two o'clock, so there was time for Jannie and Sally and Barry to roast marshmallows. Laurie and Billy went into the barn to warm up with a game of ping-pong, and Billy's father remarked that the boys certainly took this Little League setup seriously, and my husband said that it was the best thing in the world for the kids. When the boys came out of the barn after playing three games of ping-pong I asked Billy if he was feeling all right and Dot said she thought Laurie ought to lie down for a while before the game. The boys said no, they had to meet the other guys at the school at one-thirty and they were going to get into their uniforms now. I said please to be careful, and Dot said if they needed any help dressing just call down and we would come up, and both boys turned and looked at us curiously for a minute before they went indoors.

'My goodness,' I said to Dot, 'I hope they're not nervous.'

'Well, they take it so seriously,' she said.

I sent the younger children in to wash the marshmallow off their faces, and while our husbands settled down to read over the Little League rule book, Dot and I cleared away the paper plates and gave the leftover hamburgers to the dog. Suddenly Dot said, 'Oh,' in a weak voice and I turned around and Laurie and Billy were coming through the door in their uniforms. 'They look so—so—*tall*,' Dot said, and I said 'Laurie?' uncertainly. The boys laughed, and looked at each other.

'Pretty neat,' Laurie said, looking at Billy.

'Some get-up,' Billy said, regarding Laurie.

Both fathers came over and began turning the boys around and around, and Jannie and Sally came out onto the porch and stared worshipfully.

Barry, to whom Laurie and his friends have always seemed incredibly tall and efficient, gave them a critical glance and observed that this was truly a baseball.

It turned out that there was a good deal of advice the fathers still needed to give the ball players, so they elected to walk over to the school with Billy and Laurie and then on to the ball park, where they would find Dot and me later. We watched them walk down the street; not far away they were joined by another boy in uniform and then a couple more. After that, for about half an hour, there were boys in uniform wandering by twos and threes toward the baseball field and the school, all alike in a kind of unexpected dignity and new tallness, all walking with self-conscious pride. Jannie and Sally stood on the front porch watching, careful to greet by name all the ballplayers going by.

A few minutes before two, Dot and I put the younger children in her car and drove over to the field. Assuming that perhaps seventy-five of the people in our town were actively engaged in the baseball game, there should have been about nine hundred and twenty-five people in the audience, but there seemed to be more than that already; Dot and I both remarked that it was the first town affair we had ever attended where there were more strange faces than familiar ones.

Although the field itself was completely finished, there was only one set of bleachers up, and that was filled, so Dot and I took the car robe and settled ourselves on top of the little hill over the third-base line, where we had a splendid view of the whole field. We talked about how it was at the top of this hill the kids used to start their sleds, coasting right down past third base and on into center field, where the ground flattened out and the sleds would stop. From the little hill we could see the roofs of the houses in the town below half hidden in the trees, and far on the hills in the distance. We both remarked that there was still snow on the high mountain.

Barry stayed near us, deeply engaged with a little dump truck. Jannie and Sally accepted twenty-five cents each, and melted into the crowd in the general direction of the refreshment stand. Dot got out her pencil and a box score, and I put a new magazine of film in the movie camera. We could see our husbands standing around in back of the Braves' dugout, along with the fathers of all the other Braves players. They were all in a group, chatting with great humorous informality with the manager and the two coaches of the Braves. The fathers of the boys on the Giant team were down by the Giant dugout, standing around the manager and the coaches of the Giants.

Marian, a friend of Dot's and mine whose boy Artie was first baseman for the Giants, came hurrying past looking for a seat, and we offered her part of our car robe. She sat down, breathless, and said she had mislaid her husband and her younger son, so we showed her where her husband was down by the Giant dugout with the other fathers, and her younger son turned up almost at once to say that Sally had a popsicle and so could he have one, too, and a hot dog and maybe some popcorn?

Suddenly, from far down the block, we could hear the high-school band playing 'The Stars and Stripes Forever,' and coming closer. Everyone stood up to watch and then the band turned the corner and came through the archway with the official Little League insignia and up to the entrance of the field. All the ballplayers were marching behind the band. I thought foolishly of Laurie when he was Barry's age, and something of the sort must have crossed Dot's mind, because she reached out and put her hand on Barry's head. 'There's Laurie and Billy,' Barry said softly. The boys ran out onto the field and lined up along the base lines, and then I discovered that we were all cheering, with Barry jumping up and down and shouting, 'Baseball! Baseball!'

'If you cry I'll tell Laurie,' Dot said to me out of the corner of her mouth.

'Same to you,' I said blinking.

The sky was blue and the sun was bright and the boys stood lined up soberly in their clean new uniforms holding their caps while the band played. 'The Star-Spangled Banner' and the flag was raised. From Laurie and Billy, who were among the tallest, down to the littlest boy in uniform, there was a straight row of still, expectant faces.

I said, inadequately, 'It must be hot out there.'

'They're all chewing gum,' Dot said.

Then the straight lines broke and the Red Sox, who had red caps, and the Dodgers, who had blue caps, went off into the bleachers and the Giants, who had green caps, went into their dugout, and at last the Braves, who had black caps, trotted out onto the field. It was announced over the public-address system that the Braves were the home team, and when it was announced that Georgie was going to pitch for the Braves I told Marian that I was positively relieved, since Laurie had been so nervous anyway over the game that I was sure pitching would have been a harrowing experience for him, and she said that Artie had been perfectly willing to sit out the game as a substitute, or a pinch hitter, or something, but that his manager had insisted upon putting him at first base because he was so reliable.

'You know,' she added with a little laugh. 'I don't know one position from another, but of course Artie is glad to play anywhere.'

'I'm sure he'll do very nicely,' I said, trying to put some enthusiasm into my voice.

Laurie was on second base for the Braves, and Billy at first. Marian leaned past me to tell Dot that first base was a *very* responsible position, and Dot said oh, was it? Because of course Billy just wanted to do the best he could for the team, and on the *Braves* it was the *manager* who assigned the positions. Marian smiled in what I thought was a nasty kind of way and said she hoped the best team would win. Dot and I both smiled back and said we hoped so, too.

When the umpire shouted, 'Play Ball!' people all over the park began to call out to the players, and I raised my voice slightly and said, 'Hurray for the Braves.' That encouraged Dot and *she* called out, 'Hurray for the Braves,' but Marian, of course, had to say, 'Hurray for the Giants.'

The first Giant batter hit a triple, although, as my husband explained later, it would actually have been an infield fly if the shortstop had been looking and an easy out if he had thrown it anywhere near Billy at first. By the time Billy got the ball back into the infield the batter— Jimmie Hill, who had once borrowed Laurie's bike and brought it back with a flat tire—was on third. I could see Laurie out on second base banging his hands together and he looked so pale I was worried. Marian leaned around me and said to Dot, 'That was a nice try Billy made. I don't think even *Artie* could have caught that ball.'

'He looks *furious*,' Dot said to me. 'He just *hates* doing things wrong.'

'They're all terribly nervous,' I assured her. 'They'll settle down as soon as they really get playing.' I raised my voice a little. 'Hurray for the Braves,' I said.

The Giants made six runs in the first inning, and each time a run came in Marian looked sympathetic and told us that really,the boys were being quite good sports about it, weren't they? When Laurie bobbled an easy fly right at second and missed the out, she said to me that Artie had told her that Laurie was really quite a good little ballplayer and I mustn't blame him for an occasional error.

By the time little Jerry Hart finally struck out to retire the Giants, Dot and I were sitting listening with polite smiles. I had stopped saying

'Hurray for the Braves.' Marian had told everyone sitting near us that it was her boy who had slid home for the sixth run, and she had explained with great kindness that Dot and I had sons on the other team, one of them the first baseman who missed that long throw and the other one the second baseman who dropped the fly ball. The Giants took the field and Marian pointed out Artie standing on first base slapping his glove and showing off.

Then little Ernie Harrow, who was the Braves' right fielder and lunched frequently at our house, hit the first pitched ball for a fast grounder which went right through the legs of the Giant center fielder, and when Ernie came dancing onto second Dot leaned around to remark to Marian that if Artie had been playing closer to first the way Billy did he might have been ready for the throw if the Giant center fielder had managed to stop the ball. Billy came up and smashed a long fly over the left fielder's head and I put a hand on Marian's shoulder to hoist myself up. Dot and I stood there howling, 'Run run run,' Billy came home, and two runs were in. Little Andy placed a surprise bunt down the first-base line, Artie never even saw it, and I leaned over to tell Marian that clearly Artie did not understand all the refinements of playing first base. Then Laurie got a nice hit and slid into second. The Giants took out their pitcher and put in Buddy Williams, who Laurie once beat up on the way to school. The score was tied with two out and Dot and I were both yelling. Then little Ernie Harrow came up for the second time and hit a home run, right over the fence where they put the sign advertising his father's sand and gravel. We were leading eight to six when the inning ended.

Little League games are six innings, so we had five more innings to go. Dot went down to the refreshment stand to get some hot dogs and soda; she offered very politely to bring something for Marian, but Marian said thank you, no; she would get her own. The second inning tightened up considerably as the boys began to get over their stage fright and play baseball the way they did in the vacant lots. By the middle of the fifth inning the Braves were leading nine to eight, and then in the bottom of the fifth Artie missed a throw at first base and the Braves scored another run. Neither Dot nor I said a single word, but Marian got up in a disagreeable manner, excused herself, and went to sit on the other side of the field.

'Marian looks very poorly these days,' I remarked to Dot as we watched her go.

'She's at *least* five years older than I am,' Dot said.

'More than that,' I said. 'She's gotten very touchy, don't you think?'

'Poor little Artie,' Dot said. 'You remember when he used to have temper tantrums in nursery school?'

In the top of the sixth the Braves were winning ten to eight, but then Georgie, who had been pitching accurately and well, began to tire, and he walked the first two batters. The third boy hit a little fly which fell in short center field, and one run came in to make it ten to nine. Then Georgie, who was by now visibly rattled, walked the next batter and filled the bases.

'Three more outs and the Braves can win it,' some man in the crowd behind us said. 'I don't *think*,' he laughed.

'Oh, *lord*,' Dot said, and I stood up and began to wail, 'No, no.' The manager was gesturing at Laurie and Billy. 'No, no,' I said to Dot, and Dot said, 'He can't do it, don't let him.' 'It's too much to ask of the children,' I said. 'What a terrible thing to do to such little kids,' Dot said.

'New pitcher,' the man in the crowd said. 'He better be good,' and he laughed.

While Laurie was warming up and Billy was getting into his catcher's equipment, I suddenly heard my husband's voice for the first time. This was the only baseball game my husband had ever attended outside of Ebbets Field. 'Put it in his ear, Laurie,' my husband was yelling, 'put it in his ear.'

Laurie was chewing gum and throwing slowly and carefully. Barry took a minute off from the little truck he was placidly filling with sand and emptying again to ask me if the big boys were still playing baseball. I stood there, feeling Dot's shoulder shaking against mine, and I tried to get my camera open to check the magazine of film but my finger kept slipping and jumping against the little knob. I said to Dot that I guessed I would just enjoy the game for a while and not take pictures, and she said earnestly that Billy had had a little touch of fever that morning and the manager was taking his life in his hands putting Billy up there in all that catcher's equipment in that hot shade. I wondered if Laurie could see that I was nervous.

'*He* doesn't look very nervous,' I said to Dot, but then my voice failed, and I finished, 'does he?' in a sort of gasp.

The batter was Jimmie Hill, who had already had three hits that afternoon. Laurie's first pitch hit the dust at Billy's feet and Billy sprawled full length to stop it. The man in the crowd behind us laughed. The boy on third hesitated, unsure whether Billy had the ball; he started for home and then, with his mother just outside the third-base line yelling, 'Go back, go back,' he retreated to third again.

Laurie's second pitch sent Billy rocking backward and he fell; 'Only way he can stop it is fall on it,' the man in the crowd said, and laughed.

Dot stiffened, and then she turned around slowly. For a minute she stared and then she said, in the evilest voice I have ever heard her use, 'Sir, that catcher is my son.'

'I beg your pardon, ma'am, I'm sure,' the man said.

'Picking on little boys,' Dot said.

The umpire called Laurie's next pitch ball three, although it was clearly a strike, and I was yelling, 'You're blind, you're blind.' I could hear my husband shouting to throw the bum out.

'Going to see a new pitcher pretty soon,' said the man in the crowd, and I clenched my fist, and turned around and said in a voice that made Dot's sound cordial, 'Sir, that pitcher is *my* son. If you have any more personal remarks to make about any member of my family—'

'Or mine,' Dot added.

'I will immediately call Mr Tillotson, our local constable, and see personally that you are put out of this ball park. People who go around attacking ladies and innocent children—'

'Strike,' the umpire said.

I turned around once more and shook my fist at the man in the crowd, and he announced quietly and with some humility that he hoped both teams would win, and subsided into absolute silence.

Laurie then pitched two more strikes, his nice fast ball, and I thought suddenly of how at lunch he and Billy had been tossing hamburger rolls and Dot and I had made them stop. At about this point, Dot and I abandoned our spot up on the hill and got down against the fence with our faces pressed against the wire. 'Come on, Billy boy,' Dot was saying over and over, 'come on, Billy boy,' and I found that I was telling Laurie, 'Come on now, only two more outs to go, only two more, come on, Laurie, come on . . .' I could see my husband now but there was too much noise to hear him; he was pounding his hands against the fence. Dot's husband had *his* hands over his face and his back turned to the ball field. 'He can't hit it, Laurie,' Dot yelled, 'this guy can't hit,' which I thought with dismay was not true; the batter was Butch Weaver and he was standing there swinging his bat and sneering. 'Laurie, Laurie, Laurie,' screeched a small voice; I looked down and it was Sally, bouncing happily beside me. 'Can I have another nickel?' she asked. 'Laurie, Laurie.'

'Strike,' the umpire said and I leaned my forehead against the cool wire and said in a voice that suddenly had no power at all, 'Just two strikes, Laurie, just two more strikes.'

Laurie looked at Billy, shook his head, and looked again. He grinned and when I glanced down at Billy I could see that behind the mask he was grinning too. Laurie pitched, and the batter swung wildly. 'Laurie, Laurie,' Sally shrieked. 'Strike two,' the umpire said. Dot and I grabbed at each other's hands and Laurie threw the good fast ball for strike three.

One out to go, and Laurie, Billy, and the shortstop stood together on the mound for a minute. They talked very soberly, but Billy was grinning again as he came back to the plate. Since I was incapable of making any sound, I hung onto the wire and promised myself that if Laurie struck out this last batter I would never never say another word to him about the mess in his room, I would not make him paint the lawn chairs, I would not even mention clipping the hedge . . .' Ball one,' the umpire said, and I found that I had my voice back. 'Crook,' I yelled, 'blind crook,'

Laurie pitched, the batter swung, and hit a high foul ball back of the plate; Billy threw off his mask and tottered, staring up. The batter, the boys on the field, and the umpire, waited, and Dot suddenly spoke. 'William,' she said imperatively, '*you catch that ball.*'

Then everyone was shouting wildly; I looked at Dot and said, 'Golly.' Laurie and Billy were slapping and hugging each other, and then the rest of the team came around them and the manager was there. I distinctly saw my husband, who is not a lively man, vault the fence to run into the wild group and slap Laurie on the shoulder with one hand and Billy with the other. The Giants gathered around their manager and gave a cheer for the Braves, and the Braves gathered around *their* manager and gave a cheer for the Giants, and Laurie and Billy came pacing together toward the dugout, past Dot and me. I said, 'Laurie?' and Dot said, 'Billy?' They stared at us, without recognition for a minute, both of them lost in another world, and then they smiled and Billy said, 'Hi, Ma,' and Laurie said, 'You see the game?'

I realized that my hair was over my eyes and I had broken two fingernails. Dot had a smudge on her nose and had torn a button off her sweater. We helped each other up the hill again and found that Barry was asleep on the car robe. Without speaking any more than was absolutely necessary, Dot and I decided that we could not stay for the second game of the double-header. I carried Barry asleep and Dot brought his dump truck and the car robe and my camera and the box score which she had not kept past the first Giant run, and we headed wearily for the car.

We passed Artie in his green Giant cap and we said it had been a fine game, he had played wonderfully well, and he laughed and said tolerantly, 'Can't win 'em all, you know.' When we got back to our house I put Barry into his bed while Dot put on the kettle for a nice cup of tea. We washed our faces and took off our shoes, and finally Dot said hesitantly that she certainly hoped that Marian wasn't really offended with us.

'Well, of course she takes this kind of thing terribly hard,' I said.

'I was just thinking,' Dot said after a minute, 'we ought to plan a kind of victory party for the Braves at the end of the season.'

'A hot-dog roast, maybe?' I suggested.

'Well,' Dot said, 'I *did* hear the boys talking one day. They said they were going to take some time this summer and clean out your barn, and set up a record player in there and put in a stock of records and have some dances.'

'You mean . . .' I faltered. 'With *girls*?'

Dot nodded.

'Oh,' I said.

When our husbands came home two hours later we were talking about old high-school dances and the time we went out with those boys from Princeton. Our husbands reported that the Red Sox had beaten the Dodgers in the second game and were tied for first place with the Braves. Jannie and Sally came idling home, and finally Laurie and Billy stopped in, briefly, to change their clothes. There was a pickup game down in Murphy's lot, they explained, and they were going to play some baseball.

A Letter to Connie Mack

JAMES T. FARRELL

DANNY WAS TERRIFIED. He sat alone in his bedroom, thinking about what had happened. Perhaps this man was a temptation of the Devil, and God had sent this temptation as a way of telling him that he really had the call. God had often sent the Devil to saints to tempt them. But, of course, God had given the saints the strength and grace to resist temptation. But he wasn't a saint and he had never been strong enough to resist temptation.

Could he ever be a saint?

Anybody would laugh at him if they knew he even asked himself such a question.

He couldn't be too sure that this old man had been put in his path as a way of letting him know that he was really, called. He had no right to think that God was going out of His way for anybody like Danny O'Neill, did he? Of course he didn't.

Danny wandered restlessly to the parlor. He began to wonder if baseball scouts went to Washington Park. If they did, maybe one of them might see him on one of his good days. They might see how promising he was. If they did, would they get in touch with him?

But he had to give up that idea. He had to recognize that this question of the call had been on his mind for months. If it stuck in his mind so much, now mustn't it mean that it was the sign? If it kept coming back to him at so many different times, when he had so many different things on his mind or he was doing so many different things, why, didn't that mean something?

Sometimes it was like a voice inside of him talking to him, and the voice would say to him:

You know you have the call! You know you have the call! You know you got the call!

Did he? Now, there was that voice again, right now, this minute.

You know it! You know you have the call!

Suppose he did. He could first be a baseball player, and never marry, and then, when his playing days were over, he could be ordained. But if he really had the call, he wouldn't always be fighting with himself this way. If he had the call, and God had poured grace into his soul, he would want to be a priest. He wouldn't love Roslyn. He wouldn't be dreaming of being a baseball player the way he always did. Yes, he was convinced. He didn't have the call.

He jumped to his feet, happy, feeling a sudden lightness of mood.

But how could he tell Sister?

As soon as one worry left your mind, another took its place. Here was one. But then, Sister couldn't say that he had to be a priest when he didn't have the call. A person who didn't have a vocation shouldn't be a priest. That stood to reason.

Danny sat at his desk with his bedroom door closed. He was elated. Just after he had made up his mind that he didn't have the call, the idea had come to him like an inspiration. And now he had gotten the letter finished, written carefully and legibly so that it looked as if a man had written it. It ought to work, too. Connie Mack was known above all other managers as the man to pick promising players off the sand lots and develop them into stars. Well, after receiving this letter, why shouldn't Connie send a scout out to Washington Park to look him over? And maybe the scout would see him on a good day and sign him up for a tryout with the Athletics a couple of years from now when he was old enough. Players had been signed up at fifteen before. There was the case of that pitcher, Hoyt. Proud of himself, he read the letter he'd just composed.

Mr Connie Mack
Shibe Park
The Philadelphia Athletics
Philadelphia, Pennsylvania.

DEAR MR MACK:

I am writing you this letter to tip you off about a kid named O'Neill who is to be seen playing ball in Washington Park in Chicago all of the time. He isn't ripe just yet because he is only fifteen or sixteen

That was a smart idea to make out that the man who was supposed to be writing this letter didn't know too much about him, so it was best not to give his exact age.

but he is coming along fast for his age, and he will be ripe soon enough and he looks like a real comer. If you look him over you can pick up a promising youngster now for nothing and he seems destined for the big show. I am a baseball fan and like to see kids get a chance, and take pride in picking them. I picked some before and was a good picker. Years ago when George Moriarity was playing on the sand lots of Chicago I picked him, and I think you must admit I picked a big leaguer then because Moriarity is a big leaguer. You can pick this kid up now for nothing and you will never regret it. He plays out in Washington Park all the time, and you can send a scout out there to look at him and easily find out who he is.

I know you will not be sorry for this tip.

A baseball fan, a real one

T. J. WALKER

He was pleased and satisfied with his letter. All year he'd really felt that 1919 was going to be an important year for him. Maybe this letter might begin to prove that it was. He was smart to have thought up this idea.

Baseball in Mumford's Pasture Lot

SAMUEL HOPKINS ADAMS

A SMART SINGLE RIG drew up to the hitching post of No. 52 South Union Street as we three boys approached. Out of it stepped a short, red-faced, dapper man who secured his horse and then addressed us.

'Does Mr Myron Adams live here?'

'Yes, sir,' John said.

'We're just going to see him,' Sireno added. 'He's our grandfather.'

'Well, you can wait,' the stranger said. 'I've got private business with him.'

'If you're trying to sell him a colored enlargement of a photo-graph . . .' John began but got no further.

'I ain't,' the caller interrupted. 'My name is Phillips and I represent the Rochester Baseball Club.'

'There isn't any,' I said glumly.

It was cause for humiliation to every right-thinking inhabitant of the city, young and old, that in the spring of the baseball-mad year of 1879, Rochester was represented by no professional team whatever.

'There will be if I can sell fifty of these here tickets, good for the whole season and only ten dollars,' Mr Phillips said. 'D'you think he'll pony up? How's he on baseball.'

'He wouldn't know a Dollar Dead from a Young America if it hit him in the snoot,' Reno answered. The Dollar Dead was the standard amateur ball, the Young America the twenty-five-cent junior favorite.

'I'll have a crack at him anyway,' Mr Phillips decided. He vanished into the cottage, and in a few minutes we heard Grandfather, in his deep and resonant voice, putting an end to the interview. 'What?' he cried. 'Money? To witness what should be a *gentleman's* pastime? Non-sense! Fustian! Good day to you!'

The crestfallen visitor came out, silently climbed into his buggy, and drove away. We went in to pay our duty call.

A week later, the three of us ran upon Mr Phillips again, this time in Livingston Park, and heard from him tidings of great joy. In spite of Grandfather's recalcitrance, Rochester was to have its team. Mr Asa T. Soule, the patent-medicine magnate, had just come forward with an offer to finance a club out of his private pocket, provided it should bear the name of Hop Bitters, the cure-all he manufactured.

The news spread fast and, as the opening of the season drew near, Rochester glowed with restored pride. In its first game the new club swamped an amateur nine, fourteen to six.

Next, an exhibition game was scheduled against Rochester's ancient and bitter rival, the Buffalos, who were in the National League and therefore supposedly a cut above us. It was to be the event of the year, and the admission was fifty cents. John, being ten years old and our senior member, put the painful question to Reno and me.

'Where are we going to get half a dollar apiece?'

'Grandpa Adams,' I suggested doubtfully.

'In your mind, baby mine!' Reno said, using the most emphatic negation of the time.

'What other chance have we got?' I asked. Nobody had an answer. Fifty cents was unthinkably hard for a small boy to come by in those days. Grandfather was our only hope.

In preparation for the desperate attempt upon his purse, we all three devoted the next week or so to attending him with great assiduity. We mowed his lawn. We weeded the vegetable patch. We suffered errands gladly. When but two days remained before the game, we decided the time had come. We washed our hands and brushed our hair, and since none of us coveted the honor of putting the momentous question, I plucked three timothy heads for the purpose of drawing lots.

'Shortest straw pulls the skunk's tail,' I said. This was formula; no disrespect was intended.

John drew the short one, and, led by him, we went to face our grandfather. John opened cautiously, speaking of the importance of the coming event to Rochester and the Hop Bitters Club. 'You know, Grandpa, our team's named for the medicine,' he said brightly.

The old gentleman glanced at the mantel, where stood a dark-amber bottle containing the spirituous and inspiring 'Invalid's Friend & Hope.'

'Why, yes,' he said. 'A superior restorative. Very comforting to the system,' a sentiment shared by thousands of the old gentleman's fellow teetotalers.

'It's a dandy ball team,' Reno gloated.

'I assume that you refer to its costume?' Grandfather said coldly. He did not countenance slang on our lips.

'Yes, sir,' Reno agreed hastily. 'You ought to see their uniforms.'

'I am willing to believe that they present a macaroni appearance,' the old gentleman said. 'But what is the precise connection between this remedy and the projected contest?'

'Mr Soule is giving the money for the club,' John explained.

'Mr Asa T. Soule? I was not aware that he had sportive proclivities.'

'Oh, he's not really a sporting man,' John hastened to disclaim. 'No sir! He—he's quite religious. Why, he won't have a player on his team who ever played on Sunday.'

I saw that Grandfather, a strict Sabbatarian, was impressed. 'They've got a rule against Sunday games in the National League,' I said, opportunely recalling an item in the *Democrat & Chronicle*.

'Baseball is a very Christian game, sir,' John added.

'I daresay, I daresay,' the old gentleman conceded. 'But it is not, by all accounts, what it was in my day. When I first came here, the Rochester Baseball Club met four afternoons a week. We had fifty members. That was in 1827.'

'I play first base on the Livonia Young Eagles,' Reno said eagerly. 'Where did you play, sir?'

'In Mumford's pasture lot, off Lake Avenue.'

'Reno means what position, Grandpa,' I explained.

'Batter, for choice,' said the old gentleman.

'You couldn't bat all the time,' Reno demurred.

'No,' Grandfather said. 'But I preferred to. I frequently hit the ball over the fence.'

'When your side was in the field, where did you play?' John asked.

'Wherever I thought the ball most likely to be batted, naturally,' the alumnus of Mumford's pasture lot replied, manifestly annoyed at the stupidity of the question.

'That's a funny kind of a game,' Reno muttered.

'I see nothing humorous in it,' Grandfather retorted. 'The cream of Rochester's Third Ward ruffleshirts participated in the pastime.'

'Lots of the nicest boys in town go to baseball games now,' I said hopefully.

'Well, well.' Our grandfather's deep accents were benevolent. 'I see no reason why you should not attend. You are old enough to go by yourselves, I suppose.'

'It isn't that exactly, Grandpa,' John said. 'You see, sir—'

'It costs money to get in,' Reno blurted.

'So I was informed by the person with the inflamed nose,' said Grandfather dryly.

'Only fifty cents,' John said with admirable casualness; then he added, 'We thought, sir, that perhaps you would like to come along with us and see how they play it now, just for once.'

There was a breathless pause. Then Grandfather said, 'Fetch me the emergency cashbox from the desk.'

Hardly able to believe our ears, we fell over one another to obey.

During the next forty-eight hours, John, Reno and I debated long and seriously as to whether we should brief Grandfather on modern baseball, which he was about to see for the first time. All of us were, of course, experts, although we had never seen a professional game. We knew the rules and the etiquette of the diamond and could have passed perfect examinations on the quality and record of every wearer of a Hop Bitters uniform. Reno and I were for giving Grandfather the benefit of our erudition, but John outargued us. Older generations, he pointed out, did not take kindly to instruction from younger.

'He'd just tell us that he played the game before we were born,' he said.

On the great day, Grandfather and the three of us arrived early at Hop Bitters Park and found good places in the fifth row directly back of the plate. Before our enchanted eyes there stretched the greensward of the diamond bounded by the base paths. It was close cut, but the outfield was practically in a state of nature, its grass waving gently in the breeze. We had heard that the Buffalo manager had entered a protest against the outfield's unmown state, complaining that he had not brought his players all the way to Rochester to have them turned out to pasture.

The stand filled up promptly. There must have been as many as three hundred people present, mostly of the prosperous classes. Mr Mudge, the undertaker, and Mr Whittlesey, the Assistant Postmaster, took seats in front of us and were presently joined by Mr Toogood, the Troup Street livery-stable man. Two clerks from Glenny's China Emporium crowded past us, while on the aisle side the manager of Reynolds Arcade took his place, accompanied by Professor Cook, the principal and terror of No. 3 School. Back of us sat a red-necked, hoarse-voiced canalman. Mr Mudge addressed our grandfather.

'A pleasure and a surprise to see you here, Mr Adams.'

'The young must have their day,' Grandfather replied amiably, '*Maxima debetur puero reverentia*, you know.'

'Yes sir; I don't doubt it for a minute,' the liveryman said earnestly. 'I hear those Buffalos are tough.'

'We can lick 'em,' I said loyally.

'Rochester boasted a superior club in my day, also,' Grandfather said.

'Did you play on it, Mr Adams?' inquired Professor Cook.

'I did, sir, for two seasons.'

'I assume that the game as then played differs from the present form.'

'You are justified in your assumption, sir,' said Grandfather, who then entered upon an informative discourse regarding the baseball of 1827.

The play at Mumford's pasture lot, he set forth, was open to all fifty active members of the club. The pitchers, who were ex officio the captains, chose up sides. Twelve to a team was considered a convenient number, but there might be as many as fifteen. A full turnout of members would sometimes put three teams in the field. Mr Mudge expressed the belief that this must result in overcrowding. Where did they all play?

Pitcher, catcher and baseman, Grandfather said, remained in their positions. The basemen stood touching their bases with at least one foot until the ball was hit. The remainder of the out team formed a mobile defense, each man stationing himself where he foresaw the best opportunity of making catches. Mr Toogood wished to know what the third team did while two were in the field. It waited, the veteran explained. At the close of each inning, when three batters had been put out—whether on flies, fouls, or by being touched or hit with the ball—the runs were totted up and the side with the lower score was supplanted by the third team. This continued until the hour agreed upon for stopping, which was usually sunset. Then the team with the largest total was adjudged the winner.

'Sounds like three-old-cat gone crazy,' Reno muttered in my ear.

Further elucidation of the baseball of Grandfather's day was cut short by a shout of 'Here they come!' as, amidst loyal clamor, the home team strode forth in neat gray uniforms, the name of the sponsoring nostrum scarlet across their breasts. They were a terrifically masculine lot, with bulging muscles and heavy whiskers. Eagerly we boys identified our special heroes, having often trailed them through the streets to the ballpark entrance. 'That's Meyerle, the first base,' John said. 'He can jump six feet in the air and catch the ball with his left hand.'

'The little, dumpy one is Burke,' said Mr Toogood. 'He's shortstop. You oughta see him handle daisy-cutters! Oh, my!'

'McGunnigle, our right fielder, batted pretty near three hundred with Buffalo last year,' Mr Mudge told Grandfather proudly.

'Three hundred runs?' Grandfather asked with evident skepticism.

The reply was drowned by the loudest shout of all. 'There he comes! Tinker! Tinker!' A hundred voices chorused. 'What's the matter with Tinker!' and three hundred antiphonal howls responded. 'HE'S ALL RIGHT!'

The canaller leaned over and spoke confidentially in Grandfather's ear. 'You watch that fellow Tinker, Mister. If a high fly goes out to left field, he'll git under it and do the prettiest back flip ever you seen before he catches it. You wouldn't see nothing like that in the League. Used to be a circus man.'

'I shall make it a point to observe him,' Grandfather said.

Out came the enemy at a carefree trot. They were even more muscular-looking than our heroes and sported whiskers at least as luxuriant. They lined up near the plate, faced the stand, and saluted the crowd grimly, fingers to the peaks of their green caps. We boys joined lustily in the chorus of opprobrious hoots that was the response. A man in street clothes appeared and took a stand a yard behind the catcher, who stood five yards back of the plate.

'On which side does that person play?' Grandfather asked.

'He doesn't play,' Mr Mudge answered. 'He's the umpire. He makes the decisions.'

'In our game, we had no need of such intervention,' Grandfather said. 'If a point of dispute arose, the captains consulted and came to a composition.'

'Suppose they disagreed?' Professor Cook suggested.

'Then, sir, they skied a copper for heads or tails and abode by arbitrament of the coin, like gentlemen and Corinthians,' Grandfather replied. He turned his attention to the scene below. 'Why is the tall man throwing the ball at the short man?' he inquired.

'That's our pitcher, Critchley, sooppling his arm up,' Mr Toogood said.

Grandfather frowned. 'That is *throwing*, not pitching,' he said. 'He should keep his arm down.'

'He's only got to keep it as low as his waist,' Reno said.

The old gentleman shook his head obstinately. 'Knuckles should be below the knee, not the waist. A highly improper procedure.'

The Hop Bitters team had now taken their positions and were standing, crouched forward, hands upon knees, in the classic posture. A burly Buffalo player stalked to the plate, rang his bat upon it, and described threatening arcs in the air.

'High ball,' he barked at the umpire.

The umpire shouted at the pitcher, 'The batsman calls for a high ball.'

Grandfather addressed the universe. 'What in Tophet is this?'

We boys were glad to enlighten him. 'He wants a pitch between his shoulder and his belt,' John said.

'If he'd called for a low ball, it'd have to be between his belt and his knee,' Reno added.

'Do you mean to say that he can choose where the pitch is to come?' Grandfather asked incredulously.

'Yes, sir. And if it doesn't come there, it's a ball, and if he gets eight balls, he can take his base,' I said.

'I should admire to bat in such circumstances,' said Grandfather.

'Maybe it wouldn't be so easy,' Reno said. 'Critchley's got a jimdandy curve.'

'Curve?' asked the old gentleman. 'What may that be?'

'Outcurve or incurve,' Reno told him. 'It starts like this, then it goes like this or like this—sorta bends in the air—and whiff! One strike!'

'Bends in the air!' An indulgent smile appeared on Grandfather's visage. 'These young folk will accept any absurdity,' he said to Professor Cook.

'Some do hold it to be an optical illusion,' the principal said diplomatically.

'Certainly,' Grandfather said. 'Anything else would be contrary to the laws of God and nature. Let me hear no more of such fahdoodle,' he concluded sternly, turning his back upon Reno.

The first inning was uneventful, as were the second and third. Pitcher Critchley's optical illusions and those of the opposing pitcher were uniformly and dully successful. Grandfather fidgeted and commented sharply upon the torpor of the proceedings.

'Lackadaisy-dido!' he said. 'Why does not someone hit the ball?'

'A couple of goose eggs is nothing, Grandpa,' John said. 'Just let our team once get a start and you'll see.'

The last of the fourth inning supplied a momentary stir. A high foul came down just in front of us, and the Buffalo catcher raced after it. The ball slithered from his outstretched fingers. We boys shrieked with delight. He glared at us and Grandfather addressed him kindly.

'Young man, that was ill-judged. You would have been well advised to wait and take it on the first bounce.'

We held our collective breaths, but the wrath died out of the upturned face.

'Look, Mister,' the catcher said, earnestly argumentative, 'that ball was a twister. How'd I know where it would bound?'

The canaller back of us raised a jeering voice. 'Butterfingers! Whyncha catch it in your cap?'

'You can't catch a ball in your cap any more,' John said to the canaller. 'It's in this year's rules.'

'Back to the berm, fathead!' the catcher added.

The umpire walked up, lifting an authoritative hand. 'No conversation between players and spectators,' he snapped, and the game was resumed.

Later, there was a considerable delay when a foul sailed over the fence. Both teams went outside to search for the ball, and Grandfather took the occasion to expatiate upon the superiority of the old-time game.

'Our Saturdays,' he said, 'were very gala affairs. Ladies frequently attended and refreshments were served.'

'Did you have uniforms, Grandpa?' I asked.

'Uniforms? we had no need for them. We removed our broadcoats, hitched our braces, and were prepared.'

John said, 'Our nine has militia caps with brass buttons.'

'Fabricius Reynolds played catcher in a canaller's tall castor,' Grandfather recalled. 'It was of silky beaver, gray, with a picture of the *Myron Holley* passing through Lock Twenty-three painted on the front. Very bunkum.'

'I've got a fifteen-cent Willow Wand with 'Home Run' on it in red letters,' Reno said proudly.

'Hamlet Scrantom's bat was of polished black walnut with his initials on a silver plate,' the old gentleman went on. 'He was a notorious batsman.'

The quest for the lost ball was eventually abandoned, Mr Soule reluctantly tossed out a new one, the umpire called 'Play ball, gents!' and the dull succession of runless innings continued. Then, in the opening half of the sixth, with two Buffalos out and two on base, a break came. A towering fly to left field brought a yelp of anticipatory delight from the admirers of the accomplished Tinker. Fleet of foot, he got beneath the ball while it was still high in air. His back flip was a model of grace and exactitude. Down came the ball into his cupped and ready hands —and broke through. Amid howls of dismay, he chased it, scooped it up, and threw it home. It went four feet above the catcher's reach, and the Buffalo runners galloped merrily in.

'Boggle-de-botch!' Grandfather exclaimed.

John plucked at his sleeve. 'I want to go home,' he said brokenly.

'Do not show yourself such a milksop,' the old gentleman said. 'How far is our own club behind?'

'Three runs,' John groaned.

'And there's another,' I added, almost in tears, as the Buffalo shortstop sent the ball over the left-field fence.

'Pooh!' said Grandfather. 'Four runs is not an insuperable adavantage. Why, I once saw Hamlet Scrantom bat in more than that at one stroke.'

We stared at him. 'How could he, Grandpa?' John asked. 'Even if there were three men on base—'

'There were, I was one of them.'

'—that would be only four runs.'

'Seven, in this instance,' the old gentleman said cheerfully. 'Hamlet knocked the ball into a sumac thicket, and we continued to run the bases until it was found and returned.'

From then on, the Hop Bitters were a sad spectacle. They stumbled and bumbled in the field, and at bat, as the embittered Reno said, they couldn't have hit a rotten punkin with the thill of a four-horse bob. On their side, the enemy fell upon Pitcher Critchley's offerings with dire effect. They dropped short flies over the basemen's heads. They slashed swift daisy-cutters through the impotent infield. They whacked out two-baggers and three-baggers with the nonchalance of assured victory. Grandfather assayed the situation.

'The Buffalos appear to have the faculty of placing their strokes where the Rochesters are not,' he said sagely, a comment later paralleled by Willie Keeler's classic recipe, 'Hit 'em where they ain't.'

We boys and the Rochester rooters around us became silent with gloom. Only Grandfather maintained any show of interest in the proceedings. He produced a notebook from the pocket of his ceremonial Prince Albert coat and, during what was left of the game, wrote in it busily. We were too depressed even to be curious. It was a relief when the agony ended, with a pop fly to the pitcher.

'Three out, all out,' the umpire announced. 'The score is Buffalos eleven, Hop Bitters nothing. A game will be played in this park . . .'

But we had no heart in us to listen.

We went back to Grandfather's cottage, and over a consolatory pitcher of raspberry shrub in the sitting room he delivered his verdict.

'The game is not without merit,' he said thoughtfully, 'but I believe it to be susceptible of improvement.'

Surprisingly, the Hop Bitters nine beat both Worcester and Washington in the following fortnight. On the strength of their improvement, a return game with Buffalo was scheduled for August, and we boys resumed what Grandfather would have called our 'officiousness' at Union Street; we were sedulous in offers to mow, to weed, to fetch and carry. On the last Saturday in July, when a less important game, with Syracuse, was on the card, we found the front door locked and our stepgrandmother out back, tending her hollyhocks.

'Where's Grandpa?' I asked.

'You'd never guess,' the old lady said with a twinkle.

'Gone canalling,' John surmised.

'Mr Adams is attending the baseball game, if you please,' his wife said, 'and no more thought of the fifty cents expense than if it was so many peppercorns. This is the second time since he took you boys. I do believe he has ideas.'

Grandfather did, indeed, have ideas. We learned of them later. The notes made while the Buffalos were swamping the wretched Hop Bitters were the groundwork of a comprehensive plan which turned up among his papers after his death. It was a design for the betterment of baseball and was addressed to Mr Soule, the Hop Bitters Baseball Club and the Citizens of Rochester, New York. A prologue, which still seems to me to have its points, introduced it.

The purport and intent of the game of baseball, as I apprehend, is to afford healthful exercise to the participants and harmless entertainment to the spectators. In its present apathetic and supine form it fulfills neither desideratum. A scant dozen runs for an afternoon's effort is a paltry result, indeed. I have seen twice that number achieved in a single inning when the game was in its prime. I therefore have the honor, sir, to lay before you a prospectus for the rejuvenescence of the pastime and its reclamation from the slough of inertia and monotony wherein it is engulfed as practiced in your ball park.

The plan provided for an extra shortstop between first and second bases and two additional outfielders to take care of long flies. But the really revolutionary proposal dealt with the pitching. The expert of Mumford's pasture lot approved of one innovation he had witnessed, the right of the batter to call his ball. But this did not go far enough. Grandfather's rule proscribed the pitcher from 'any motion or pretense delusive of or intended to delude the eye of the batter.'

'Such practice,' he wrote, 'savors of chicanery and is subversive of true, Corinthian sportsmanship.' So much for curves!

Whether Mr Soule ever received the memorial I don't know. Certainly he did not act upon it. A Rochester team took the field in the following spring with the usual complement of nine players and Grandfather never went to another ball game.

'Miracle' Braves Humble Athletics

NEW YORK TIMES

BOSTON, OCT. 13, 1914—Johnny Evers, nervous and irritable, faced Bob Shawkey in the momentous fifth inning at Fenway Park this afternoon. Rudolph and Moran were crouched on the dusty base paths ready to dash for home. The score was tied, 1 to 1, and two Braves were already out.

Crash! Evers' bat smacked the ball solidly and it whistled its way to center field. Two Braves flashed across the plate with the baseball championship of the world. The veteran Evers, as tricky a batsman as ever worried a pitcher, had matched his years of experience against Connie Mack's last hope. Evers had coaxed Shawkey into giving him just the kind of ball he wanted, so he whanged it to his heart's delight.

With this one blow the Boston Braves won their fourth straight victory over the Athletics in the world series and won the biggest prize in American sports. George Stallings' makeshift team, compactly welded together with a unity of purpose and a perfect harmony of action, had triumphed over one of the greatest ball clubs the game has known.

The all-conquering spirit of this Boston team carried it through the stormiest campaign baseball has ever known. Inspired by its own ability, the Braves accomplished something no team has achieved before in a world series since the National Commission assumed charge in 1905. It captured four straight games in as many played. It has turned the whole realm of baseball upside down. In a year of reversals in sport the Boston team accomplished a task which a few days before looked impossible. A ball club which started the season as a joke reached the perch de luxe in baseball in a blaze of glory.

A crowd of 34,365 saw the Athletics make their final stand. They did nothing which calls for praise. Their resistance was reduced. The

Mackian Maulers—they used to call them that—were whipped before they started. Broken in spirit and despondent after Monday's heart-breaking game, the Athletics sorely lacked enough spunk to make the Braves do their best to beat them. They were overawed by the superb reserve strength of Stallings' men. In the last four innings of their dying chance they didn't make a single hit off Rudolph.

A great change has come over baseball. There is no longer a $100,000 infield in Philadelphia, the far-famed 'Home Run' Baker is no more. Today he is plain Frank Baker. Collins, 'the greatest player in the world,' is now a private in the ranks. The masterful Bender and the marvel of all southpaws, Plank, are through with world series. They have had their day; all the gifts baseball can give were once theirs, but a new generation of ball players has grown up. The mighty have fallen. Old Father Time has gently laid his hand on the shoulders of the disciples of the old school and has shown them to a back seat, where they can sit back comfortably and watch youngsters like Maranville, the Boston Rabbit; Bill James, Dick Rudolph, and Hank Gowdy go through their paces, with the bloom of youth still on them and latent strength hidden in their muscles, all ready to be called into action, just as it has been in this wonderful world series struggle which has just ended.

Before today's game even the most optimistic admirer of the Mackmen admitted that the great machine squeaked in places and that the engine missed fire. Today it was just a hopeless fight against an irresistible force. What with Rudolph's perfectly controlled pitching and the snappy, concentrated batting outbursts of Boston, there was nothing for the Athletics to do but take their medicine.

Rudolph was the same pitching magician that he was when he conquered the Mackmen at Shibe Park on Friday. He whisked a mystifying variety of tangents at the rival batsmen. Each time he pitched Rudolph went through the preparations of throwing his moist ball. The trick worked famously. He tossed everything he had from this same deceptive wind-up. Mack's battery of .300 batters waved their bats foolishly at a slow lob or an outcurve which brought shrieks of laughter from the closely packed stands of Boston rooters. He gave them seven hits, but in only one inning, the fifth, were they able to group their smashes in a way which was productive of runs.

In the fifth inning Jack Barry beat out a high bounder between third and short. He went along a station while Evers was busily cutting down Schang at first base. The man supposed to be the weakest hitter on the club was responsible for the Athletics' lonesome run. Bob Shawkey, probably despondent over the weak hitting of his teammates, took it all upon himself and swung savagely on the ball. He produced a screaming two-base hit which encouraged Jack Barry home and saved the team from a disgraceful shutout. Every time the Athletics seemed to be gathering strength the Braves' defense would suddenly loom up before them and stop the advance short. Gowdy threw the ball with the speed of a rifle and twice he cut down men at second.

The Boston infield was picketed by the sharpest kind of defenders. Maranville executed the real glittering fielding gem in the sixth inning. McInnis drove a ball over second base. Maranville, with superhuman fleetness, lunged to one side and speared the singing, screaming ball with one hand. He didn't wait to set himself to throw. While poised on his toes he smilingly flipped the ball in the general direction of first base, and his quick, jerky heave beat the romping McInnis to the bag with seconds to spare. When the 'Rabbit' walked to the bench after that inning every man and woman stood up and the human jumping-jack got the longest and most sincere greeting of any player in the whole show.

The teams went along for three innings with no excitement in sight. In the fourth Evers got a pass. Looking back through the story of the Braves' wonderful rise this year, you will find staring you in the face that name of Evers. He won't be downed. Well, in the fourth he got a pass. He went down to second while Collins was tossing Connolly out at first. Whitted hit a smart hopper at Collins. The ball bounced playfully off his outstretched hands and rolled just far enough away to permit Whitted to camp comfortably at first and Evers at third.

Evers took a big lead down the third base line. Big Schmidt pushed a slow roller to Barry. Before Barry was set to throw to first the alert Evers had jumped over the plate with a run.

It was again that bugaboo name of Evers that confronted the Mackmen in the fifth inning. Whenever there is trouble in a ball game you can place your finger on Evers and you will find that trouble. It was that way when he was the keystone of the great Cub team that Frank Chance had in Chicago.

Maranville and Deal were quick outs in the fifth inning. Dick Rudolph hit Shawkey for a clean single to centerfield. Moran slapped the first ball to the fence between left and center and pulled up at second base, with Rudolph at third.

Evers is up! A veteran swatter pitted against a young flinger. Shawkey tried to cut the corners of the platter. It would be just as easy to try to fool a fox. The count went to 3 and 2. Evers knew that the next ball must be a 'cripple,' right in the middle of the plate.

Johnny made a short, snappy half swing at the ball and it went down through a hole at second that was big enough to drive a haywagon through. Rudolph and Moran both scored and the game was won. From that moment the Braves were champions of the world and the Athletics had slipped back into the ruck.

With the last put-out in this colossal baseball reversal, Boston's enthusiasm exploded. The Royal Rooters, with their band and their painted braves and their 'Honey Fitz,' stormed the Boston bench. The players were dragged out by willing hands, and the baseball diamond became black with a bubbling mass of 20,000 idolizing fans. Stallings was placed on exhibition as Exhibit A, the 'Miracle Man'. He was cheered and cheered, and nobody could hear him as he softly said 'Thank you' a dozen times. Yes, he had accomplished wonders.

He made a fine ball club out of a crazy quilt of baseball remnants. He made them play for all that was in them. On the bench he was no more gentle than Simon Legree, but he's been able to get his men all keyed up, and has kept them at that stage through thick and thin. He brought them to the fine edge of top form all at the same time. George Tweedy Stallings deserves all that is being said about him. He fooled all the wise ones, George did.

The Thrill of the Grass

W. P. KINSELLA

1981: THE SUMMER THE baseball players went on strike. The dull weeks drag by, the summer deepens, the strike is nearly a month old. Outside the city the corn rustles and ripens in the sun. Summer without baseball: a disruption to the psyche. An unexplainable aimlessness engulfs me. I stay later and later each evening in the small office at the rear of my shop. Now, driving home after work, the worst of the rush-hour traffic over, it is the time of evening I would normally be heading for the stadium.

I enjoy arriving an hour early, parking in a far corner of the lot, walking slowly toward the stadium, rays of run dropping softly over my shoulders like tangerine ropes, my shadow gliding with me, black as an umbrella. I like to watch young families beside their campers, the mothers in shorts, grilling hamburgers, their men drinking beer. I enjoy seeing little boys dressed in the home-team uniform, barely toddling, clutching hotdogs in upraised hands.

I am a failed shortstop. As a young man, I saw myself diving to my left, graceful as a toppling tree, fielding high grounders like a cat leaping for butterflies, bracing my right foot and tossing to first, the throw true as if a steel ribbon connected my hand and the first baseman's glove. I dreamed of leading the American League in hitting—being inducted into the Hall of Fame. I batted .217 in my senior year of high school and averaged 1.3 errors per nine innings.

I know the stadium will be deserted; nevertheless I wheel my car down off the freeway, park, and walk across the silent lot, my footsteps rasping and mournful. Strangle-grass and creeping charlie are already inching up through the gravel, surreptitious, surprised at their own ease. Faded bottle caps, rusted bits of chrome, an occasional paper clip, recede into the earth. I circle a ticket booth, sun faded, empty, the door closed by an oversized padlock. I walk beside the tall, machinery-green, board fence. A half mile away a few cars hiss along the freeway; overhead a single-engine plane fizzes lazily. The whole place is silent as an empty classroom, like a house suddenly without children.

It is then that I spot the door-shape. I have to check twice to be sure it is there; a door cut in the deep green boards of the fence, more the promise of a door than the real thing, the kind of door, as children, we cut in the sides of cardboard boxes with our mother's paring knives. As I move closer, a golden circle of lock, like an acrimonious eye, establishes its certainty.

I stand, my nose so close to the door I can smell the faint odor of paint, the golden eye of a lock inches from my own eyes. My desire to be inside the ballpark is so great that for the first time in my life I commit a criminal act. I have been a locksmith for over forty years. I take the small tools from the pocket of my jacket, and in less time than it would take a speedy runner to circle the bases I am inside the stadium. Though the ballpark is open-air it smells of abandonment; the walkways and seating areas are cold as basements. I breathe the odors of rancid popcorn and wilted cardboard.

The maintenance staff were laid off when the strike began. Synthetic grass does not need to be cut or watered. I stare down at the ball diamond, where just to the right of the pitcher's mound, a single weed, perhaps two inches high, stands defiant in the rain-pocked dirt.

The field sits breathless in the orangy glow of the evening sun. I stare at the potato-colored earth of the infield, that wide, dun arc, surrounded by plastic grass. As I contemplate the prickly turf, which scorches the thighs and buttocks of a sliding player as if he were being seared by hot steel, it stares back in its uniform ugliness. The seams that send routinely hit ground balls veering at tortuous angles are vivid, grey as scars.

I remember the ballfields of my childhood, the outfields full of soft hummocks and brown-eyed gopher holes.

I stride down from the stands and walk out to the middle of the field. I touch the stubble that is called grass, take off my shoes, but find it is like walking on a row of toothbrushes. It was an evil day when they stripped the sod from this ballpark, cut it into yardwide swathes, rolled it, memories and all, into great green-and-black cinnamonroll shapes, trucked it away. Nature temporarily defeated. But Nature is patient.

Over the next few days an idea forms within me, ripening, swelling, pushing everything else into a corner. It is like knowing a new, wonderful joke and not being able to share. I need an accomplice.

I go to see a man I don't know personally, though I have seen his face peering at me from the financial pages of the local newspaper, and the *Wall Street Journal*, and I have been watching his profile at the baseball stadium, two boxes to the right of me, for several years. He is a fan. Really a fan. When the weather is intemperate, or the game not close, the people around us disappear like flowers closing at sunset, but we are always there until the last pitch. I know he is a man who attends because of the beauty and mystery of the game, a man who can sit during the last of the ninth with the game decided innings ago, and draw joy from watching the first baseman adjust the angle of his glove as the pitcher goes into his windup.

He, like me, is a first-base-side fan. I've always watched baseball from behind first base. The positions fans choose at sporting events are like politics, religion, or philosophy: a view of the world, a way of seeing the universe. They make no sense to anyone, have no basis in anything but stubbornness.

I brought up my daughters to watch baseball from the first-base side. One lives in Japan and sends me box scores from Japanese newspapers, and Japanese baseball magazines with pictures of superstars politely bowing to one another. She has a season ticket in Yokohama; on the first-base side.

'Tell him a baseball fan is here to see him,' is all I will say to his secretary. His office is in a skyscraper, from which he can look out over the city to where the prairie rolls green as mountain water to the limits of the eye. I wait all afternoon in the artificially cool, glassy reception area with its yellow and mauve chairs, chrome and glass coffee tables. Finally, in the late afternoon, my message is passed along.

'I've seen you at the baseball stadium,' I say, not introducing myself.

'Yes,' he says. 'I recognize you. Three rows back, about eight seats to my left. You have a red scorebook and you often bring your daughter . . .'

'Granddaughter. Yes, she goes to sleep in my lap in the late innings, but she knows how to calculate an ERA and she's only in Grade 2.'

'One of my greatest regrets,' says this tall man, whose moustache and carefully styled hair are polar-bear white, 'is that my grandchildren all live over a thousand miles away. You're very lucky. Now, what can I do for you?'

'I have an idea,' I say. 'One that's been creeping toward me like a first baseman when the bunt sign is on. What do you think about artificial turf?'

'Hmmmf,' he snorts, 'that's what the strike should be about. Baseball is meant to be played on summer evenings and Sunday afternoons, on grass just cut by a horse-drawn mower,' and we smile as our eyes meet.

'I've discovered the ballpark is open, to me anyway,' I go on. 'There's no one there while the strike is on. The wind blows through the high top of the grandstand, whining until the pigeons in the rafters flutter. It's lonely as a ghost town.'

'And what is it you do there, alone with the pigeons?'

'I dream.'

'And where do I come in?'

'You've always struck me as a man who dreams. I think we have things in common. I think you might like to come with me. I could show you what I dream, paint you pictures, suggest what might happen . . .'

He studies me carefully for a moment, like a pitcher trying to decide if he can trust the sign his catcher has just given him.

'Tonight?' he says. 'Would tonight be too soon?'

'Park in the northwest corner of the lot about 1.00 a.m. There is a door about fifty yards to the right of the main gate. I'll open it when I hear you.'

He nods.

I turn and leave.

The night is clear and cotton warm when he arrives. 'Oh, my,' he says, staring at the stadium turned chrome-blue by a full moon. 'Oh, my,' he says again, breathing in the faint odors of baseball, the reminder of fans and players not long gone.

'Let's go down to the field,' I say. I am carrying a cardboard pizza box, holding it on the upturned palms of my hands, like an offering.

When we reach the field, he first stands on the mount, makes an awkward attempt at a windup, then does a little spring from first to about half-way to second. 'I think I know what you've brought,' he says, gesturing toward the box, 'but let me see anyway.'

I open the box in which rests a square foot of sod, the grass smooth and pure, cool as a swatch of satin, fragile as baby's hair.

'Ohhh,' the man says, reaching out a finger to test the moistness of it. 'Oh, I see.'

We walk across the field, the harsh, prickly turf making the bottoms of my feet tingle, to the left-field corner where, in the angle formed by the foul line and the warning track, I lay down the square foot of sod. 'That's beautiful,' my friend says, kneeling beside me, placing his hand, fingers spread wide, on the verdant square, leaving a print faint as a veronica.

I take from my belt a sickle-shaped blade, the kind used for cutting carpet. I measure along the edge of the sod, dig the point in and pull carefully toward me. There is a ripping sound, like tearing an old bed sheet. I hold up the square of artificial turf like something freshly killed, while all the time digging the sharp point into the packed earth I have exposed. I replace the sod lovingly, covering the newly bared surface.

'A protest,' I say.

'But it could be more,' the man replies.

'I hoped you'd say that. It could be. If you'd like to come back . . .'

'Tomorrow night?'

'Tomorrow night would be fine. But there will be an admission charge . . .'

'A square of sod?'

'A square of sod two inches thick . . .'

'Of the same grass?'

'Of the same grass. But there's more.'

'I suspected as much.'

'You must have a friend . . .'

'Who would join us?'

'Yes,'

'I have two. Would that be all right?'

'I trust your judgement.'

'My father. He's over eighty,' my friend says. 'You might have seen him with me once or twice. He lives over fifty miles from here, but if I call him he'll come. And my friend . . .'

'If they pay their admission they'll be welcome . . .'

'Indeed they may. But what will we do with this?' I say, holding up the sticky-backed square of turf, which smells of glue and fabric.

'We could mail them anonymously to baseball executives, politicians, clergymen.'

'Gentle reminders not to tamper with Nature.'

We dance toward the exit, rampant with excitement.

'You will come back? You'll bring others?'

'Count on it,' says my friend.

They do come, those trusted friends, and friends of friends, each making a live, green deposit. At first, a tiny row of sod squares begins to inch along toward left-centre field. The next night even more people arrive, the following night more again, and the night after there is positively a crowd. Those who come once seem always to return accompanied by friends, occasionally a son or young brother, but mostly men my age or older, for we are the ones who remember the grass.

Night after night the pilgrimage continues. The first night I stand inside the deep green door, listening. I hear a vehicle stop; hear a car door close with a snug thud. I open the door when the sound of soft-soled shoes on gravel tells me it is time. The door swings silent as a snake. We nod curt greetings to each other. Two men pass me, each carrying a grasshopper-legged sprinkler. Later, each sprinkler will sizzle like frying onions as it wheels, a silver sparkler in the moonlight.

During the nights that follow, I stand sentinel-like at the top of the grandstand, watching as my cohorts arrive. Old men walking across a parking lot in a row, in the dark, carrying coiled hoses, looking like the many wheels of a locomotive, old men who have slipped away from their homes, skulked down their sturdy sidewalks, breathing the cool, grassy, after-midnight air. They have left behind their sleeping, grey-haired women, their immaculate bungalows, their manicured lawns. They continue to walk across the parking lot, while occasionally a soft wheeze, a nibbling, breathy sound like an old horse might make, divulges their humanity. They move methodically toward the baseball stadium which hulks against the moonblue sky like a small mountain. Beneath the tint of starlight, the tall light standards which rise above the fences and grandstand glow purple, necks bent forward, like sunflowers heavy with seed.

My other daughter lives in this city, is married to a fan, but one who watches baseball from behind third base. And like marrying outside the faith, she has been converted to the third-base side. They have their own season tickets, twelve rows up just to the outfield side on third base. I love her, but I don't trust her enough to let her in on my secret.

I could trust my granddaughter, but she is too young. At her age she shouldn't have to face such responsibility. I remember my own daughter, the one who lives in Japan, remember her at nine, all knees, elbows and missing teeth—remember peering in her room, seeing her asleep, a shower of well-thumbed baseball cards scattered over her chest and pillow.

I haven't been able to tell my wife—it is like my compatriots and I are involved in a ritual for true believers only. Maggie, who knew me when I still dreamed of playing professionally myself—Maggie, after over half a lifetime together, comes and sits in my lap in the comfortable easy chair which has adjusted through the years to my thickening shape, just as she has. I love to hold the lightness of her, her tongue exploring my mouth, gently as a baby's finger.

'Where do you go?' she asks sleepily when I crawl into bed at dawn.

I mumble a reply. I know she doesn't sleep well when I'm gone. I can feel her body rhythms change as I slip out of bed after midnight.

'Aren't you too old to be having a change of life,' she says, placing her toast-warm hand on my cold thigh.

I am not the only one with this problem.

'I'm developing a reputation,' whispers an affable man at the ballpark. 'I imagine any number of private investigators following any number of cars across the city. I imagine them creeping about the parking lot, shining pen-lights on licence plates, trying to guess what we're up to. Think of the reports they must prepare. I wonder if our wives are disappointed that we're not out discoing with frizzy-haired teenagers?'

Night after night, virtually no words are spoken. Each man seems to know his assignment. Not all bring sod. Some carry rakes, some hoes, some hoses, which, when joined together, snake across the infield and outfield, dispensing the blessing of water. Others, cradle in their arms bags of earth for building up the infield to meet the thick living sod.

I often remain high in the statium, looking down on the men moving over the earth, dark as ants, each sodding, cutting, watering, shaping. Occasionally the moon finds a knife blade as it trims the sod or slices away a chunk of artificial turf, and tosses the reflection skyward like a bright ball. My body tingles. There should be symphony music playing. Everyone should be humming 'America The Beautiful'.

Toward dawn, I watch the men walking away in groups, like small patrols of soldiers, carrying instead of arms, the tools and utensils which breathe life back into the arid ballfield.

Row by row, night by night, we lay the little squares of sod, moist as chocolate cake with green icing. Where did all the sod come from? I picture many men, in many parts of the city, surreptitiously cutting chunks out of their own lawns in the leafy midnight darkness, listening to the uncomprehending protests of their wives the next day—pretending to know nothing of it—pretending to have called the police to investigate.

When the strike is over I know we will all be here to watch the workouts, to hear the recalcitrant joints crackling like twigs after the forced inactivity. We will sit in our regular seats, scattered like popcorn throughout the stadium, and we'll nod as we pass on the way to the exits, exchange secret smiles, proud as new fathers.

For me, the best part of all will be the surprise. I feel like a magician who has gestured hypnotically and produced an elephant from thin air. I know I am not alone in my wonder. I know that rockets shoot off in of half-a-hundred chests, the excitement of birthday mornings, Christmas eves, and home-town doubleheaders, boils within each of my conspirators. Our secret rites have been performed with love, like delivering a valentine to a sweetheart's door in that blue-steel span of morning just before dawn.

Players and management are meeting round the clock. A settlement is imminent. I have watched the stadium covered square foot by square foot until it looks like green graph paper. I have stood and felt the cool odors of the grass rise up and touch my face. I have studied the lines between each small square, watched those lines fade until they were visible to my eyes alone, then not even to them.

What will the players think, as they straggle into the stadium and find the miracle we have created? The old-timers will raise their heads like ponies, as far away as the parking lot, when the thrill of the grass reaches their nostrils. And, as they dress, they'll recall sprawling in the lush outfields of childhood, the grass as cool as a mother's hand on a forehead.

'Goodbye, goodbye,' we say at the gate, the smell of water, of sod, of sweat, small perfumes in the air. Our secrets are safe with each other. We go our separate ways.

Alone in the stadium in the last chill darkness before dawn, I drop to my hands and knees in the center of the outfield. My palms are sodden. Water touches the skin between my spread fingers. I lower my face to the silvered grass, which, wonder of wonders, already has the ephemeral odors of baseball about it.

Baseball and Writing

MARIANNE MOORE

Fanaticism? No. writing is exciting
and baseball is like writing.
　You can never tell with either
　　how it will go
　　or what you will do;
　generating excitement—
　a fever in the victim—
　pitcher, catcher, fielder, batter.
　　　　　Victim in what category?
Owlman watching from the press box.
　　　　To whom does it apply?
　　　　Who is excited? Might it be I?

It's a pitcher's battle all the way—a duel—
a catcher's, as, with cruel
　puma paw, Elston Howard lumbers lightly
　　back to plate. (His spring
　　de-winged a bat swing.)
　They have that killer instinct;
　yet Elston—whose catching
　arm has hurt them all with the bat—
　　when questioned, says, unenviously,
　　'I'm very satisfied. We won.'
　　　Shorn of the batting crown, says, 'We;'
　　　robbed by a technicality.

When three players on a side play three positions
and modify conditions,
   the massive run need not be everything.
     'Going, going . . .' Is
     it? Roger Maris
     has it, running fast. You will
     never see a finer catch. Well . . .
     'Mickey, leaping like the devil'—why
       gild the cliché, deer sounds better—
   snares what was speeding towards its treetop nest,
     one-handing the souvenir-to-be
     meant to be caught by you or me.

Assign Yogi Berra to Cape Canaveral;
he could handle any missile.
     He is no feather. 'Strike! . . . Strike *two* !'
     Fouled back. A blur.
     It's gone. You would infer
     that the bat had eyes.
     He put the wood to that one.
Praised, Skowron says, 'Thanks, Mel.
     I think I helped a *little* bit.'
         All business, each, and modesty,
       Blanchard, Richardson, Kubek, Boyer.
       Who in that galaxy
       of nine won the pennant. Each. It was he.

Those two magnificent saves from the knee—throws
by Boyer, finesses in twos—
   like Whitey's three kinds of pitch and pre-
     diagnosis
     with pick-off psychosis.
   Pitching is a large subject.
   Your arm, too true at first, can learn to
   catch the corners—even trouble
       Mickey Mantle. ('Grazed a Yankee!
   My baby pitcher, Montejo!
       With some pedagogy,
       you'll be tough, premature prodigy.')

They crowd him and curve him and aim for the knees.
  Trying
indeed! The secret implying:
  'I can stand here, bat held steady.'
    One may suit him;
    none has hit him.
Imponderables smite him.
Muscle kinks, infections, spike wounds
require *food*, rest, respite from ruffians. (Drat it!
    Celebrity costs privacy!)
Cow's milk, 'tiger's milk', soy milk, carrot juice,
    brewer's yeast (high-potency)—
    concentrates presage victory

sped by Luis Arroyo, Hector Lopez—
deadly in a pinch. And 'Yes,
  it's work; I want you to bear down,
    but enjoy it
    while you're doing it.'
Mr Houk and Mr Sain,
if you have a rummage sale,
don't sell Roland Sheldon or Tom Tresh.
    Studded with stars in belt and crown,
the Stadium is an adastrium.
    O flashing Orion,
    your stars are muscled like the lion.

Baseball

JACQUES BARZUN

WHOEVER WANTS TO know the heart and mind of America had better learn baseball, the rules and realities of the game—and do it by watching first some high school or small-town teams. The big league games are too fast for the beginner and the newspapers don't help. To read them with profit you have to know a language that comes easy only after philosophy has taught you to judge practice. Here is scholarship that takes effort on the part of the outsider, but it is so bred into the native that it never becomes a dreary round of technicalities. The wonderful purging of the passions that we all experienced in the fall of '51, the despair groaned out over the fate of the Dodgers, from whom the league pennant was snatched at the last minute, gives us some idea of what Greek tragedy was like. Baseball *is* Greek in being national, heroic, and broken up in the rivalries of city-states. How sad that Europe knows nothing like it! Its Olympics generate anger, not unity, and its interstate politics follow no rules that a people can grasp. At least Americans understand baseball, the true realm of clear ideas.

That baseball fitly expresses the powers of the nation's mind and body is a merit separate from the glory of being the most active, agile, articulate and brainy of all group games. It is of and for our century. Tennis belongs to the individualistic past—a hero, or at most a pair of friends or lovers, against the world. The idea of baseball is a team, an outfit, a section, a gang, a union, a cell, a commando squad—in short, a twentieth-century setup of opposite numbers.

Baseball takes its mystic nine and scatters them wide. A kind of individualism thereby returns, but it is limited—eternal vigilance is the price of victory. Just because they're far apart, the outfield can't dream or play she-loves-me-not with daisies. The infield is like a steel net held in the hands of the catcher. He is the psychologist and historian for the staff—or else his signals will give the opposition hits. The value of his headpiece is shown by the ironmongery worn to protect it. The pitcher, on the other hand, is the wayward man of genius, who others will direct. They will expect nothing from him but virtuosity. He is surrounded no doubt by mere talent, unless one excepts that transplanted acrobat, the shortstop. What a brilliant invention is his role despite its exposure to ludicrous lapses! One man to each base, and then the freelance, the trouble shooter, the movable feast for the eyes, whose motivation animates the whole foreground.

The rules keep pace with this imaginative creation so rich in allusions to real life. How excellent, for instance, that a foul tip muffed by the catcher gives the batter another chance. It is the recognition of Chance that knows no argument. But on the other hand, how wise and just that the third strike must not be dropped. This points to the fact that near the end of any struggle life asks for more than is needful in order to clinch success. A victory has to be won, not snatched. We find also our American innocence in calling 'World Series' the annual games between the winners in each big league. The world doesn't know or care and couldn't compete if it wanted to, but since it's us children having fun, why, the world is our stage. I said Baseball was Greek. Is there not a poetic symbol in the new meaning—our meaning—of 'Ruth hits Homer?'

Once the crack of the bat has sent the ball skimming left of second between the infielders legs, six men converge or distend their defense to keep the runner from advancing along the prescribed path. The ball is not the center of interest as in those vulgar predatory games like football, basketball, and polo. Man running is the force to be contained. His getting to first or second base starts a capitalization dreadful to think of: every hit pushes him on. Bases full and a homer make four runs, while the defenders, helpless without the magic power of the ball laying over the fence, cry out their anguish and dig up the sod with their spikes.

But fate is controlled by the rules. Opportunity swings from one side to the other because innings alternate quickly, keep up spirit in the players, interest in the beholders. So does the profusion of different acts to be performed—pitching, throwing, catching, batting, running, stealing, sliding, signalling. Blows are similarly varied. Flies, Texas Leaguers, grounders, baseline fouls—praise God the human neck is a universal joint! And there is no set pace. Under the hot sun, the minutes creep as a deliberate pitcher tries his feints and curves for three strikes called, or conversely walks a threatening batter. But the batter is not invariably a tailor's dummy. In a hundredth of a second there may be a hissing rocket down right field, a cloud of dust over first base—the bleachers all a-yell—a double play, and the other side up to bat.

Accuracy and speed, the practiced eye and hefty arm, the mind to take in and readjust to the unexpected, the possession of more than one talent and the willingness to work in harness without special orders —these are the American virtues that shine in baseball. There has never been a good player who was dumb. Beef and bulk and mere endurance count for little, judgment and daring for much. Baseball is among group games played with a ball what fencing is to games of combat. But being spread out, baseball has something sociable and friendly about it that I especially love. The ball is not shuttling in a confined space, as in tennis. Nor does baseball go to the other extreme of solitary whanging and counting stopped on the brink of pointlessness, like golf. Baseball is a kind of collective chess with arms and legs in full play under sunlight.

How adaptable, too! Three kids in a back yard are enough to create the same quality of drama. All of us in our tennis days have pounded balls with a racket against a wall, for practice. But that is nothing compared with batting in an empty lot, or catching at twilight, with a fellow who'll let you use his mitt when your palms get too raw. Every part of baseball equipment is inherently attractive and of a most enchanting functionalism. A man cannot have too much leather about him; and a catcher's mitt is just the right amount for one hand. It's too bad the chest protector and shinpads are so hot and at a distance so like corrugated cardboard. Otherwise, the team is elegance itself in its striped knee breeches and loose shirts, colored stockings and peaked caps. Except for brief moments of sliding, you can see them all in one eyeful, unlike the muddy hecatombs of football. To watch a football game is to be in prolonged neurotic doubt as to what you're seeing. It's more like an emergency happening at a distance than a game. I don't wonder the spectators take to drink. Who has ever seen a baseball fan drinking within the meaning of the act? He wants all his senses sharp and clear, his eyesight above all. He gulps down soda pop, which is a harmless way of replenishing his energy by the ingestion of sugar diluted in water and colored pink.

Happy the man in the bleachers. He is enjoying the spectacle that the gods on Olympus contrived only with difficulty when they sent Helen to Troy and picked their teams. And the gods missed the fun of doing this by catching a bat near the narrow end and measuring hand over hand for first pick. In Troy, New York, the game scheduled for 2 p.m. will break no bones, yet it will be a real fight between Southpaw Dick and Red Larsen. For those whom civilized play doesn't fully satisfy, there will be provided a scapegoat in a blue suit—the umpire, yell-proof and even-handed as justice, which he demonstrates with outstretched arms when calling 'Safe!'

And the next day in the paper: learned comment, statistical summaries, and the verbal imagery of meta-euphoric experts. In the face of so much joy, one can only ask, Were you there when Dodger Joe parked the pellet beyond the pale?

ACKNOWLEDGEMENTS

The Publishers wish to thank the following for permission to reprint previously published material. Every effort has been made to locate all persons having any rights in the stories appearing in this book but appropriate acknowledgement has been omitted in some cases through lack of information. Such omissions will be corrected in future printings of the book upon written notification to the Publishers.

Chicago Tribune for "Baseball is a Dream That Can't Go Away" by Phil Hersh. Copyright © 1985 *Chicago Tribune*.

Houghton Mifflin Company for excerpts from SHOELESS JOE by W.P. Kinsella. Copyright © 1982 by W. P. Kinsella. Jacket design © 1982 by Wendell Minox.

Macmillan Publishing Company for "The Milk Pitcher" by Howard Brubaker from SHORT STORIES 1 edited by Virginia Alwin © 1961.

The Washington Post for "'Best' Team Won Even It Wasn't The Most Talented" by Thomas Boswell. Copyright © 1985 *The Washington Post*.

Little, Brown and Company for "Line-up for Yesterday, An ABC of Baseball Immortals" by Ogden Nash from VERSUS. Copyright © 1949 by Ogden Nash. First appeared in *Sport*.

The Atlantic Monthly Press for "The Barbarians" by Patricia Highsmith from ELEVEN copyright © 1945, 1962, 1964, 1965, 1967, 1968, 1969, 1970. "The Barbarians" copyright © P. Highsmith and Agence Bradley, 1968 was originally published in French in No. 17 of *La Revue de Poche* published by Robert Laffont, and in English in BEST MYSTERY STORIES edited by Maurice Richardson, copyright Introduction and Selection by Faber & Faber 1968.

Don Congden Associates, Inc. for "The Big Black and White Game" by Ray Bradbury. Originally published in *American Mercury* © 1945.

Alfred A. Knopf, Inc. for "The First Kiss" by John Updike from HUGGING THE SHORE copyright © 1979 by John Updike.

Scott Meridith Literary Agency, Inc. and Ellery Queen for "Man Bites Dog" from SPORTING DETECTIVE STORIES copyright © 1946.

The American Play Company Inc. for "Baseball Hattie" by Damon Runyon from TAKE IT EASY. Copyright © 1938.